The Other Helpers

The Other Helpers.

Paraprofessionals and Nonprofessionals in Mental Health

Michael Gershon
Henry B. Biller
University of Rhode Island

Lexington Books
D.C. Heath and Company
Lexington, Massachusetts
Toronto

Library of Congress Cataloging in Publication Data

Gershon, Michael.
    The other helpers.

    Bibliography: p.
    Includes index.
    1. Allied mental health personnel. 2. Community psychology. I. Biller,
Henry B., joint author. II. Title. [DNLM: 1. Allied health personnel.
2. Community mental health services—Manpower—United States. WM21
G381o]
RC440.2.G47   362.2'04'25   76-55535
ISBN 0-669-01317-x

Copyright © 1977 by D.C. Heath and Company.

Published simultaneously in Canada.

Printed in the United States of America.

International Standard Book Number: 0-669-01317-x

Library of Congress Catalog Card Number: 76-55535

To Linda and MaryAnn

Contents

Preface

The original concept of this volume was to include a brief review of the nonprofessional mental health literature as a framework for the development and execution of a paraprofessional training program for volunteer homemakers. However, as the authors explored the research, the diversity, expansiveness and disorganization of the literature became apparent. While others have attempted to create some order to the literature of this field, their reviews tend to be either too limited in scope or insufficiently critical of methodological flaws. Therefore, what began as a brief review evolved into a volume guided by three basic goals: 1) to critically examine selected programs in the literature on nonprofessionals; 2) to provide a sourcebook for readers interested in the many aspects of this immense field; and, 3) to suggest a model for conceptualizing, implementing, and evaluating nonprofessional programs.

Certainly, this examination does not include all the publications dealing with nonprofessional programs. It is a sample of an ever growing area. For example, the authors have excluded nonprofessional related programs in the following areas: correctional facilities, day care centers, crisis-intervention and suicide-prevention centers, health clinics, and dental offices. Nevertheless, the present sample of programs is a fair representation of the exciting and innovative nonprofessional revolution occurring throughout the country.

The authors are indebted to many individuals at the University of Rhode Island for their encouragement and ideas, particularly Drs. Allan Berman, George Fitzelle, Lawrence Grebstein, Peter Merenda, and Alan Willoughby. The publication of this book also owes much to the consistent support of Ellen Glisker, Michael McCarroll, and Margaret Zusky of Lexington Books.

1

The Nonprofessional Revolution

A review of the mental health literature dramatically demonstrates the occurrence of a "nonprofessional revolution" (Sobey 1970). There has been a vast and variegated response to the recommendation of the Joint Commission on Mental Illness and Health (1961) that alternatives to traditional psychiatric treatment and training for the delivery of mental health services be explored, particularly with regard to nonprofessional resources. The plethora of recent edited volumes, articles, and surveys reflects this strong growing interest in the use of nonprofessional talent and the wide variety of roles which are increasingly evolving for such individuals (e.g., Cowen, Gardner, and Zax 1967; Golann 1970; Grosser, Henry, and Kelly 1969).

A survey of 80 federally funded community mental health centers revealed projections that at least 42 percent of all full-time positions would be occupied by nonprofessional mental health personnel (Levenson and Reff 1970). As this growth is taking place there will be a great diversity of types of nonprofessionals broadening their roles and responsibilities to serve a wide variety of client populations (Cowen 1973).

A problem in reviewing the nonprofessional literature is that most of the writers are too concerned with the uniqueness of their programs, often describing their projects in glowing terms with little concern for theoretical rationale, operational definitions, selection methods, nature of training, appropriate assessment, and adequate methodology (Durlak 1971; Fraleigh 1971; Gruver 1971; Siegel 1973). It is difficult for the interested reader to clearly determine both the efficacy of this movement and its essential ingredients in terms of types of nonprofessionals, assumed roles, nature of training, and actual subsequent impact.

Before the four prime factors underlying the present nonprofessional movement are described, it should be emphasized that non-psychiatrically trained mental health helpers have been with us for quite some time, providing a range of services. The early use of nonprofessionals is seen most clearly in the very nature of some psychiatric hospitals during the late eighteenth and early to mid-nineteenth centuries. These facilities were characterized by a highly enlightened therapeutic approach called "moral treatment," which was in sharp contrast to the earlier bedlamlike madhouse that used torture and chains as well as the state hospital of the later nineteenth and twentieth centuries which featured ECT (Electroconvulsive Therapy), strait jackets, and general emotional and physical stagnation (Bockhoven 1963).

1

The basic premise in moral treatment was that a positive change in a patient's milieu and a recognition of the reciprocal interaction between patients and hospital personnel would consequently lead to therapeutic change. Specifically, the following were stressed: healthy and clean living standards, respect for a patient's rights, high expectations for patient performance, and much group interaction between lay/professional staff and patients in work, social, and academic activities.

Unfortunately, by the mid-nineteenth century the moral treatment movement began to wane, but this trend in psychiatric care was actually the forerunner of the present "third revolution" in mental health (Bloom 1973). There are many modern psychiatric developments which parallel former moral treatment features, including the therapeutic milieu, group therapy and support systems, emphasis on self-help and environmental management, educational and social skills training programs, and the utilization of nonprofessional personnel as key members of the treatment team.

Workforce Shortage

A prime reason for the increased use of nonprofessionals has been the growing personnel shortage faced by all the mental health professionals which, over time, is expected to worsen (Hersch 1968; Matarazzo 1971; Skovholt 1973).

Albee's (1959) early investigations into professional workforce resources clearly indicated the severity of personnel shortages in the face of increasing demands for services by the public. Later surveys and analyses have continued to confirm these predictions (Albee 1967, 1968a, 1968b; Matarazzo 1971; Schindler-Rainman 1971).

Despite dramatic increases in the core mental health professions, the nation continues to fall behind in meeting its mental health needs, and many professional positions remain unfilled. This trend may be a function, in part, of our accelerating population growth concomitant with increased urbanization, mobility, and multiple social changes at work and at home. Changes in modern life-style have resulted in more people with emotional problems across all age, ethnic, and socioeconomic categories (Sobey 1969).

In general, the definitional scope of the mental health field has broadened considerably to include more diverse types of individuals, groups, and settings. An outcome of this increasing demand for services has been the hard realization that there are not now, nor will there be in the future, enough professionally trained individuals to meet these mounting needs. Other solutions have to be sought in resolving these problems, and certainly the use of nonprofessional personnel may be the most cogent answer to the supply-demand problem.

Changes in Mental Health Ideology

Even if there were sufficient numbers of professional personnel, changing concepts of mental health, treatment, and prevention continue to point to new workforce requirements and roles (Albee 1968b; Arnhoff 1968a; Matarazzo 1968).

Hobbs (1964) described a "third revolution" in mental health characterized by a movement away from a traditional individual therapy model toward a greater community approach, so as to extend mental health services to more members of the general population. This community psychiatry approach challenges the highly individualistic, intrapsychic orientation toward cause and treatment of troubled people and replaces it with a stronger emphasis toward environmental and sociological considerations (Hersch 1968; Finestone and Sobey 1969).

Again it should be underscored that "revolution" is an apt description of the newer ideology. New collaborative roles need to be developed and clarified by professionals as do the conceptual models utilized in approaching the community from this new perspective (Cohen 1973; Regester 1974).

Perhaps the major problem in need of a creative, yet realistic, solution is the supply-demand dilemma that faces both traditional and newer mental health approaches (Riessman 1970). Briefly, the situation is this: as the community is offered effective programs, the demand for such services accelerates, eventually outdistancing the supply of available services and personnel. Even though the newer, indirect services, such as consultation, are instituted in order to lessen the demand for services through prevention of future problems, the exposure of such programs in the community initially tends to inflate the direct service load. This is only one of the many problems that community mental health practitioners are striving to grapple with. Whether the struggle is with conceptual or workforce issues, it appears that suggested possible solutions point more and more to collaborative professional-nonprofessional efforts. The utilization of nonprofessionals fits well within the new ideological perspective. This is reflected in the changes occurring in and out of psychiatric settings and in the new coordinated efforts in multiservice community agencies.

In discussing the moral treatment movement, the concept of the therapeutic community was touched upon as the modern manifestation of that earlier therapeutic approach. Day care, outpatient, or inpatient psychiatric facilities are characterized by a therapeutic milieu emphasizing group therapy programs and activities, short-term involvement, environmental changes, and highly practical training (e.g., job hunting, budgeting). This model lends itself very naturally to the greater inclusion of other change and helping agents besides professionals (e.g., psychiatric attendants, occupational and activity therapists, pastoral counselors) who can readily learn and implement these more concrete and practical services now being provided to clients.

Turning away from the more clinical, psychiatric types of settings and focusing instead on some of the newest mental health innovations occurring within the community, one is struck by the recent developments of the "human services" or "human resources" concept (Bourne 1974; March 1968). The human services model has developed within the last few years as a direct result of the expanding range and perspective around mental health activities and the realization that any comprehensive helping service for people in trouble can only come about with systematic linkage between a variety of caregiving agencies which, if operating alone, would usually provide fragmented, perhaps irrelevant, help.

Five general themes emerge from the human services orientation: "systematic integration of services; comprehensive services and accessibility; client troubles defined as problems in living; generic characteristics of helping activities; and accountability of service providers to clients" (Baker 1974).

Whereas the multiproblem family seeking help from a particular agency might previously have received aid for a specific difficulty and then have had to be referred elsewhere for further assistance for its problems, now it will be able to contact one consortium of closely linked facilities where the needed comprehensive care will be available. Coordinated helping systems will only be possible as mental health professionals learn to work effectively with one another, with other caregiving, allied professionals, and with the nonprofessional personnel increasingly represented in most of these agencies (Schulberg 1972).

Inequality of Services

The fact that professionals are not meeting the mental health needs of a large number of people has been amply documented and cited as a strong determinant for the nonprofessional workforce boom (Arnhoff, Rubenstein, and Speisman 1969). This lack has been particularly apparent in the limited, often irrelevant, clinical services offered to the poor and minority groups where the approach too frequently fits the needs of the professionals and not those of their clients (Carkhuff 1971b; Carter 1973; Cobb 1972; Goldstein 1973; Jones 1974; Pearl and Riessman 1965; Riessman, Cohen, and Pearl 1964; Riessman and Schribner 1965; Selig 1973).

Lower-class clients tend to be less verbal and more action-oriented; more concerned with symptom change and not dramatic personality changes; and expectant of direct, concrete, immediate results when dealing with helpers rather than some vague, ongoing therapeutic process (Durlak 1971). While various writers have addressed themselves to this necessary change in professionals' personal ideology and strategy regarding the needs of low-income and minority groups, it is also apparent that utilizing nonprofessional mental health workers, who come from backgrounds similar to those of the clients they serve, may best provide the realistic and effective services so badly needed (e.g., Beit-Hallahmi 1974; Iscoe 1974; Reiff 1966, 1968, 1969, 1971; Reiff and Riessman 1965; Riessman 1967a; Runquist and Behar 1974). The indigenous nonprofessional may be more optimistic about his interventions and be better able to identify, empathize, and communicate with low-income groups. Also, they can be efficiently trained to provide directive and supportive counseling approaches which are quite meaningful when working with the disadvantaged (Goldstein 1973; Riessman, Cohen, and Pearl 1964).

Examples of indigenous nonprofessional programs are fully described in Chapter 8, but the basic issue being discussed here, namely the inequality of professional services, applies equally well to the problems of helping other groups of people such as addicts, alcoholics, the aged, and the mentally retarded. Here again nonprofessional workers may have filled the professional service void by providing meaningful contact and programs.

Already Available Nonprofessional Helping Resources

Another reason for the developing interest in and utilization of nonprofessionals is the extensive use of lay helpers and non-mental health professional people. For example, troubled people are likely to first turn to close friends and relatives (Armstrong 1969; Eddy, Paap, and Glad 1970; Zolik and Stotsky 1966); helpful neighbors (Collins 1972); natural community caregivers such as clergy, physicians, lawyers, public health nurses, and teachers (Arnhoff 1968a; Eddy, Paap, and Glad 1970; Gurin, Veroff, and Feld 1960; Mandeville and Maholick 1969; Mueller, Cameron, and Joransen 1971); and even newspaper advice columns (Dibner 1974) before seeking help from mental health professionals.

Despite the increasing recognition of the importance of these formal and informal natural support delivery systems (see Caplan 1974a; Levy 1973), such important community counselors are still sometimes difficult to identify. Drum and Figler (1973) suggest four reasons for this phenomenon: (1) the individual may disclaim his helping skills as he does not wish to pretend that he is a professional counselor; (2) the helper may feel that being so identified will overlegitimize him and possibly cause him to lose the support and trust between himself and his helpees; (3) the individual may be fearful that his mode of helping behavior might be criticized; and (4) the person may actually not be aware that he is functioning in a helping role in providing his particular services.

Nevertheless, these people do exist and they are used extensively by psychologically troubled individuals. Once contact has been made with such people, they will generally take on the responsibility of intervening at some level, for they commonly share a reluctance to refer to mental health professionals (Durlak 1971; Mueller, Cameron, and Joransen 1971).

Thus, there are a variety of community resources to which people may initially turn in time of need, and it may be rather late, if at all, in a person's help-seeking itinerary that contact is made with actual professional or even specifically designated nonprofessional mental health personnel.

2 Goals and Organization

Some of the reasons underlying the increasing utilization of nonprofessionals have been outlined, and a more focused literature review considering the work of the various groups of nonprofessional mental health helpers is systematically presented in the following chapters. Various classification systems have appeared in the literature that attempt to give some order to the voluminous data as well as organize the types of helpers and their respective functions (Atkeson 1967; Phelan 1966; Richan 1961; Finestone and Sobey 1969). A particularly useful model was developed by Hartog (1967). The present schema is, in part, based on Hartog's eight-category system and some of the ideas suggested by this model.

The nonprofessional groups critiqued here include the paraprofessionals, community agents, medical and allied health professionals, urban agents, self-help organizations, "exotic" professionals, mental health volunteers, and selected parents. There is actually considerable overlap among these categories with a given helper often being simultaneously a member of a number of these groups. For clarity of discussion, however, these specific categories seem to make sense. In addition, despite their overlap and commonality, these groupings do tend to have a particular identity.

It should be noted that there is a highly interdisciplinary interest in the nonprofessional mental health workforce as seen in such diverse fields as psychology, psychiatry, child development and family relations, general medicine, nursing, social work, sociology, anthropology, guidance and counseling, education, economics, police science, business management, and political science. Even within a single professional discipline such as psychology, a variety of subspecialties—including developmental psychology, social psychology, clinical/counseling/community psychology—have all contributed data regarding the conceptualization, training, and use of nonprofessional personnel. What is most striking is the frequent convergence in ideas and approaches across disciplines. These points are clarified in later chapters.

Definition of Terms

The term *professional mental health worker* is used here to indicate the traditional core of mental health personnel (i.e., psychiatrist, psychologist, social worker, psychiatric nurse). Such a definition of *professional*, which is presumably a rubric signifying competence and high standards, may in fact be irrelevant

7

and perhaps at times harmful in the mental health field, serving only to set up a protective guildlike barrier (Reiff 1969).

Nonprofessional helpers, as used here, is a rather broad concept primarily denoting any individuals who may be involved in some mental health or related activity who do not belong to the above-mentioned professional groups and who have generally not received any formalized professional training.

Five different levels of individuals are included under the title *nonprofessional*. They are merely noted below, as they will be more fully discussed in subsequent chapters.

Community Caretakers

Comprising this group are those key individuals providing essential community services such as the police, clergy, lawyers, physicians, (nonpsychiatric) nurses, and teachers. While such people are considered professional within their given fields, they are viewed here as nonprofessional only in that they are not formally trained in mental health work.

Paraprofessionals

Included here are a variety of paid, middle-level mental health workers either formally or informally trained in newly emerging nontraditional training models.

Volunteers

This largest group of nonprofessional personnel consists of a variety of people such as interested homemakers, college students, and high school students. Such individuals provide tremendous workforce resources for such settings as psychiatric hospitals, community mental health centers, programs and institutions for the retarded, and crisis intervention facilities.

Self-Help Nonprofessionals

Such individuals may be paraprofessionals or volunteers, but also they often consist of lay members of various groups who are striving to create a mutual support system for one another so as to meet their particular needs and problems which the professional community has either ignored, underserviced, or inappropriately handled. Included in this category are members of Alcoholics Anonymous and Gamblers Anonymous.

Natural Nonprofessionals

These exotic types of community healers (e.g., witch doctors, faith healers) are frequently found in both urban and rural settings and may be quite esteemed and are often sought out for numerous physical and emotional ailments. Of note is the increasing use being made of these natural healers by their professional counterparts.

Not included in any of the above nonprofessional categories are the various subspecialty or "subprofessional" workers found within the very ranks of the mental health professions themselves such as the bachelor-level psychologist, social worker technician, and psychiatric nursing aide.

All the nonprofessionals are being referred to as *helpers*, as opposed to counselors or therapists. Although their duties may include some form of counseling or therapy, the term *helper* is more broadly descriptive and encompasses the many different services provided by nonprofessionals. Brammer (1973) described a model which fits well with this broad description of a nonprofessional mental health helper. Basically the paradigm suggests that a given helper's personality in combination with particular skills can lead to particular growth conditions in a helpee (i.e., the recipient of the service or intervention) which in turn may lead to specific individual, group, or societal changes. Terms such as *helper-helpee* can easily be translated into *therapist-patient* or *counselor-counselee*, but may also describe some of the same basic interpersonal processes occurring in parent-child and teacher-student relationships.

Level of Evaluation and Research Adequacy

This term refers to the degree of research sophistication reported in a particular study. This dimension approximates a continuum from no research at all to relatively high-level methodology. When the data are evaluated within the framework of such a continuum, the relative lack of research support for both professional and nonprofessional programs becomes apparent. Perhaps the frequently poor empirical efforts in the mental health helping area may simply reflect the limits of present methodological technology and not just careless evaluation. However, it is one goal of this book to show that reasonably sophisticated research is not only desirable, but in fact possible.

Descriptive

This term is self-explanatory: it refers to reports that basically present the background, activities, and results of a lay program with minimal or no thought about research. Unfortunately, such reports are abundant in the literature with "results" often presented in glowing terms, but with little or no concern for any kind of objective evaluation of the performance of nonprofessionals.

Inadequate Research

This term will hereafter be applied to studies of programs which evidence some attention to research but seemingly as an afterthought rather than as an adequate, preconceived empirical design. For example, some articles discuss the use of premeasures and postmeasures or self-report instruments. However, because the instruments are used in an unsystematic manner, any "results" are quite questionable.

Suggestive Research

Reports classified as "suggestive research" comprise a large number of the articles examined for this review. In such reports the investigators have made some legitimate research efforts. One problem, however, is that such variables as the particular design, types of measures, success and outcome criteria, and nature and number of individuals or groups trained may be found wanting. This is enough to cast some doubt on even the most positive findings as well as on the generalizability of the results.

Adequate Research

The term is used to designate only those investigations which approach quality-level research. Typical features might include appropriate statistics; random assignment of clients to interventions and/or helpers; clear descriptions of the nature of the interventions; inclusion of matched no-intervention control groups, placebo control groups, and other intervention comparison groups; reliable and valid preintervention and postintervention criteria measures; and follow-up. Such studies have important implications in empirically determining nonprofessional training and effectiveness. Unfortunately they are in the minority.

Outcome evaluation is another important factor which must be considered when determining the adequacy of research in this field. It should be noted that there are two kinds of outcome reported in nonprofessional articles. First, there are those programs emphasizing the "process" variable of the training experience, which is specifically concerned with the program effects on the attitudes, feelings, and helping skills of the nonprofessional trainees themselves. This type of study does not evaluate the impact of the nonprofessional on his helpees either during or following the program. Other studies demonstrate a second emphasis, namely, the direct effects of the helper's intervention activities on his target population, with less interest in any concomitant helper changes occurring in the process. A minimum number of studies simultaneously consider both helper process and helpee outcome results. In order for a study to be considered adequate, effects on the helpee must be systematically examined.

Preview

A description of how the material has been organized in ensuing chapters will now be presented. Chapter 3 begins the actual literature review, starting with an examination of the trained or semitrained paraprofessionals, defined as those paid mental health workers such as psychiatric aides or attendants. The services rendered by these individuals, current developments and training trends, and available research are all discussed. These same issues are similarly examined for other types of helpers in subsequent chapters. Chapter 4 focuses on the community agents or caretakers, such as lawyers, clergy, teachers, and police. Chapter 5 examines the mental health work of nonpsychiatric medical and related personnel. Included here are physicians and nurses.

Chapter 6 reviews the work of the urban agents, those particular nonprofessional community members who are in frontline positions, which gives them key access to people in actual or potential emotional trouble. Such people as union foremen and stewards, bartenders, beauticians, taxicab drivers, and "good" neighbors comprise this group.

Chapter 7 centers on a large body of nonprofessionals, examining examples of individuals involved in the many self-help programs which seem to have emerged in response to both the lack of adequate professional services and poor quality of care. Such groups are the retired and aged; mentally retarded; psychiatric patients and ex-patients; addicts; single, widowed, and divorced individuals; and the many men and women currently engaged in consciousness-raising activities as a self-help healing process.

Chapter 8 continues the examination of mutual-help groups, this time specifically focusing on the indigenous mental health worker. These individuals are essentially from working-class and minority groups, and they have been a growing force in view of the apparent inability of traditional mental health personnels to provide sufficient and meaningful services. Included in this chapter is a particularly fascinating group of indigenous lay helpers, the "exotic professionals." These are individuals residing in rural and urban settings who are the "primitive" healers providing for a wide variety of emotional and physical ailments. Whether referred to as faith healers, shamans, or witch doctors, such people apparently meet many needs of their community constituents. Although little hard research has been done on the activities of such people, some very interesting parallels have been drawn between their attitudes and skills and those of their professional counterparts. This discussion provides a basis for beginning to explain why lay and professional mental health workers may similarly be quite effective (or ineffective) in their helping ability in spite of wide cultural, educational, philosophical, and economic differences.

Chapter 9 primarily focuses on parents as an increasing key nonprofessional ally. Emphasis here is on the role of parents as major interveners either with other parents or in handling their own personal problems.

The largest group of nonprofessionals is examined in Chapter 10, which takes a critical look at the mental health volunteer. This category refers to such people as homemakers, students, and other community individuals interested in sharing their time and skills in such settings as psychiatric hospitals, day hospital programs, mental health clinics, and other related agencies.

Chapter 11 summarizes the conclusions reached in the previous chapters and draws some implications from these results. The problems in the research are outlined as well as the positive and negative findings which have emerged. Some discussion is aimed at determining possible factors explaining how the relatively untrained, presumably unsophisticated lay personnel may at times be rather successful in their helping interventions. Then the underlying issues inherent in nonprofessional program development, training, and evaluation are presented. Finally, some implications for professional mental health are examined in terms of the professional's relationship with lay personnel as well as with respect to his own academic and professional development.

3

The Paraprofessionals

This broad term *paraprofessional* generally refers to those paid subprofessionals working in a variety of capacities in clinics, mental health centers, various community agencies, and, most frequently, private and state psychiatric hospitals. Wherever they are employed, their job descriptions are numerous and overlapping, with these nonprofessionals being referred to as any of the following: mental health workers, psychiatric aides, technicians, technologists, mental health assistants, attendants, expediters, advocates, associates, preprofessionals, new professionals, middle-level workers, human service workers, and child care specialists.

Despite the fact that this large workforce has been available for quite a while, only recently have training programs been created and the therapeutic value and potential of these workers been more fully appreciated (e.g., Pattison and Elpers 1972). The growing awareness of the significance that such workers can have is seen currently in expanded job descriptions, duties, and career ladders.

Current Educational and Training Trends

The most important development in the present utilization of paraprofessionals has been the establishment of inservice training programs in clinics or hospitals. There has also been the creation of actual mental health training programs, leading to degrees at the associate, bachelor, and even masters levels. Such training programs are aimed at developing a new level of mental health workers who are often referred to as "middle-level workers." Individuals may be trained as mental health generalists or specialists with expertise in, for example, community organization (Krasnoff 1970) and behavior modification (Lee and Znachko 1968). The major training emphasis seems to be on developing generalists whose primary focus is on working with individuals, families, and groups and providing whatever services are needed for the welfare of their helpees (McPheeters, King, and Teare 1972).

A number of recent articles attest to the remarkable growth of these different types of paraprofessional programs (Collins 1971; Hadley, True, and Kepes 1970; Lief 1966; True, Young, and Packard 1972). For example, there are now 174 colleges in 44 states offering associate-degree mental health training programs. These programs already have over 11,000 graduates, and the number

13

is expected to exceed 20,000 in the near future (True and Young 1974). About 50 percent of these graduates are employed in positions relevant to their training; 40 percent work in state hospitals; 30 percent in mental health centers; and the remainder work in a variety of other treatment and educational facilities.

Matarazzo (1971) emphasized that community colleges became important as paraprofessional training centers because of the failure of professional schools to create appropriate subprofessional training to meet the workforce shortage. Previous to the development of associate degree programs, hospital attendants and aides often had only meager inservice training. Although varying much in their objectives and format, these hospital-based programs were intended to promote better understanding of the etiology and treatment of emotional problems, greater interest and enthusiasm of staff, the enhancement of the aides' fairly poor self-image (Lawton and Goldman 1965), and the improvement of communication between professional and nonprofessional staff (Euster 1971; Kilburn, McDole, and Smith 1970; Vaughn, Teitelbaum, and Kumpan 1962; Wollersheim 1973).

These institutional programs were gradually supplemented by a few courses or other educational experiences offered either at the community college or by invitation at the hospital itself. As demands for more courses and training increased, the opportunity for more formalized programs sponsored by academic facilities consequently expanded. As Baker (1972) suggests, the problem with agency- or institution-sponsored inservice training is that such programs are too often designed to meet more immediate needs of the host setting and are not broad enough to enable trainees to develop a wider range of generalizable skills.

One of the first major steps at collaboration between mental health facilities and educational institutions was the NIMH-sponsored associate pilot program at Purdue University, initiated in 1965 with its first graduating class in 1967 (Hadley, True, and Kepes 1970). Spurred on by this program and a series of subsequent conferences between mental health professionals and southern community colleges (Southern Regional Education Board 1966), the interest in training mental health paraprofessionals greatly accelerated. Although NIMH has continued to sponsor selected training programs, the majority of programs are being funded by a combination of college and/or institutional funds. For example, the Veterans Administration offers two possible training tracts to interested and qualified trainees: (1) a 48-week hospital-based program that is equally divided between didactic and clinical training and is geared for VA employees seeking career advancements; and (2) a VA stipend-supported mental health technician program for students who receive their practicum training in VA facilities and community agencies and seek an Associate of Arts degree (Siegel 1974).

An example of a typical Associate of Arts training program is described by Danzig (1970). This two-year program, jointly sponsored by the Kingsborough

Community College and the New York State Department of Mental Hygiene, provides a didactic and highly practical program resulting in a graduate whose title was "mental health assistant." The curriculum offers training and courses in basic liberal arts, philosophy of behavioral sciences, human growth and development, social problems and aging, sociology of the family, introductory psychopathology, behavior modification, group dynamics, and clinical fieldwork practices.

A similar extensive program developed at the Brentwood VA Hospital in California has been described by Felton and his associates (Felton 1973; Felton, Wallach, and Gallo 1974a, b). This program provides an educational-clinical new career pattern, and it involves either one- or two-year training tracts. It is primarily aimed at lower-echelon hospital employees and noncollege community members.

The Danzig (1970) and Felton (1974a) programs are fairly typical of the current crop of associate degree programs. McPheeters (1972) suggests the following as common ingredients underlying most of the community college programs: (1) generally small programs with selected enrollment and few full-time faculty members; (2) classwork curriculum fairly equally divided among liberal arts courses, mental health or related courses, and practicum and field experiences; (3) a strong emphasis on process and experiences requiring active participation coupled with the acquisition and practice of a wide range of skills; (4) a wide assortment of students drawn from interested homemakers, high school graduates, indigenous community members, and experienced psychiatric aides; and (5) graduates capable of providing an array of direct and indirect service skills in psychiatric and related community agencies.

Mental health worker training has also begun to be available from educational facilities other than community colleges. Fink and Zerof (1971) described the paraprofessional program developed at Hahnemann Medical College. This program leads to a Bachelor of Science degree and prepares trainees in highly skilled specific areas with high-level responsibility for patient care. The focus in this program is to develop specialists rather than generalists, and trainees may specialize in the following areas: child care, family therapy, psychiatric research, group therapy, community activity, rehabilitation services, outpatient psychiatric clinic work, school consultation, inpatient hospital work, criminology, and geriatric intervention.

Powell (1969) described a highly specialized work-study program leading to a Master of Science degree in community mental health offered at Northern Illinois University. Students are placed in various agencies throughout the community after 300 hours of supervision. The graduate is then considered qualified to serve in a number of capacities: as the linking agent between returning hospitalized patients and appropriate after-care community resources; as the developer of preventive community programs through contact with schools, agencies, and local mental health associations; as an assessor of local agency needs; and as an expediter in helping formulate and carry out the recommendations of mental health center personnel. Perhaps the most comprehensive approach to college-based paraprofessional training is Maryland's human services career programs (Vidaver 1969; Vidaver and Carson 1973). This program utilizes three 2-year modules extending from the community college mental health associate degree through the baccalaureate and master's degree.

Nondegree Paraprofessional Programs

Despite the recent rapid growth of these educationally oriented mental health worker training programs, relatively little evaluative data regarding these projects have appeared in the professional literature. Typically the usual paraprofessional programs that are described in the literature include aides or attendants, with minimal or no formal training beyond on-the-job experience, who are involved in a number of helping services.

The activities in which these largely hospital-trained workers have been involved include the following: individual, group, or milieu therapy (Anker and Walsh 1961; Appleby 1963; Ishiyama, McCulley, and Rodriguez 1967; Mendel and Rapport 1963); intakes and evaluations (Golland 1971); language development training (Guess, Smith, and Ensminger 1971); supervision of other aides (Mehr 1971); outreach work and community representation (Halpern 1969); and behavior modification in psychiatric wards (Lee and Znachko 1968; Hollander and Plutchik 1972; Pomerleau, Bobrove, and Smith 1973).

Recent years have also seen changes in attendants' status and functioning in residential centers for the retarded, with greater emphasis on the acquisition of assessment skills (Barnett and Bensberg 1964; Bensberg, Barnett, and Hurder 1964). Two other key roles more frequently served by aides in these settings have been as behavior modifiers (Panyan, Boozer, and Morris 1970) and as communication and language skills trainers (Shubert and Fulton 1966).

Evaluation of Paraprofessional Programs

Although most of the above programs report successful outcomes, such evaluation tends to be global and descriptive rather than based on hard data. In our analysis we considered 26 paraprofessional programs which had at least some research aspects. Paraprofessional interventions were directed at both individuals and groups, in this case essentially inpatient adults in psychiatric settings. The goals for any interventions were almost exclusively for remedial purposes, utilizing direct or supportive services or some combination of the two.

The paraprofessionals, then—at least as seen in this sample of programs—are performing many of the same helping activities as professionals, namely, individual, group, or milieu counseling. It should be noted that twenty of the articles reviewed refer to the hospital-based, psychiatric aide type of program that often involves little formal training or educational background.

The remaining articles were those more comprehensive degree programs discussed above (i.e., Baker 1972; Danzig 1970; Felton 1973; Fink and Zerot 1971; Powell 1969; Vidaver and Carson 1973). These programs are discussed separately to note their distinctive features, such as the variety of helpee recipients receiving services and the range of approaches utilized in providing these services. It often appears that a main distinction between this level of paraprofessional helper and his professional colleague is that the paraprofessional is primarily involved in direct, remedial activities while the professional has more and more branched out into developmental and preventive services.

It is important to analyze the depth of training and research incorporated into all of the above programs. It is apparent that eighteen of the reported programs are of either a descriptive or an inadequate research nature, thus neutralizing their generally favorable reported "findings." Six programs qualify for a suggestive research rating. Only one study (Paul, McInnis, and Mariotto 1973) out of the entire sample met the criteria for an adequate research study.

In terms of kinds of training experiences, all types are represented with two particular training modalities standing out more than others. These are the informal and didactic-experiential training approaches.

In eight articles there was a description of minimal training experiences and evidence of few or, at best, poor attempts at evaluation. This is not surprising, for such programs seem to entail little planning and hence there is generally a concomitant lack of concern for accountability of services rendered. It seems that there is simply a felt need to have aides provide a particular service, and this becomes the immediate goal to be achieved in the least costly and involved manner.

While this problem may be understood for the above hospital-based types of programs, it is somewhat disconcerting to find that the most extensive (didactic-experiential) training packages, including the associate degree programs, that do involve much planning and resources, similarly have failed to be adequately researched. This is unfortunate as these programs appear quite promising and innovative in producing a highly qualified nonprofessional mental health worker. McPheeters (1972) suggests that the very newness and continuing burgeoning growth of these programs may have temporarily prevented serious research efforts. Baker (1972) adds that their very innovative, flexible, and comprehensive nature may also have mitigated against systematic evaluation and control. Up until this point it appears that much of the available data have been directed more at the trainee's employability, job satisfaction, and types of services provided than at his particular helping effectiveness (e.g., Baker 1972, 1973).

Only three articles out of this sample of paraprofessional programs presented sufficient data on helpee outcome (Anker and Walsh 1961; Appleby

1963; Mendel and Rapport 1963). These studies report significant improvement in psychiatric inpatients (Anker and Walsh 1961; Appleby 1963) and outpatients (Mendel and Rapport 1963) as a result of paraprofessional intervention.

In the Anker and Walsh (1961) study, 134 hospitalized male patients were assigned either to activity therapy groups led by paraprofessionals or to more formal group therapy provided by professional personnel. These interventions lasted for one year, with the criteria for change consisting of such variables as periodic six-week assessments on behavioral rating scales and discharge rates from the hospitals. Reported results indicated significantly greater behavioral adjustment for activity group patients than for group therapy patients. Also important was the fact that, although they received some supervision, the paraprofessional helpers had apparently not received any specific training for their roles. Problems in the research are apparent, however. First, the specific nonprofessional and professional interventions, as described, were somewhat vague, as were the relatively gross behavioral change criteria. Second, the lack of a minimal or no-treatment control group cautions against assuming any automatic relationship between intervention and patient improvement since change may just as well have resulted from spontaneous recovery. Third, it is difficult to determine whether nonprofessionals were actually more effective than professionals since the type of therapy was not held constant across groups. Thus, the particular intervention may have been the key variable rather than the level of helper training.

Appleby (1963) randomly assigned 53 chronic hospitalized female patients to the following four groups: (1) a 10-patient treatment group where psychiatric aides were the primary therapists providing whatever direct services were needed and coordinating any other resources; (2) two 10-patient treatment groups offering intensive treatment (i.e., groups, individual, milieu) and administered by professional staff and comprising typical hospital-based teams; and (3) a no-treatment control group receiving no formal intervention. The program lasted nearly three years and was assessed by independent evaluators who rated the patients on a number of behavior rating scales, which were primarily scored at pretreatment, 4-month intervals, and 8 and 20 months following treatment. The results of this study indicate that the nonprofessional treatment group significantly improved on behavioral ratings over the no-treatment control group. Also important is the finding that the minimally trained nonprofessionals were equally effective as the two other professional-led groups.

Despite these reported positive findings, an examination of the Appleby study also raises important methodological questions. For example, the meaning of a "no-treatment control group" is questionable. Even though 23 patients did not receive intensive treatment, they did have other advantages such as improved physical facilities, bus rides, and ward government meetings. Hence the control of the essential variable of intervention versus no intervention was not tested in this study. Another criticism applied to the Anker and Walsh (1961) article is just as relevant here. Specifically, since treatment approach across disciplines differs, one cannot appropriately compare the effectiveness of nonprofessional and professional groups. A final point that was unclear in the Appleby study was whether nonprofessional and professional helpers were actually being contrasted regardless of services provided. An implication in this study was that the two professionally administered treatment groups may have consisted of interdisciplinary teams involving *both* professional and nonprofessional helpers. As such, the nonprofessional treatment group actually may have been compared to "contaminated" control groups.

The third study, reported by Mendel and Rapport (1963), dealt with an outpatient treatment program for a group of 166 females which utilized both professional and experienced nonprofessional helpers. The program consisted of an existentially-oriented, individual therapy approach, with 58 patients being treated by psychiatrists, 47 patients by psychiatric aides, 31 by social workers, and 30 by psychologists. The major goal of this 51-month program was to determine whether such treatment would be effective in maintaining these patients outside the hospital. Actual helper-patient contact during this time consisted of monthly 20- to 30-minute interviews consisting of concrete and specific adjustment issues and an avoidance of dynamic interpretations, fantasy and hallucinations, and previous life history data.

Evaluation of the program consisted of the very global judgments of social workers not connected with the program who assessed patients' nonhospital level of functioning. In this study the need to return to the hospital was interpreted as a therapeutic failure. The capacity to remain out of the hospital was interpreted as evidence of adequate organization and functioning (Mendel and Rapport 1963). Based on these data, the effectiveness of the professional and nonprofessional workers was compared. The nonprofessional and professional groups did not differ greatly in their effectiveness. For example, of the patients treated by psychiatrists, 34 percent returned to the hospital, while 36 percent of the patients treated by the psychiatric aides similarly returned.

As with the previous two investigations, the Mendel and Rapport (1963) study also has serious methodological shortcomings. For example, the criteria and means of evaluating patients are rather vague. Mendel and Rapport are not at all clear as to what behavioral variables the social workers were using, just how they went about measuring these criteria, nor at what particular point a patient was considered in need of hospital readmittance. The readmission criterion itself is quite global and does not include the numerous other behavioral changes which may be manifested by patients whether in or out of the hospital.

In addition, various factors appear to have contaminated all the control groups. For example, although in this study both professional and nonprofessional personnel were all presumably providing the same model of individual therapy, there seems to have been no control for several important factors: (1) some of the patients were on medication while others were not; (2) a number of patients had been previously seen by the same therapist who continued with them during the program, while other patients started with entirely new therapists at the start of the program; (3) even during the program itself some therapists apparently dropped out and were replaced by new ones while other therapists provided consistent patient contact throughout the entire program period; and (4) there was even inconsistency about the presumably constant, once a month, 20- to 30-minute session interviews since occasionally some patients were seen on a more frequent basis.

Such methodological drawbacks only confound the data and strongly undermine the positive findings reported in the Mendel and Rapport (1963) paper. Uncontrolled factors may have contributed to the end results; thus one cannot assume the viability of this type of intervention as utilized by these particular helpers.

In summary, these studies leave much to be desired despite the fact that these reports were, relatively speaking, the more methodologically sound outcome studies in the sample of paraprofessional research reviewed here. Although these three articles do indicate positive benefits for inpatient and outpatient adults as a result of a variety of direct services, more and better controlled studies are needed to substantiate these findings. Similarly, the training issue remains unsettled since the level of training was not a specific variable which was manipulated, controlled, and measured so as to accurately appraise differential training effectiveness. The issue of nonprofessional versus professional impact was also not adequately examined. While in these articles the nonprofessional personnel are reported as being as effective as, if not superior to, their professional colleagues, the various research flaws in these studies bring into question such conclusions.

Training Paraprofessionals

The issue of training is important in paraprofessional development, but there has been little relevant research either in terms of specific trainee effectiveness or in the relative differential impact of various training methodologies. The most comprehensive training approaches (and quite possibly the most exciting) are the associate degree, college-based programs which, unfortunately, have provided little hard research data.

What appears to be most reported in the literature are general, descriptive accounts of training programs for inpatient paraprofessional hospital staff. These usually deal with one particular training modality with the immediate focus being on the trainees' attitudes and skills and not necessarily on a consideration of the trainees' subsequent effectiveness with patients. The programs themselves vary widely in the number of participants, informal and formal training experiences, and the sponsoring hospital's attitudes regarding such program development.

The types of training offered have typically involved T-group training (Pino 1971), brief communication courses (Pryer, Distefano, and Poe 1966), extended programs in group therapy (Ebersole, Leiderman, and Yalom 1969), and group process (Bernstein and Herzberg 1970; Lee and Znachko 1968; Panyan, Boozer, and Morris 1970). Most of these programs have tended to incorporate a more structured, often didactic, focus along with some degree of practice. Training tools frequently used have been lecturettes, role playing and modeling, group and supervisory feedback, live and videotape demonstrations, and reading materials.

Common criteria for trainee change have emphasized specific skill development as well as some measure of appropriate attitude change. Typical criterion measures have varied and have included such variables as amount of aide-patient contact (Ishiyama, McCulley, and Rodriguez 1967), degree of self-disclosure and empathic ability (Pino 1971), objective tests on course/workshop content (Mehr 1971), preratings and postratings in therapy skills (Ebersole, Leiderman, and Yalom 1969), attitudinal changes regarding job satisfaction and mental health (Pryer, Distefano, and Poe 1966), increased communication between trainees and professional staff (Bernstein and Herzberg 1970), and psychological tests (Pino 1971). Such behavioral and attitudinal criteria run the gamut from gross to highly specific measures and similarly range from quite subjective assessment to rather objective measurement. Too often these criteria are rather questionable because of their lack of precision (i.e., in terms of reliability and validity) and the very way in which the data were obtained (e.g., untrained or biased raters).

There has been some attempt to research these training programs and at least introduce some element of control (e.g., Cochran and Steiner 1966; Ebersole, Leiderman, and Yalom 1969; Mehr 1971; Pryer, Distefano, and Poe 1966; Vaughn, Teitelbaum, and Kumpan 1962). However, such efforts have been rather poor and have generally lacked sufficient control groups. Little attention has been given to properly matching or randomly assigning training group members, reporting demographic variables, supplying information regarding previous informal and formal training experiences, and taking into account possible practice effects resulting from pretesting and posttesting.

Exceptions to this trend of inadequate research are seen in two recent articles which have systematically attempted to investigate the effects of various training modalities on the performance of psychiatric aides (Cook, Kunce, and Sleater 1974; Paul, McInnis, and Mariotto 1973).

In the Cook, Kunce, and Sleater (1974) study, 33 psychiatric aides were randomly assigned to participate in one of three special training program formats. These consisted of a discussion group, a combination didactic and discussion group, and a vicarious induction group. This latter innovative group was derived from learning/modeling theory and consisted of three basic steps: (1) determination of the specific behaviors and attitudes desired in the trainees; (2) selection of appropriate models to depict the development of these behaviors and attitudes via videotaped vignettes; and (3) observation of the videotapes by the trainees and discussion of their meaning.

After assignment to one of these groups, the paraprofessionals attended nine meetings, each lasting 30 minutes and extending over a two-week period. The particular content presented in these programs concerned the development of facilitative interpersonal skills (i.e., listening and attending behaviors, giving and receiving help). Evaluation and comparison of the three training modalities involved first, an appraisal of the personal reactions of both the trainees and their instructors, and second, a comprehensive assessment of the aides' competency (via rating scales by independent judges). These evaluations were made immediately at the end of the training program and following 6 weeks of actual performance on the hospital ward. Among the behaviors rated were exhibiting nonjudgmental attitudes toward the patients and consulting appropriate staff resources when needed. While there were no clear-cut differences regarding personal reactions to the three training programs, sizable differences were found in the ratings of the ward performance of the aides, with the vicarious induction (modeling) group trainees receiving the highest ratings and being significantly superior to the discussion group psychiatric aides.

Paul, McInnis, and Mariotto (1973), in a methodologically tight study, reported the training effects on two groups of paraprofessional psychiatric aides who underwent different training approaches to develop skills in milieu and social learning hospital treatment programs. The first training format consisted of a sequential/professional approach in which academic instruction was completed prior to the initiation of on-the-job clinical training, with all aspects of training being conducted by the professional staff. The second group, in contrast, was trained in an integrated/technical mode whereby a shortened form of the professionally provided academic instruction was coupled with on-the-job clinical observation.

After this initial training phase, aides then began on-the-job training which was conducted and supervised by experienced paraprofessionals, not by professional personnel. Evaluation focused on two six-week periods of clinical performance, one while still under supervision and the other when the trainees were functioning as independent certified "change agents." Numerous written and behavioral assessment procedures were utilized to evaluate the training effects of these two programs. Assessment included academic tests, attitudinal and personality measures, and extensive trainee-patient interactional ratings. Overall results of this research project and related studies (e.g., Lentz and Paul 1971) indicated that the sequential/professional group of trainees had higher academic test performance and greater understanding of principles and procedures while the integrated/technical training group had faster acquisition and, in general, better on-the-floor performance.

Both the Cook, Kunce, and Sleater (1974) and the Paul, McInnis, and Mariotto (1973) articles address themselves to the issue of types and effectiveness of various training modes. Whereas many of the previous studies in this section either explicitly or implicitly suggested that a didactic-experiential approach might be the most viable tact in nonprofessional training, only these two programs lend some solid support to this view. Specifically, these programs emphasize a type of didactic-experiential blend in which acquired knowledge is heavily reinforced with observation, very practical and concrete concepts and experiences, and frequent modeling and feedback. While there are some methodological limitations in both these articles (e.g., the lack of a nontrained aide control group), they still hold up well in providing important leads to paraprofessional training. The Paul, McInnis, and Mariotto (1973) article is but one of a series of studies which have comprehensively examined both trainee and patient outcome as a result of these particular training/therapeutic programs (for further details see Lentz and Paul 1971; Lentz, Paul, and Calhoun 1971).

Additional Issues in Paraprofessional Training

Among other concerns facing paraprofessional programs, in addition to those previously discussed, are the issues of selection and recruitment, job satisfaction, placement, appropriate utilization, and career opportunities.

Whereas many of the earlier hospital-based programs relied primarily on any available workers, recent training program efforts have increasingly concentrated on the importance of selection criteria, particularly on how the quality of the paraprofessional worker is related to training and subsequent job performance (e.g., Cochran and Steiner 1966; Goldman and Lawton 1962; Kilburn, McDole, and Smith 1970). For example, in reviewing the literature regarding attendant selection Cleland (1962) concluded that the very nature of a facility's training program may in part be determined by such considerations as the aides' intelligence, personality, and initial skills, suggesting the necessity for some preliminary screening and criteria procedures.

In addition to the acquisition of basic skills another commonly sought objective in most of the training programs discussed earlier appears to be a concomitant change in trainee aides' attitudes and feelings toward their work in general, their perceptions toward patients, and their own self-image. The implicit assumption seems to be that an essential ingredient for successful paraprofessional programs is the availability of experiences that may bolster aides' enthusiasm, level of self-esteem, feelings of confidence, and attitudes toward their work. Often these experiences have taken the form of some type of group experience such as human relations training (Mehr 1971; Pino 1971), group counseling (Felton 1973), or small unstructured ongoing group meetings (Bernstein and Herzberg 1970). Results of studies investigating this issue have, however, been somewhat conflicting.

For example, although aides have been shown to demonstrate high initial enthusiasm for their work, there is nevertheless a likelihood for positive attitudes to fade or "burn out" (Ishiyama, McCulley, and Rodriguez 1967). Similarly, despite data indicating that aides initially adopt more modern, progressive mental health attitudes (e.g., Smith 1969), other reports have failed to demonstrate such changes at follow-up subsequent to training (Pryer, Distefano, and Poe 1966; Vaughn, Teitelbaum, and Kumpan 1962). In a recent study of the effects of long-term attitudes of psychiatric aides, Perry (1974) observed a negative progression whereby the more experienced an aide, the more likely he was to evidence unfavorable (e.g., more restrictiveness and authoritarianism) attitudes.

Possible explanations of the above trend may be found in those articles examining the role concepts, career ladders, and job satisfaction of paraprofessional personnel. Baker (1972) followed 30 employed graduates from nine different degree training programs. Among the variables examined were personal data, attitudes and job satisfactions, services provided, career objectives, and obstacles encountered. Findings suggested that in general the paraprofessionals receive relatively low pay, do not have sufficient opportunity for advancement, experience some dissatisfaction with their job specifications, and perceive a lack of cooperation from traditional trained professionals. A second study further assessed this same group of paraprofessionals as well as a more recent group of graduates. Some of the same pessimistic findings were again obtained (Baker 1973).

There are important implications from these results. For example, they suggest that, regardless of whether a paraprofessional program is informal or fairly comprehensive, positive attitudes and feelings of worth and ambition will not be enhanced (and may even be discouraged) unless the trainee is provided some modicum of respect, responsibility, and career opportunities. All the T-group training available will only temporarily embellish an aide's self-esteem if he is not subsequently provided a deservedly positive environment involving true respect for his skills. Perhaps the key factor in this issue is that of professional-nonprofessional relationships and the new demands on identity, territoriality, and provided services which such interactions are creating. Such difficulties arise not only for paraprofessional workers but also for all other emerging nonprofessional personnel as they continue to join the accepted ranks of helping personnel. This important issue will be discussed in more detail later.

Fortunately, some changes are now beginning to emerge in various institutional settings (Mehr, Truckenbrod, and Fisher 1973; Vidaver 1969). The trend is for the development of competitive career ladders for capable, motivated paraprofessionals with increasing financial and occupational benefits. Such a change is imperative; otherwise these talented workers are likely to drop out of these programs, seek jobs or training in other fields, or possibly feel a need to pursue longer, more traditional mental health training. All these steps would, of course, defeat the very purpose of the paraprofessional movement—the development of a cadre of highly effective new workers to help fill the increasing void of professional services.

Summary

The following points summarize the review of paraprofessional articles.

(1) Paraprofessionals appear to be providing most of the services traditionally offered by professionals both in hospital and in community settings. Their work at this point, however, has tended to be in psychiatric settings, often dealing with adult patients while providing a variety of individual, group, or milieu counseling.

(2) The development of associate degree college-based programs has begun to heavily expand the ranks of paraprofessional personnel as well as ensure a higher level of academic and practical training. Recent graduates have emerged with either speciality or generalist skills in most areas of mental health services.

(3) While nearly all the studies reviewed in this chapter report positive results, most of these findings have been based on impressionistic or questionable data rather than on "hard facts."

(4) Only three articles dealt specifically with helpee outcome, and all reported positive results. Minimally trained paraprofessionals were reported to perform as well as, if not better than, their professional counterparts. However, various methodological drawbacks in each of these studies brought into question such generally positive conclusions.

(5) Various training strategies and techniques were also reported in the paraprofessional literature, but there was little research support either in terms of specific subsequent effects on helpees or with respect to the differential impact of particular training approaches on the paraprofessional helpers themselves. There was, however, some indication that a didactic-experiential training approach may be most viable, especially if it is practical and concrete in both content and experience and if it also includes a good deal of observation, modeling, feedback, and continued practice and further skill refinement.

(6) Additional issues with which paraprofessional programs have been concerned are selection criteria, attitude and personality changes in paraprofessionals, subsequent duties and skill utilization, career opportunities and job satisfaction, and interactions between professional and nonprofessional staff.

4 Community Agents

This group consists of the natural community caretakers discussed earlier: nonhealth and nonscience professionals such as lawyers, clergy, and teachers; community officers such as the police; and other community figures such as business executives, supervisors, and union leaders. Hartog (1967) states that this essential group is often frustrated in their training, knowledge, and supervision despite their frequent contact with front-line mental health crises.

Lawyers as Mental Health Helpers

Although it is probable that many of the issues facing clients in psychiatric settings (both in and out of the hospital) are legal in nature rather than psychological or medical, lawyers are rarely utilized as actual staff members. Instead, legal counsel tends to be sought on an occasional consultative basis for general issues (e.g., malpractice suits, hospitalization) while the day-to-day client concerns are left for social work staff to deal with (Weilhofen 1972).

This lack of close collaborative efforts between mental health and legal personnel is similarly paralleled in lawyers' general reluctance to seek psychiatric consultation. A poll conducted by Selzer and Benedek (1965) indicated that the legal profession tended to use psychiatry sparingly because of the frequently high expense to clients, the common feelings of discomfort or resentment of clients toward mental health services, and the too frequent unavailability of effective professional helping resources. In fact, there has been a vehement challenge to traditional psychiatric services for not advocating patients' rights and liberties (Ennis 1972; Ennis and Siegel 1973).

Meyer (1969) described a new program in a New York State mental hospital in which lawyers have set up offices that are accessible to patients. Issues dealt with are patient civil liberties, rights concerning involuntary commitment, property, marital problems, taxes, pensions, and drivers' licenses. Similarly, Weilhofen (1972) emphasized the importance of employing lawyers in community mental health centers (particularly if located in the inner cities) and the impact legal counselors would have for clients, administration, and the community. Client problems may be closely tied to marital, employment, financial, and housing difficulties. A lawyer would be available to offer advice regarding possible divorce, child custody and visitation rights, job discrimination, workmen's benefits, welfare rights, and unfair housing practices. A lawyer could also

27

offer information to the center staff regarding these issues and professional liabilities. In terms of the greater community, the lawyer would serve as an important link to the courts, police, other lawyers, and appropriate state legislators.

Bernstein (1974) makes a strong case for an interdisciplinary team consisting of mental health personnel and lawyers in handling marital/divorce/family problems. Specifically, he suggests that in family counseling too often the professional counselor may be faced with legal issues which transcend his expertise. Similarly, the lawyer confronting a troubled marriage should face the considerable emotional strain that separation or divorce might have for the parties involved in addition to simply dealing with the mechanics of the law. The team approach is one alternative, then, in providing a dual helping perspective to family difficulties.

The ideas generated in these few articles seem exciting and consistent with the new mental health ideology. They basically represent the attorney as being a provider of supportive mental health services for individual, family, or group of clients; a consultant for mental health and other community agencies; and as a cocounselor with fellow mental health professionals. Unfortunately, such programs cannot be evaluated for they are essentially descriptive of actual or potential helping activities. Hopefully, data will emerge in future articles that will help to evaluate the role of lawyers as mental health helpers.

Little information is provided regarding the training of these attorneys in their new mental health roles with clients and their interface with other professionals. One program was developed with the specific intention of providing selected law students with a psychiatric clerkship to develop basic mental health knowledge and interviewing skills (Clancy, Brodland, and Fahr 1972). Dissatisfied with the typical psychiatric law course as part of the basic law school curriculum, these writers outlined the development of a didactic-experiential year-long program where law students are exposed to theory and actual supervised practicum experiences as they rotate through inpatient and outpatient psychiatric services. The goals of the clerkship include the following: a basic awareness of the principles of normal and pathological human behavior; a familiarity of the methods of diagnosis and treatment; actual practice in and skill development of interviewing techniques; and facility in determining the need for referral as well as in appropriately utilizing other resources. The results of this program are reported as favorable but are based on rather gross, open-ended questionnaire data.

Clergy as Mental Health Helpers

The essential mental health role played by clergy was suggested by one survey showing that 42 percent of adults seeking help with personal problems consult a clergyman while only 18 percent visit professional mental health personnel (Gurin, Veroff, and Feld 1960). Weiner (1966) and Wagner and Dobbins (1967) obtained similar findings, particularly noting the wide variety of individuals with psychiatric problems who seek help from clergymen.

Brodsky (1968) outlined a number of features unique to the clergyman's role which help explain both these findings and lay people's reluctance to seek out traditional mental health workers. In particular, the clergyman often has an intimate familiarity with his parishioners and key people in their lives, and he can offer stigma-free assistance.

Such observations have led to a greater appreciation of the mental health care clergy provide and the increasing development of training and consultation programs to further inhance this skill (Caplan 1972; Eberdt 1970). An additional key factor influencing this expanding ministerial role has been the greater commitment of many clergy to social and political issues (i.e., race, war, poverty) and the pressing needs of the immediate community (Sata, Perry, and Cameron 1970; Sloane and Horvitz 1971; Westberg 1970). This movement toward greater secular involvement easily lends itself to new role relationships between clergy and parishioners.

Typical Mental Health Activities of the Clergy

Given the above statistics, unique role characteristics, and recent changes in ministerial ideology and practices, it is not surprising to find clergy performing such key mental health roles as individual and group psychotherapy and consultation (Brodsky 1968; Pasework, Hall, and Grice 1969).

For example, in a 10-year study of the nature of counseling services provided by a sample of clergymen, Stephan (1971) found the following: (1) clergymen were doing more counseling over the 10-year span with no changes in the particular types of problems they had been dealing with; (2) marital difficulties were the major problem area; (3) alcoholism, drug abuse, and personality disorders were the most difficult problems to counsel, yet they were also least often brought to their attention; (4) the majority of clergymen counseled with individuals rather than families or groups and perceived their theoretical approach as most consistent with client-centered therapy; and (5) most of the sample group were desirous of further mental health training experiences.

Counseling and other direct helping services are but one mental health area in which clergy have become involved. Hiltner (1972) sees another important role in ministerial consultation within psychiatric hospitals, community clinics, and other institutions. Typical consultative roles for clergy might involve training in clinical pastoral education programs, participating in multiprofessional case conferences, lending a pastoral perspective to administrative decisions, and meeting with selected individuals or groups of patients struggling with theological issues. Bruder (1971) emphasizes the consultative role as particularly that of a key liaison person to other clergymen and other groups of professionals such as physicians and teachers, as well as in developing mental health-related programs.

Current Educational and Training Trends

The goal of this section is not to concentrate on those clergy who have received training in the more formalized pastoral counseling graduate programs. Rather the emphasis is on those individuals who may not want, or have the time, to pursue formalized graduate training yet who are nevertheless desirous of becoming involved in briefer training experiences to either develop or further refine their mental health helping skills.

An article by Strom (1973) describes the historical and current developments in clinical education and training programs for clergy. The present direction appears to be traditional and dynamically based, generally emphasizing the personal and professional growth of the pastor. A problem with these programs, however, is that the needs of the patient or parishioner are not often directly considered. Strom (1973) urges that the clinical pastoral field focus on actual treatment-patient effects as well as training and educational results. Unfortunately, the clergy studies have generally not heeded suggestions such as Strom's and appear to consider helpee outcome almost incidentally while focusing more on clergy-trainee developments.

The mental health training opportunities available to interested clergy intending to develop their counseling skills have been varied. For example, clergy have participated in: a ten-week didactic and experiential program in basic community mental health principles and practices (Hammer 1965); ongoing case conference groups (Rockland 1969); weekly seminars on a variety of mental health-related topics (Mesmer et al. 1971); courses in crisis intervention (Oetting, Cole, and Adams 1969); a series of workshops in developing assessment, intervention, and referral skills (Maholick, Shapiro, and Crumbaugh 1960; Mandeville and Maholick 1969; Shapiro and Maholick 1962; Shapiro, Maholick, and Robertson 1967); and more intensive counseling training courses and fieldwork (Jansen and Garvey 1973, 1974; Jansen, Robb, and Bonk 1972; Sloane and Horvitz 1971).

The characteristics and qualifications of these ministerial trainees have also been quite diverse, ranging from fundamentalists to universalists, from lay preachers to highly educated pastors, and from individuals with minimal counseling experience or training to those with considerable clinical experience. Not only have the program participants differed, but so have their training programs. Training has taken anywhere from 3 days (Hiltner 1972) to 10 months (Hammer 1965) and has relied on any one of a variety of teaching techniques from simple case presentations (e.g., Rockland 1969) to more elaborate role-playing videotape training and supervision (e.g., Dworkin 1974).

Results of Clergy Training Programs

The eleven articles analyzed seem to be fairly representative of the types of activities, training, and evaluation reported in the literature. The major mental health thrust by clergy is that of individual intervention, which is basically provided via direct counseling skills buttressed by various supportive services. The target populations, whether in hospital or in community settings, are apt to be troubled adults or adolescent helpees rather than children, although in his natural role of caregiver/ombudsman the clergyman may serve as a multiservice resource person for the numerous problems facing all his parishioners. As evidenced in these articles, the typical counseling interventions provided by clergy are individual, group, and milieu services. Supportive duties commonly involve companion, liaison, and referral roles. The purposes of such interventions are generally for remedial goals, although Mesmer et al. (1971) suggest the value in clergy-sponsored courses and discussion groups (i.e., developmental/preventive approaches) while Hammer (1965) and Bruder (1971) see mental health benefits developing as clergy assume consulting roles.

Out of the eleven articles, eight of the training programs involved some type of didactic-experiential focus. Clergy trainees are never reported as receiving little or no training experience and being left to their own devices, as was so often the case with paraprofessionals. This is not surprising in view of the greater professional and educational status of clergy and their increasing acceptance by professionals as collaborative mental health workers.

All these articles reported positive findings. However, three of the programs reported simply descriptive impressions (Brodsky 1968; Hammer 1965; Rockland 1969) while another four described inadequately researched data (Mesmer et al. 1971; Oetting, Cole, and Adams 1969; Pasework, Hall, and Grice 1969; Shapiro, Maholick, and Robertson 1967). Another four studies achieved at least a suggestive methodological level of research, and this included the Dworkin (1974) program and a series of investigations stemming from the ongoing work of Jansen and his associates (Jansen and Garvey 1973, 1974; Jansen, Robb, and Bonk 1972).

Typical methodological problems in most of these programs include poor design, lack or insufficient use of control procedures (i.e., randomization, matching, alternative or no-training control groups, etc.), biased ratings, and questionable measures and criteria for change. For example, among the criteria used to infer the effectiveness of pastor training have been subjective feedback from participants (Rockland 1969), increased number of client contacts (Hammer 1965), and postprogram follow-up questionnaires (Mesmer et al. 1971). Only in the more methodologically sophisticated studies are multiple measures (e.g., personality tests, peer and supervisor rating, etc.) and more appropriate pretest-posttest designs employed. But even here the lack of both comparative and nontraining control groups suggests caution in interpreting the predominantly reported positive effectiveness of these training modalities. Quite possibly the reported group-measured attitudinal and behavioral changes may reflect external training program influences occurring during the training period (e.g., other coursework and helpee contact) or the differences among program participants in their demographic characteristics, personalities, and previous clinical experience and training.

The common explanation for the too frequent lack of adequate design (when assessment is even mentioned as an issue) is that practical considerations such as time and resources ruled against systematic evaluative efforts. Nevertheless, Oetting, Cole, and Adams (1969), while describing the various difficulties which may certainly arise in researching such action programs, do insist that meaningful research is still possible and, in fact, suggest a number of guidelines for such strategies.

Two ministerial training programs will now be presented and reviewed in depth as they exemplify well all the points made in the previous discussion. They typify the array of program objectives, techniques, training and research methodology, and strengths and weaknesses of many of the programs cited above.

The 15-year training program developed at the Bradley Center in Georgia is an excellent example of the professional community's recognition of the actual and potential mental health role clergy (and other caregivers) may assume as well as a creative means for meeting this training challenge (Maholick, Shapiro, and Crumbaugh 1960). The basic features of this program are: to teach caregivers such as clergy a theoretical perspective in comprehending social and psychological processes; to provide them with a standardized method for collecting comprehensive information about a person's past and present functioning; to teach them a systematic approach to organizing, summarizing, and evaluating the collected data; and to encourage them to utilize their own intervention skills or use other available resources when indicated (Shapiro, Maholick, and Robertson 1967). Actual training in counseling and interviewing techniques is limited, the focus instead being on enhancing already existing skills with the option for advanced specialized training for interested individuals.

The major emphasis of this program is on ways to pinpoint essential data presented by a troubled individual. This has been systematically achieved via the use of a brief Personal Data Kit consisting of a biographical, open-ended questionnaire, a more specific informational checklist, the Mooney Problem Check List, and the Cornell Index. Once this information has been obtained, the trainee uses a special summary form for organizing and evaluating the data so as to make appropriate judgments for intervening personally and/or making referrals. The positive results of the program have been essentially impressionistic (e.g., questionnaire), as attested to by the several articles emerging from the Bradley Center program (i.e., Maholick, Shapiro, and Crumbaugh 1960; Mandeville and Maholick 1969; Shapiro and Maholick 1962; Shapiro, Maholic, and Robertson 1967).

The data reported in these articles were based on such criteria as the highly favorable response of prospective clergy wishing to participate, the increased number of counseling activities undertaken by trainees, their greater use of referral resources, the development of preventive courses and programs by the trained clergy, and the increased communication and cooperative contacts between the clergy and other community caregivers. While this type of training package appears to be quite useful as a means for delivering new mental health tools to a variety of nonprofessional personnel, continued evaluation appears necessary. Particularly in need of further evaluation is just what type of impact the trainee graduates have on their increasing helpee contacts via their counseling or program services. In addition, follow-up data on all the above criteria might indicate whether the reported positive effects hold up over time.

Another example of an innovative ministerial training program was recently described by Dworkin (1974). This project was specifically aimed at providing inservice training so as to increase knowledge of counseling approaches and community settings, further develop empathy-listening skills, and facilitate effective peer communication and consultation. The eighteen participants in this program included eight clergy, five religious educators, and five social workers.

The program consisted of ten biweekly, 3-hour sessions; it involved an orientation to Erikson's psychosocial theories, exposure to crisis theory and intervention techniques, and introduction, discussion, and practice with transactional, behavioral, and humanistic models of counseling. The particular techniques and materials utilized in teaching the above skills were extremely varied and included role playing, empathy training, small group activities, reading handouts, and analyzing audio tapes (Dworkin 1974).

Results of the training program were derived from comparisons of the total group's pretest and posttest differences as well as individual comparisons between the clergy, professionals, and clergy educator subgroups. Dworkin (1974) reported that informal success of the program was suggested by the good turnout of participants, the high interest in the program's content and process, as well as the requests for additional training experiences. Results from the premeasures and postmeasures also suggested positive, although somewhat equivocal, trends.

The failure of clergy to significantly increase their empathic communication skills is seen by Dworkin (1974) as possibly a result of personality factors and religious training, both of which may be inhibiting to the professional and personal growth of the trainees. Before evaluating this intriguing point further, it is important to note that the Dworkin findings appear to be positive trends rather than hard results. The particular design used in this study (i.e., one group pretest-posttest) has various inherent problems, such as not having sufficient control groups. For example, apparently lacking were randomly assigned or matched comparative groups and no-treatment (training) control groups of either nonprofessionals or professionals. In addition, because of relatively small sample sizes, it is difficult to pinpoint significant subgroup differences. Also, the fact that all the participants were members of the larger, common training group makes it impossible to determine whether any significant changes were due to the actual training approach itself, and/or were a function of some interaction effect resulting from mixing professionals and nonprofessionals.

It may be concluded that clergy are providing direct mental health services akin to those offered by professionals, both in psychiatric hospitals and in community mental health agencies. Even if such services are not offered at the above type of facilities, then certainly clergy are functioning as key caregivers within their own parishes. It also appears that the helping focus, at least as depicted in these articles, is aimed primarily at troubled adolescents and adults rather than at children. However, as noted earlier, the clergyman might very well be the ombudsman for many types of troubled people in dealing with mental health or related issues.

Regardless of the target population helped, it appears that clergy are being prepared for their newer helping roles by means of a wide variety of long- and short-term training programs which generally attempt to provide both didactic and experiential techniques. Unfortunately good-quality research appears to be lacking in most of the studies. Even though the writers almost consistently report significant training effects on clergy trainees' attitudes, feelings, and acquired skills, such findings are suspect until further research is forthcoming. Lacking are studies which systematically compare the differential effects of various training modes on clergy trainees so as to delineate which combination of didactic and experiential elements comprises the best training package.

A final, and perhaps most important, problem is that none of these articles systematically assessed the subsequent outcome of these training programs in terms of the actual impact clergy have had on their helpee recipients. While these reports certainly discuss the numerous mental health roles of clergy and presumably the effectiveness of these activities, these statements are not supported by research findings. Rather, these investigations have focused more on the effectiveness of training on the participants than on the subsequent effect on troubled people. This is particularly unfortunate since the ultimate question concerning nonprofessional clergy work (i.e., are they indeed effective helpers?) remains essentially unanswered.

Despite the recognition that professionals are increasingly according clergy for both traditional and newer helping roles, the research supporting this optimism is at best equivocal, buttressed by essentially subjective, albeit enthusiastic, support. Certainly, this highly regarded workforce source will continue to be utilized and trained regardless of the questionable results of a few studies. However, future sophisticated research would clarify the most viable training models for clergy trainees. It could provide a more precise picture as to what mental health services they are best equipped to deliver.

Personality Traits of Clergy and Pastoral Training

An issue raised in the Dworkin (1974) study was whether certain factors inherent in the clergy's very makeup and role were counterproductive to effective mental health training and later performance. Traditionally, clergy have been typed as being somewhat authoritarian, dogmatic, and rigid and not as evidencing those personal liberal qualities presumably shared by mental health practitioners (Mason, Holt, and Newsome 1969). For example, an important question is whether clergy can be open, flexible, and accepting of a given helpee's values and beliefs particularly when these might be strongly in contrast to the clergy's own moral and value system. Such freedom and tolerance would seem to be an essential ingredient in successful mental health endeavors.

Various empirical investigations have yielded generally conflicting results. Two earlier studies, for example, failed to find significant differences between clergy and counselors in training on various personality and attitudinal measures (Mason, Holt, and Newsome 1969; Phillips 1970). An article by Naftulin, Donnelly, and Wolkon (1974) similarly found that those clergy who become mental health trainees tend to have personality traits or attitudes (i.e., low levels of rigidity and authority) which are quite consistent with counseling interests. Williams and Kremer (1974) compared the values and beliefs of 90 secular counseling students with those of 58 pastoral counseling students. Although results did indicate that the clergy trainees were more dogmatic, less open, and less flexible, they nevertheless responded at a higher level of client acceptance than secular trainees.

Jansen and Garvey (1974) criticize studies such as these for their failure to make appropriate use of actual measures of counseling competency and for the lack of any evaluation of the clinical skills of clergy in comparison with other groups of counselor trainees. The research has focused more on attitudinal and belief differences which may or may not have relevance to subsequent performances. Jansen and his colleagues have conducted research comparing clergy and secular counseling trainees who were rated by supervisors and peers as high, average, or low in clinical competence. Overall results indicated various intellectual and personality differences with clergymen apparently more similar to those counselors rated lower in competence by their peers than to counselors rated higher in competence (Jansen and Garvey 1973, 1974; Jansen, Robb, and Bonk 1972).

There are many unanswered questions regarding the effects of pastoral personality and training on subsequent clinical performance. Perhaps more studies of the Jansen and Garvey (1973) variety, which specifically begin to examine actual helping competency, will clarify the issue.

Additional Training Issues

The success of any of these programs, either during or following training, also appears to be strongly contingent upon (1) whether the clergyman is able to accept his new secular mental health position and (2) whether other mental health professionals really feel comfortable with this new brand of counselor (e.g., Sloane and Horvitz 1971). Clergy must work out for themselves how their new counselor role fits with their traditional spiritual-religious training and function. Coming to terms with this duality of role necessitates a clear, perhaps painful, examination of one's values, beliefs, and mission (Bentz 1968; Brodsky 1968; Scarlett 1970).

Similarly, for fruitful collaboration between clergy and professionals to occur, there must be both an awareness of their mutually overlapping functions as well as an appreciation of the different perspectives and skills each legitimately offers (Brodsky 1968; Nelson and Torrey 1973; Streeter and Owens 1970; Wilson 1973). Of note is the fact that these issues of identity and relationship with mental health professionals are two key problem areas experienced by the paraprofessional personnel discussed in Chapter 3. It thus appears that important elements in successful nonprofessional mental health work involve feeling comfortable with this new role as well as being accepted by professional personnel.

School Personnel as Mental Health Helpers

The Joint Commission on the Mental Health of Children (1970) emphasized that only about one-third of the children in need of psychiatric care are receiving even minimal clinical services. Given these alarming figures, it is not surprising that there is a heightened awareness of the need for upgrading mental health services in schools (e.g., Cowen, Gardner, and Zax 1967) and the realization that a preventive approach at the school level may be the only meaningful way to deal with the spiraling incidence of emotional problems (Schulman et al. 1973b). Preventive programs can be implemented readily in school settings since various aspects of youngsters' growth and development can be monitored and manipulated over a period of years (Stringer 1973a). Historically school systems have been involved with preventive health measures such as physical checkups, compulsory dental care, and immunizations (Schulman, Ford, and Busk, 1973).

By virtue of their extensive contact with the children the key figures in any school mental health program must be classroom teachers. They can have a pervasive influence by their impact on their pupils' attitudes, emotions, and behaviors. They also have the ability to successfully carry out various mental health-related interventions on an ongoing basis (e.g., Biller 1974; Davis and Mann 1973; Guerney and Flumen 1970; Stringer 1973b).

Increasing professional attention has focused on various consultative and training avenues through which to enhance the already existing helping ability of teachers as well as provide them with new mental health skills (e.g., Berlin 1965a; Davis and Mann 1973; Grundle, Emiley, and Webb 1973; Myrick and Moni 1972a; Weissman and Steward 1973). Traditionally mental health professionals may have been called in to deal directly with problem children confronting a given teacher. Currently, there is beginning to be more of a consultation focus toward teachers. This involves a continuum of aiding teachers to deal themselves directly with problem children, providing a given teacher or group of teachers with certain skills to handle other currently or potentially difficult children, and developing learning and growth experiences for teachers in which they explore their own attitudes and interactions with pupils as well as learn particular facilitative skills that may be conducive to effective interactions with healthy as well as problematic children. Apparent in this continuum is the utilization of teaching personnel in a variety of possible helping roles ranging from direct services to preventive programs.

Many articles have dealt with the traditional deficits in teacher training, and they reflect an exciting trend in inservice opportunities for educators. Their general aim is to increase teachers' understanding of the meaning of pupils' classroom activities as well as affect their responses and reactions to them. Teachers have been involved in mental health training experiences involving sex education and awareness (Bennett, Taylor, and Ford 1969), case conference discussion groups (Gordon 1967; Oxhorn 1965), workshops in teacher and student psychodynamics (Cozzarelli and Silin 1974; Laemmel 1969), group process and sensitivity training (Beach, Levine, and Goldberg 1973; Grossman and Clark 1967), listening workshops (Crabbs 1972), achievement motivation development (Alschuler, Tabor, and McIntyre 1971), and intensive human relations training (Gazda et al. 1973).

While nearly all these programs reported highly favorable results, most of these articles are of a descriptive nature with only two evidencing a research level sufficient to warrant some positive conclusions; but even these are relatively weak from an empirical perspective (Beach, Levine, and Goldberg 1973; Bennett, Taylor, and Ford 1969). Although the teaching levels of trainees involved in these programs have run the gamut from nursery through high school, they most typically are based in elementary schools. The depth and extent of the programs themselves have varied with training experiences ranging from 1 hour 15 minutes (Crabbs 1972) to two-year ongoing weekly seminars

(Gordon 1967). Of note is that regardless of the actual structure of these programs, they have tended to focus primarily on experiential or combined didactic-experiential formats. Typical tools utilized have included lecturettes, case discussions, films, role playing, and small group exercises.

The general goals for teacher trainees inherent in all the above programs have involved self-understanding and personal growth, actual skill acquisition, the development of a group identity and support system, and the comfortable acceptance of a legitimate mental health helping role.

Client-Centered Training for Teachers

A more focused program has been developed for teachers whereby participants are trained and supervised in client-centered play therapy to work with underachieving and withdrawn children (Guerney and Flumen 1970). Teachers (or students or parents) learn the basis of Rogerian therapy, examine techniques of play therapy, observe demonstrations by trainers, practice these skills themselves with children, and receive supervisory feedback from trainers and other group participants (Guerney 1964; Andronico and Guerney 1967).

Andronico and Guerney (1967) emphasized the necessity of adopting such didactic-experiential training programs. Mental health professionals currently working in school systems are much too overloaded with administrative and clinical responsibilities to adequately meet the many demands facing teachers. Appropriately trained and supervised educators might just as well provide the desperately needed direct counseling services to students.

Guerney and Flumen (1970) trained and supervised 11 elementary school teachers to be client-centered play therapists. Trainees received about 20 weeks of instruction with 1½-hour meetings covering the presentation of theory, demonstration, practice, feedback, and participation in actual play sessions prior to beginning the therapy program.

Each teacher had previously chosen two children from the classroom who were considered either withdrawn or unassertive, and these pupils were subsequently randomly assigned to either an experimental treatment (4 boys, 5 girls) or nontreatment (4 boys, 2 girls) control group. Treatment sessions were conducted weekly for 45-minute meetings for 14 sessions over 17 weeks. The criterion for student change consisted of an objective coding system for evaluating classroom behavior.

Trained raters assessed pupils and teachers according to behavioral criteria, and the results showed a significant rise in the assertiveness of the experimental group of students, but no such change was evident for the similarly withdrawn control group pupils. Guerney and Flumen (1970) also reported a significant correlation between the degree of pupils' assertiveness and their teacher's therapeutic role performance. The investigators suggested that this was indicative of the specific therapy intervention by the teacher. Furthermore, they noted that of the four components comprising assertive behavior, the greatest change was seen in student-student interactions, which suggested a general improvement in a given child's behavior and not one just limited to the teacher-student counseling relationship.

While this study is methodologically superior to any of the previous articles so far reviewed in this section, a number of questions arise which need additional consideration before one can draw any definitive conclusions. For example, how do we know without attention-placebo or other treatment control groups whether the reported rise in student assertiveness was really a function of client-centered counseling and not simply a reflection of the special individualized attention these teachers were providing their withdrawn pupils? Specific control groups appear to be needed to tease out just what elements in the teacher-student relationship facilitated the obvious positive gains achieved by the experimental pupils.

Further controls are also needed to examine teachers' general in-class behavior aside from their counseling roles. Outside- and inside-classroom teacher behaviors are very likely not separate influences affecting the behavior of the child. Presumably we are dealing with teachers who have been trained in new therapeutic skills and attitudes that do not suddenly disappear following a teacher's individual counseling session, but rather are attributes which to some degree are apt to be evident in their overall classroom functioning. The experimental group child may be receiving a combination of helping interventions including individual counseling *and* a healthier classroom atmosphere. Such a possibility might help explain why the experimental and control groups in the study were not dramatically different in terms of overall changes; it might be that the control group pupils were not really devoid of any treatment but were in fact benefiting from a more mentally healthy classroom situation. Additional research is indicated in both the particular counseling meetings and the classroom environment itself to determine more specifically what helping elements actually facilitated the apparent growth of the experimental children.

The high interest level expressed by trainees and their apparently easy acquisition of the requisite skills might be especially attributable to the particular didactic-experiential training mode used in teaching filial therapy principles. The training format involves concretely breaking down the skill into its component parts, viewing ample demonstrations of the desired behavior which are later rehearsed, receiving intensive individual and group feedback regarding performance level, and subsequently further practicing and refining these skills until an acceptable competency is achieved. This approach is almost exactly the same as the didactic-experiential training model noted in Chapter 3 that was reported as probably being the most viable vehicle for paraprofessional mental health training (e.g., Paul, McInnis, and Mariotto 1973).

Teachers as Behavior Modifiers

Teachers are also increasingly becoming involved in behavior modification training in dealing with particular problem children, around the overall enrichment of their classrooms, or in some form of general inservice training to acquire new skills for either current or future application. The upsurge of interest in this approach stems from the very real need of teachers for concrete and effective measures for coping with large numbers of children exhibiting learning and behavior problems. The recent flood of behavior modification training manuals for educators attests to the wide application being made of this approach in the classroom (e.g., Carter 1972; Homme et al. 1970; Lundell 1972; Neisworth, Deno, and Jenkins 1973; Palumbo and Kurtz 1973; Patterson and Gullion 1968; Sheppard, Shank, and Wilson 1972; Smith and Smith 1966; Vernon 1972; Wiener 1972; Zifferblatt 1970).

Altman and Linton (1971) see three major reasons why teachers and classrooms are ideal targets for behavioral approaches. (1) Classrooms traditionally have been the place where a good deal of a child's academic and social behavior has been modified. (2) Teachers have always been functioning as behavior modifiers using a variety of contingency sanctions (such as praise, grades, punishment) except they have been generally unaware that these principles can have real impact if used in a more consistent and deliberate fashion. (3) These techniques offer much promise for the possible prevention of the types of problem behaviors that have usually led to later special class placement and eventual rejection by the school system.

Inservice workshops have been aimed at training teachers in such areas as basic learning principles, behavioral analysis, classroom observation, control techniques such as contingency management and token reinforcement, and the skills to be resource people for other teachers seeking behavioral management assistance (e.g., Andrews 1970; Halfacre and Welch 1973; Hall 1971a; McNamara and Diehl 1974; Madsen et al. 1970; Martin 1973; Snow and Brooks 1974).

Generally, in using a combined didactic-experiential focus, these programs intend to quickly provide teachers with a variety of conceptual and practical tools in behavior modification. These programs have usually dealt with a relatively small number of trainees who are expected during the workshop to actually apply these new skills. Typically a variety of concrete behavioral observations are taken by trained raters of both the teachers' and pupils' in-class behaviors and often of the interactions between the two. Usually the intervention sequence involves taking a baseline (i.e., current level of functioning), then instituting some behavioral program, after which new observations are taken to see if there are any changes according to the observed criteria.

Most of these programs are at a suggestive research level and report positive findings indicating that teaching personnel can easily acquire the tools and principles of behavior modification and can effectively apply these skills within their classrooms. However, experimental controls are occasionally lacking. For example, there is often an absence of untrained-teacher comparison groups which would provide a control for nontraining/intervention effects on both teachers and pupils. Madsen et al. (1970) did employ experimental and control groups and found that behaviorally trained teachers increased their positively reinforcing behavior (with a resulting decrease in negative student behavior) more than was evident in a matched control group of teachers.

Also in need of further empirical attention are studies directly comparing different approaches to training teachers in behavior modification principles. While all the above programs generally have the same goals, the particular format utilized tends to differ (i.e., content, time, exercises, practice, etc.), and the question arises as to which approach might be most effective and efficient. Fortunately, recent work on comparative effects of differential behavior modification training of teachers has begun to appear in the literature (see McNamara and Diehl 1974).

School-Based Behavior Modification Programs

Whereas the previous section dealt with programs primarily concerned with preparing teachers for behavior modification work, the present section deals with the more usual type of study, namely, where the emphasis is not on training but rather on the application of behavior modification principles. That is, after some minimal and brief preparation, teachers are then dealing with specific child/classroom situations. The literature is replete with case studies in which teachers have used various behavioral approaches (usually under the guidance and supervision of professionals) to handle a wide range of problems in the classroom.

Typical examples of specific situations where behavioral programs have been successfully applied are with educationally handicapped children exhibiting poor self-control and low frustration tolerance (Stiavelli and Shirley 1968); self-destructive, blind, and retarded adolescents (Greene and Hoats 1971); emotionally disturbed boys with learning and behavior problems (Zimmerman and Zimmerman 1962); and disruptive children in normal elementary school classes (Becker et al. 1967).

An earlier review by Altman and Linton (1971) did critique and integrate relevant studies, and their conclusions are applicable to any of the current crop of teacher-based behavioral programs. These reviewers divided the available research into several areas of behavior modification work that had been conducted within the classroom setting. These included teacher attention effects, token reinforcement, and vicarious reinforcement.

Studies dealing with teacher attention effects have systematically examined such variables as positive and negative attention and its concomitant effects on student behavior. Altman and Linton (1971) concluded that the available research sufficiently demonstrated that positive attention from the teacher does significantly affect behavior while teacher disapproval (verbal or physical) may either serve as a reinforcement of the negative behavior or have no effect on the classroom behavior upon which it is made contingent.

Token reinforcement is defined here as the use of tangible objects or symbols (e.g., stars) which may be exchanged for a variety of other objects (e.g., candy, privileges) and serve to increase positive behaviors. Altman and Linton (1971) found too few studies which have systematically investigated the effects of token reinforcements, but what they did find demonstrated generally positive results, suggesting a largely untapped resource for behavior modification classroom work.

Vicarious reinforcement or *modeling effects* refers to the increase of target behaviors as a result of one pupil observing another student being rewarded for that same behavior. Altman and Linton (1971) failed to find enough adequate research to make a final judgment on the viability of vicarious reinforcement approaches within the classroom.

The research examining teacher attention effects and use of token reinforcement principles demonstrates that educators can become effective contingency managers in a variety of settings. Certainly more research is needed in these areas to further substantiate this conclusion. What seems most required are future studies systematically including attention-placebo or other intervention control groups as well as nontreatment control groups.

What particularly seems to facilitate teachers becoming effective behavioral helpers is their apparent ease in grasping the principles and acquiring the necessary skills. A primary factor for the success of a classroom behavior modification program is gaining the trust and cooperation of teachers and demonstrating to them that behavioral control measures can be quite consistent with their humanistic philosophy and approach to teaching (Cote 1973; Hall 1971a; Smith 1973).

Teachers and Mental Health Curricula

An exciting trend in school intervention which utilizes the teacher in a greater preventive role is seen by the numerous attempts to develop curricula and programs in psychological and human relations training within the classroom (Levine and Graziano 1972). School courses can be evaluated for their detrimental or therapeutic effects on students' emotional growth (Ashbaugh 1965), and basic coursework in mental health principles can be added to even the elementary school curriculum (Roen 1967).

The focus is increasingly on teachers as the most appropriate change agents to provide such experiences. Presumably little necessary preparation or supervision by professionals is needed, provided that the programs are easily understandable and enjoyable by both teachers and their pupils (Levine and Graziano 1972; Peck 1967).

Such programs are highly experimental in nature, dealing with a variety of areas such as effective listening and communicating, identifying and expressing feelings, small group processes, self-concept, friendship, honesty, fear, and relations to adults (Borton 1969; Gerler 1973; Lombardo 1968; Nadler 1973; Van Camp 1973; Schulman, Ford, and Busk 1973; Schulman et al. 1973a). A variety of techniques have been utilized in teaching children mental health concepts such as group and individual discussions and experiential exercises, plays and role playing, audiovisual aids and filmstrips (e.g., Haak 1972; Nadler 1973; Myrick and Moni 1972b, 1972c; Van Camp 1973).

For example, Gerler (1973) describes the Magic Circle program, consisting of a group of eight to ten pupils and their teachers, all of whom are seated in a circle with a variety of issues and feelings to discuss. Every Magic Circle session lasts 20 minutes, and the objectives and nature of the program are related to increasing awareness of feelings, self-confidence, and social interaction. Teachers can apparently learn the Magic Circle technique easily. Their major goals are to model the essential sharing and listening skills, provide each child who wants to talk with the opportunity to express something, and facilitate interpersonal communication among the group members. Positive outcomes from such programs have been reported, but these efforts have tended to be anecdotal or of rather limited research value (e.g., Limbacher 1967; Lombardo 1968).

Somewhat better evaluative efforts have evolved from the work of Schulman and his associates, who have developed a series of teacher-taught educational materials that promote knowledge of and experience with a variety of mental health concepts while experimenting with individual and group interaction (e.g., Schulman, Ford, and Busk 1973; Schulman et al. 1973a). Typical units have ranged from six to twelve lessons and have focused on such personality aspects as friendship, honesty, self-concept, fear, and relationships with adults. Since this approach requires very little teacher preparation, children are easily included in in-class and out-of-school assignments involving small group discussions, role playing, written work, and film clips.

In one study, twenty experimental and eighteen control classrooms in the fourth, sixth, and eighth grades were given presociometric and postsociometric tests to determine the impact of the friendship unit. Results indicated that fourth-grade experimental classrooms, and experimental boys in the sixth and eighth grades, achieved significant gains in mutual friendship (Schulman et al. 1973a). These writers recognize the need for more adequately researching such programs but conclude that their work suggests that educators can provide an important mental health function.

Another related program is the Developing Understanding of Self and Others (DUSO) project developed by Dinkmeyer (1970) to promote a positive self-concept and feelings of adequacy in children. The DUSO materials include problem-solving experiences, puppetry, music, and role playing, all geared for facilitating a child's awareness of himself and others. A recent study by Eldridge, Barcikowski, and Witmer (1972) investigated the effects of a teacher-led DUSO program on second-grade children and utilized various measures of self-concept. While not all the instruments were sensitive to changes in self-concept, some did suggest a significant difference in self-concept for children who participated in the DUSO programs, with a group of experimental children scoring more positively than a control group. However, important methodological defects such as an inappropriate design and improper use of prescales and postscales, dampen the positive findings reported in this study.

Continuing basic research is particularly indicated for evaluating the effects of these programs on both teachers and students. If Levine and Graziano (1972) are correct in their contention that mental health curricula development can have the most far-reaching preventive effects within the school system, then it seems imperative that further programs of this nature be developed along with well-controlled research studies.

A key issue in the success of such programs is the capacity of the teacher to effectively implement these projects (Long 1974). Levine and Graziano (1972) contend that such curricula may be worthless unless carried out by sensitive and skilled teachers. Of note is the fact that in most of the programs there was apparently little time spent on selection and training of teaching personnel, the assumption probably being that the materials could carry themselves, buttressed with some informal preparation and supervision. This is really an empirical issue, and research might systematically evaluate the specific interaction effects of various teacher personalities and styles, mental health curricula, and subsequent outcome effects on the children. It may well be, for example, that certain types of educators might be better suited for more structured curriculum experiences while other teachers might be particularly effective in providing more open-ended programming. Such empirical questions are important, for even though generally untrained teachers are reported as effectively providing mental health curricula programs, a review of these studies demonstrated somewhat questionable research results.

Borton (1969) discussed other pertinent professional and ethical considerations. Specifically, he sees a basic problem in such studies concerning the inherent expectation that the students' uncovered feelings will be sensitively handled by both other students and the teachers. Borton suggests that, to avoid difficult problems, teachers not involve students in emotional areas where they are not personally comfortable and not push students to disclose anything they might be reluctant to reveal. This would appear to be an essential issue in the mental health curriculum programming area. It is hoped that further program efforts will consider this issue more carefully and also examine other important variables such as teacher selection, training, and supervision.

Other School-Related Personnel as Helpers

In addition to teachers, there are other available allied school personnel who may also serve mental health helping roles. Among these are student teachers (Campbell 1967), school administrators, principals (Carlson 1972; Lykke 1972), and librarian-counselors (Kelly and Midgette 1972).

Carlson and Pietrofesa (1971) suggested a trilevel guidance structure within the school setting so as to maximize available helping resources. This is essentially a "guidance team" consisting of professional mental health workers, guidance workers, and paraprofessionals, each differing in terms of educational background, training, and role requirements. As conceived here, the professional would primarily provide direct counseling and consultation; the guidance worker would function as a support person assisting the professional in various indirect services; the paraprofessional would serve more like a teacher's aide, performing any auxiliary paper and clerical duties while possibly assisting in school-community relations and home visits.

This model attempts to systematically employ a wide range of caregivers within the school setting, but it is limited in that it minimizes the depth of helping skills that can be acquired by these educated and trained personnel. Later chapters will show how individuals such as retired people (e.g., Cowen, Leibowitz, and Leibowitz 1968) and volunteer homemakers (e.g., Terrell, McWilliams, and Cowen 1972; Zax et al. 1966) have directly intervened with emotionally disturbed children in school.

Results of School Personnel Helping Programs

Although most of the studies relevant to the previous discussion on the use of teachers as mental health personnel have been reviewed and critiqued, the present section will reemphasize certain aspects of the findings. While some work has been done with individual children (e.g., in behavior modification and client-centered therapy), most of the work has been concerned with the overall classroom environment. The goals have been more developmental and preventive in purpose rather than aimed at direct remediation. This is consistent with the less clinical and more supportive posture being assumed by teachers as they are endeavoring to create healthy classroom situations.

Some programs have described teachers providing behavioral or client-centered counseling skills. More work, however, is being developed in which educators are providing indirect support and preventive services. Thus, if teachers do not treat problematic situations directly, they may at least effectively diagnose problems before they erupt or know when to make appropriate referrals. Some of the most exciting services teachers are currently providing are through mental health types of curricula. Such programs ideally will promote the personal and behavioral growth of students, while possibly enriching the lives and preventing further deterioration of problematic children. Quite possibly such curricula will be diagnostic in pinpointing vulnerable children who may need either additional work by the teacher or the services of other qualified resource people.

Although nearly 60 percent of the studies reviewed achieve at least a suggestive empirical rating, their findings are still equivocal enough to draw somewhat guarded conclusions about the efficacy and real impact of teachers as helpers. Training has tended to combine didactic and experiential features. Where there has been more emphasis on lecturing and discussion, this has involved behavioral management training. The only area where teachers have received little or no formal preparation for their helping tasks has been in mental health curricula development work.

Summary

Teachers have been increasingly involved in a variety of mental health training or related activities aimed at fostering self-growth and knowledge as well as providing new skills that may be applied in the classroom. While such activities reported as subjectively rewarding and effective for teachers, little adequate research has been done (e.g., lack of other treatment, attention-placebo, and nontreatment control groups). Further investigations are needed to clarify the best training approaches, and the subsequent outcome and endurance of program effects on both teachers' and students' functioning.

Teachers have been trained in client-centered therapy techniques and reportedly have provided effective help to withdrawn children. At this point only one study systematically investigated the efficacy of teachers providing such direct services; and, as was pointed out above, various methodological problems in this study preclude clear-cut conclusions. Additional studies are needed to carefully examine variables such as method of training, comparative effects of professionals and nonprofessionals, and the possibility of applying this approach to the overall classroom rather than to specific children.

Behavior modification training is another area in which teachers have been increasingly involved. Most of the articles reviewed here described both the easy acquisition by teachers of behavioral skills and their effective application of these tools within the classroom. But, as is the case with general training workshops and client-centered training, good research in this area is rather scarce, with much of the research having insufficient controls and questionable methodology. While the available data certainly point to the effectiveness of teachers as successful behavioral engineers, further research is needed to more fully understand the specific variables involved. Particularly promising areas for further study concern teacher attention effects and token economy approaches.

Also needed are comparative training studies which examine the best approach to teaching educators behavioral principles.

Regardless of the presumably vast differences between the behavioral and client-centered schools of therapy, the training of teachers in both these approaches was nevertheless quite similar. Both involve first clearly defining and discussing the desired skill, breaking it down, modeling it, practicing it, evaluating it, and then refining it. Perhaps, then, regardless of the particular content or philosophy inherent in a training program, the vehicles through which these principles are presented and learned might be basically the same. There is again support for some type of didactic-experiential training model as being a general approach for all types of nonprofessional training—regardless of the particular target skills involved.

Perhaps teachers interested in the mental health area are becoming most involved in providing psychological education within the classroom. From a preventive perspective, this appears to be the most exciting and innovative helping role for teachers. While there have been some reasonable research attempts in support of this type of helping endeavor, much of the work in this area has tended to be anecdotal. Aside from further researching the actual short-term and long-term effects on the children participating in these programs, issues of teacher selection, supervision, and training must also be dealt with.

Ultimately the efficacy of teacher helping effectiveness must rest with the actual effects of the program on the children regardless of whether the intervention utilized is behavioral, client-centered, or psychological education. The tightest, most well-designed training programs will only answer how well teachers acquire or implement particular skills, not how effective they ultimately are. Unfortunately, many of the articles reviewed here totally neglect, informally discuss, or poorly evaluate the pupil outcome issue. There were four studies that were of at least a suggestive research level and that did specifically examine student outcome effects. These articles have already been reviewed and critiqued, and the point was made that despite their positive findings and relatively superior empirical efforts, more and better research is needed to systematically evaluate training and outcome effects.

Police as Mental Health Helpers

The numerous mental health functions provided by police are increasingly being recognized by the professional community. In fact, it is estimated that between 80 and 90 percent of police officers' work does not involve law enforcement, but rather deals with individual, family, and community problems (Bard 1971a; Bard and Berkowitz 1967; Cumming, Cumming, and Edel 1965; Kadish 1966; Shane 1974; Whittington, 1971).

The police are increasingly placed in this role since they are the major public agency open 24 hours a day, 7 days a week. People in severe emotional crises can quickly turn to them without a fear of waiting lists and long evaluations (Barocas 1972). Available evidence has documented this trend, showing that a high percentage of disturbed individuals and their families (as well as their physicians, employers, lawyers, or friends) make some contact with police along the route to the state hospital because other possibly more appropriate resources are unknown, unavailable, or unwilling to get involved with the troubled person, particularly if he is reluctant about hospitalization (Bittner 1967; Bard and Berkowitz 1967; Cumming 1962; Ephross and French 1972; Liberman 1969).

A variety of programs have been recently developed that are aimed at establishing collaborative relationships between police and mental health facilities. Such endeavors may be successful, however, only if consulting professionals do the following: (1) recognize the numerous potential problems inherent in entering the police system; (2) familiarize themselves thoroughly with police roles and functions (Mann 1971; Reiser 1970); (3) implement any subsequent involvement or training programs with a sensitivity to the authoritarian and hierarchical nature of the organization (Kadish 1966), the need for a reciprocal, respectful relationship (Beigel 1973; Friedman 1965), and the development of programs whose content is concretely action-oriented and applicable to actual police work (Friedman 1965; Kadish 1966; Matthews and Rowland 1960).

General Mental Health Training Approaches

Once such considerations are dealt with, it is then possible for mental health facilities to generate meaningful relationships between themselves and law enforcement agencies. Such an interface is being spurred on particularly by the awareness that the mental health and behavioral science training of the police has been abysmally limited. Whittington (1971) urged that mental health centers need to approach law enforcement in a comprehensive way, addressing such essential issues as selection and training of police officers, providing facilities for the study and modification of disordered behavior, including police in community planning, and consulting with police concerning social problems. A pioneering mental health program involving police was described by Friedman (1965). Clinic representatives met with a group of police officers for a series of 2-hour seminar meetings extending over a 5-week period. The sessions were primarily didactic in nature, utilizing a series of films (on pathology, delinquency, suicide, and aggression) followed by discussion periods.

Mann (1971) outlined a more extensive project in which a mental health center was active in offering a variety of services to an urban police department. For example, the center's 24-hour emergency telephone service was made available to any police officers needing assistance and advice. Another facet of the program involved 8 to 10 hours of training for a small group of police recruits in techniques for recognizing disordered behavior and then making appropriate referrals. Subsequent endeavors involved inservice training for command-level officers, human relations training for the police and various community groups, and program planning for incorporating psychological knowledge into the regular law enforcement training curricula.

A particularly ambitious program was developed by Rolde and his associates (Rolde et al. 1973) for the training of thirty participants representing ten different law enforcement agencies. The unique aspect of this program was that unlike the other projects which focused primarily on police officers, this program also included probation and parole officers. With the general goal of increasing understanding, communication, and cooperation among these types of law enforcement officers and other community agencies, the training groups met every other week for about a year, each session lasting for 2 or 3 hours. Since the primary focus was on youth and delinquency problems, various relevant guest agencies participated each week, the first half of the meeting being devoted to presentations by these guest speakers and the second half consisting of intensive small group meetings including both community agency staff and law enforcement officers.

Community settings are not the only areas where mental health and law enforcement facilities are attempting to develop working relationships. Similar collaborative efforts are being considered for more specialized minicommunities, such as the college campus. Kramer and Barr (1974) described a training model for meeting the special needs of the campus security force at Cornell University. A survey had revealed that these police officers needed assistance and training in the same areas as their counterparts in local community enforcement agencies. Kramer and Barr developed a program geared for facilitating both the personal growth and the actual skill development of the trainees. The three major areas considered were general education and personal development (e.g., listening and interviewing skills), development and maintenance of communication skills (e.g., ways of opening channels of communication within the university), and community building activities (e.g., talks by officers in academic classes). Among various training techniques utilized in this program were instructional skill modules, discussion and/or learning groups, and video and audio tape programs. The entire program appears to have balanced didactic and experiential features with much of the emphasis being on practical training and a learning-by-doing format.

The above four programs should help to provide an adequate picture of the types of interactions occurring between law enforcement and mental health agencies. They demonstrate general approaches by clinics in helping police officers recognize and enhance their mental health helping skills as well as becoming familiar with the relevant services offered by other caregiving agencies. An essential ingredient in these programs is that this collaboration is not a one-way process, but rather a mutually accepting relationship whereby professionals also spend a considerable amount of time learning about the police officer's world, role, and skills.

All the accounts of these programs were descriptive, with no objective data to back up favorable impressions. Positive outcome was often based on such general criteria as numbers of trainees attending and completing the program. That positive effects are indeed being achieved is certainly suggested by the high enthusiasm law enforcement agencies displayed during and following these programs. This is particularly striking since the police officer is considered one of the more difficult community caretakers with whom one could form a meaningful consultative relationship. The goal of these studies was to carefully describe the important rapport building process so essential for mental health professionals entering the law enforcement system. Once such admittance had been achieved, rather innovative training approaches were then devised for personal growth, skill-building, and interagency cooperative efforts.

Police and Human Relations Training

Whereas the previously described programs were of a broader scope, the projects that are discussed in this section are more focused in nature, providing training in a more specialized area—human relations training for improving community relationships. Typically called sensitivity or T-group training programs, their major objective is enhancing the police officer's knowledge, attitudes, and behavioral repertoire. Many of the techniques described earlier may be incorporated into human relations training, but the major focus is experiential, on the "here and now." Particular techniques utilized tend to be small group discussion sessions, a variety of verbal and nonverbal exercises, and much focused feedback and role playing.

The tremendous social unrest within the last ten years, particularly in the inner cities, has necessitated some type of planned cooperative effort among community members. The increasing tension between community residents and police in particular demanded some means by which members of these two groups could work out some reasonable dialogue and mutual understanding.

To counteract such tension in the community, a variety of human relations programs have been developed, all following some type of sensitivity training model with differences apparently stemming from the particular needs of the given community (e.g., Allen, Pilnick, and Silverzweib 1969; Bell et al. 1969; Jones 1972; Sikes and Cleveland 1968; Talbott and Talbott 1971).

Despite the positive results reported for these programs, the findings are really suspect because of the general lack of adequate experimental procedures. It is impossible to determine whether positive effects are actually due to the training program or to some other outside, uncontrolled influences. Similarly, there is no way of knowing just what features of the training program were actually facilitative of the reported changes. For example, were specific techniques (e.g., role playing) particularly helpful or was some combination of techniques most effective? Finally, although these articles described some criteria (however vague) for change during the program, little follow-up information is presented as to the short- and long-term subsequent program effects. Specifically, what are the nature and duration of any changes evidenced by the community member and police program participants?

A somewhat better (although still methodologically weak) research effort is seen in the human relations program developed by Lipsitt and Steinbruner (1969). This report also typifies this kind of training program in terms of goals and format. These investigators studied the effectiveness of small-group discussion meetings in reducing tension and facilitating appropriate interaction between a group of Boston ghetto residents and police officers. Two 15-member groups comprised of police and community members met once a week for 2½- to 3-hour sessions over a period of 12 weeks. Evaluation was based on three sets of data consisting of the content analysis of written logs of the meetings, a set of preproject and postproject attitude scales (i.e., community identification and authoritarianism), and a subjective assessment of personal experiences during the program.

The researchers reported that initially hostile participants developed increased understanding and empathy and became more willing to constructively interact with others. This optimistic outcome was not buttressed by well-researched facts. The design, lack of control, nature and measurement of dependent variables, possible rater bias, and lack of follow-up are but a few of the methodological shortcomings in this project warranting caution in interpreting the results.

Proponents of human relations programs typically argue that good objective evaluation of such projects is contraindicated because of the practical limitations such action projects engender. For example, these programs usually arise out of immediate emotional needs and deal with serious current or potential community conflicts. There is little time in such crisis circumstances to design tight research as well as come up with the costs and related resources that might be needed. Another issue raised in explaining the lack of adequate empiricism is one of confidentiality and rapport. Most participants entering these programs are usually apprehensive and suspicious either of members of the "opposing faction" or of the project as a whole. A problem in conducting good research is that it is often hard to win the respect and trust of program participants to begin with, let alone risk threatening them further by asking them to become research subjects. Nevertheless, taking into account the practical constraints of action research, it is still possible to make a reasonably good empirical effort in spite of the very real practical limitations. The following program demonstrates this and also underscores the complexity of evaluating and interpreting human relations training for police officers.

Kroeker, Forsyth, and Haase (1974) conducted and assessed a T-group training program aimed at fostering communication between inner-city youths and police officers in the Rochester Police Bureau. There were 78 youths who participated in the program, 47 of them attending the experiential workshop while 31 served in control groups. Similarly, 47 police officers participated in the evaluation with 24 attending the training groups and another 23 serving as a control group. The average number of training sessions attended by the youths and by police was 4.5 and 3.5 respectively. All program participants were volunteers although there was slight pressure on the police to participate.

Several positive trends emerged from this program: (1) The youths became more confident in their own abilities to effectively interact with the police as opposed to feeling that they were victims of their environment. (2) After the workshop experience, both the police and youths felt less aggressive to one another, with the greatest reduction in overt aggressive statements occurring in the youth group. (3) Both the police and youths, when describing one another, used fewer stereotypic terms.

The authors critiqued their own study by pointing out a number of empirical problems in the design plus the finding that pretesting differentially affected subject responses to both the program and the criteria measures. For example, it appeared that retesting sensitized the police more than the youths in this study. Other limitations in this program, according to these writers, were the lack of random assignment of participants to both experimental and control groups, the sporadic attendance by both youths and police such that often participants would wander in and out of the training sessions, and the failure to assess the influence of relevant, major disruptive events occurring in the home community during the actual program period.

The best developed and designed human relations program, however, will not be effective unless particular attention is paid by professionals to initial trust building and careful entry into the system. Stressed in some of the prior articles is that the professional trainer must be very sensitive to his own personality and skills as well as to those of his trainees (e.g., Elkins and Papanek 1966). According to O'Connell (1969), the trainer must assume an active, directive role for police trainees will be unresponsive to a nondirective approach. Similarly, he must be comfortable leaving the protection of his professional office and be willing to expose himself to the harsh realities of the police officer's world.

Boer and McIver (1973) further suggest that an effective program must emphasize a clear, specific direction and behaviorally stated goals. Such a concrete approach, they feel, will facilitate the translation of human relations principles into actual police work. Too often the focus is made on encountering and emotional catharsis of the participants rather than on practical application. A related issue of which the prospective trainer needs to be aware is the feeling on the part of many law enforcement officers that human relations training might make their work more dangerous by acquiring "soft" attitudes and skills which might interfere with the aggressive approach so often needed in police work.

An additional issue that needs to be dealt with in future studies is a closer examination of the content of the human relations program itself. While all these programs described a similar process and techniques (e.g., role playing), it is never clear just what particular elements (or combinations) produced the generally enthusiastic response in trainees. In other words, research is needed to study the comparative effects of different human relations training approaches.

Huseman (1973) has attempted some work in this area. Utilizing 23 law enforcement officers, Huseman evaluated the effects of three communication training methods. These approaches were videotaped role-playing exercises, group conflict problem solving, and film-based case studies. Evaluation following the end of the program consisted of trainee ratings of the effectiveness of the different teaching instruments, the change in the amount of a participant's knowledge, and the relevancy to the trainee's actual job functioning. Results failed to indicate the superiority of one method over another, but rather demonstrated that the majority of the trainees found all the approaches informative, helpful, and relevant. However, while they may actually be equally effective, these three methodologies were insufficiently researched in this study. There was a failure to employ basic control groups which would more clearly measure differential or equivalent training effects.

Police as Family Crisis Intervention Specialists

Another major area receiving much attention from mental health professionals is police training in family crisis intervention. Because of the on-call, front-line contact of the police with the community (particularly in an urban setting), the police are in a unique position to observe and intervene in many child and marital crisis situations. It is estimated that 80 percent of a police officer's work involves settling family disturbances (Kaplan 1972). Responding to calls for assistance during family disturbances has become a rather routine assignment— although some of the most dangerous situations for police frequently evolve from such interventions (Barocas 1973). Bard (1971a) cites statistics indicating that 22 percent of police officers killed in the line of duty are slain in intervening in family crises, with another 40 percent injured in the same manner.

Despite this highly dangerous yet crucial role, police are seldom competently trained to deal with family crisis situations with other than their traditional approach of counterforce, and control (Driscoll, Meyer, and Schanie 1973; Ephross and French 1972; Katz 1973). In fact, it has been suggested that unless police are given new skills and a broader base of awareness, understanding, and sensitivity to emotional problems, they might heighten rather than alleviate the emotionally charged family situation (Bard 1971b; Barocas 1973). That such steps are beginning to be taken is seen in improved screening and selection of police candidates (e.g., Rhead et al. 1968) as well as in actual training in recognizing their own emotional upset and loss of control (Danish and Brodsky 1970; Sokol and Reiser 1971).

Extensive programs have been developed providing police with specific training in how to effectively intervene directly in family crises—either as front-line helpers or as referral sources. Overall, these programs tend to be highly practical and action-oriented, combining the principles and techniques gleaned from crisis intervention and family therapy. The general underlying assumption of these programs is that during the crisis period the potential for change is greatly increased, and hence an effective police intervention at this point might successfully stabilize family functioning as well as produce durable results (e.g., Kaplan 1972).

A typical program aimed at achieving this mission was developed by Katz (1973) for the city of Lowell, Massachusetts. Ten experienced police officers were intensively trained in the knowledge and skills appropriate for family crisis intervention. The program was divided into two parts. Phase 1, consisting of 8 days of varied experiences involving active participation by the police trainees, emphasized the development of tactics to ensure physical safety, interviewing skills, understanding of family dynamics, knowledge about community resources, and self-insight.

Presentations specifically avoided the traditional lecture-question format, for this mode of instruction was found to be both boring and irrelevant to trainee needs. Instead the emphasis was experiential in nature and included active, tandem teaching by trainers, provocative films on relevant subjects, visits with social agency personnel to open up lines of communication, and simulated intervention scenarios role-played by professional actors. This last teaching tool seemed particularly helpful in that police had live demonstrations of typical family conflicts with which to practice interventions, receive videotape feedback from both their peers and themselves, and then refine and further practice their new helping skills. Perhaps most important was not simply a police officer's learning of these helping skills but rather an understanding of his own motivations and interpersonal style. Such knowledge will hopefully provide the police officer with a basic awareness of what needs and personality characteristics (and possible problems) he brings to the many conflict situations involved in his job.

Phase 2, the follow-up period, was initiated as soon as the police officers returned to their duties. Part of this 26-week period was devoted to biweekly group meetings where police officers received supervision of their work and consolidated their skills. An additional feature of phase 2 consisted of the trainer actually accompanying some of the police officers in their fieldwork. This provided the trainer with an opportunity to view firsthand the interventions of the police officers as well as modeling alternative strategies for them.

A similar program is reported in a series of articles by Barocas (1972, 1973, 1974). He describes a 6-month family crisis intervention project carried out in cooperation with the Dayton, Ohio, police department. Over 43 carefully selected patrolmen were involved in this training program. Typical selection criteria considered were motivation, aptitude for crisis intervention work, flexibility, and frustration tolerance. Selected police officers then underwent an initial 3-week full-time training program involving 1 week of police investigative training, 1 week of live-in experience with a ghetto family, and 1 week of group training in crisis intervention. This third week consisted of intensive laboratory work involving simulated family/community conflicts role-played by professional actors, practice intervention by teams of trainees, focused videotape feedback, and continual small group interaction. From this experience trainees appeared to emerge with more flexible approaches in their intervention techniques.

Following this training period, police were then assigned to a mixed ethnic experimental district. At the same time they continued follow-up group supervisory sessions, meeting for 15 weekly 2-hour periods. A number of changes among the police were reported, such as a greater repertoire of skills in handling crises, a change in attitudes and stereotypes regarding community residents, increased awareness of their own personal and familial psychodynamics, and a generally improved self-image and sense of adequacy.

The goals, procedures, and outcomes described in both the Katz (1973) and the Barocas (1973) articles are very impressive. But the studies are also similar in that they did not empirically validate any of their supposed results. The studies thus exemplify the too frequent principle of creating highly innovative programs to meet immediate needs with little time or thought for evaluation.

However, similar but somewhat better validated programs have been instituted in West Harlem by Morton Bard and his associates (Bard 1969, 1970, 1971a; Bard and Berkowitz 1967, 1969). This two-year demonstration project was cooperatively developed by the psychology clinic of City College and the police precinct adjacent to the campus. The target area of the program was a residential apartment complex housing nearly 85,000 mostly lower-class black residents. The project consisted of three specific phases: selection and training, on-the-job work functioning plus continual supervision, and evaluation (Bard 1970).

Phase 1. The first month of the program involved the selection of eighteen patrolmen from a total of 45 volunteers. Criteria included recommendation by the patrolman's commanding officer, at least three years of patrol experience, and a reasonable motivation and aptitude for the program goals. Also, the men were sought to make up a complement of nine biracial teams who could man a special family crisis intervention patrol.

The second part of the first phase was a month-long intensive training program. This part of the program entailed 160 hours of training spaced over 5 full days per week. Morning sessions were spent on lectures, films, slides, and tapes; and the afternoon sessions were experiential in format. Included in the afternoon sessions were human relations training aimed at sensitizing participants to their own personality styles and specific laboratory training modules concerning family crisis intervention skills. This model was quite similar to training approaches described in the previous programs. That is, professional actors role-played a series of family conflict scenes to which the police trainees practiced their usual and modified intervention techniques. Following the role playing, there was a period of group feedback providing an opportunity to fully explore and, if necessary, modify the manner of handling family conflicts.

Phase 2. This was the operational period of the program during which police trainees actually assumed their new intervention helping roles. Specifically, the Family Crisis Intervention Unit (FCIU) manned their special patrol car which was always on-call for all requests involving family assistance for disturbances anywhere in the precinct. The unit personnel were still fully responsible for carrying out their typical police duties in addition to their intervention work.

Concomitantly with their crisis fieldwork experiences, program participants were split into three discussion groups, of six men each, which met for weekly sessions with their own group leader for approximately 1½ hours. These sessions appeared to have involved both supervisory and further sensitivity training experiences. In addition to the ongoing group meetings, trainees were individually assigned supervisor/consultants for 1-hour weekly sessions.

Phase 3. This phase consisted of the evaluation of the program. Throughout the entire project, there was systematic data collection primarily involving simple tabulations on a number of variables for both the experimental training precinct and a comparative, nontreatment control precinct. Data were collected and analyzed over a period of 21 months. The specific focus of assessment was restricted to program effectiveness in relation to crime control and police safety in both the experimental and the control communities.

The results were at best equivocal. There were some positive findings, including a decrease in family assault in the demonstration precinct with none of the FCIU unit sustaining any injuries. On the other hand, in the demonstration precinct there was a significant *increase* in family disturbance complaints, repeat cases, and the number of general and family homicides. Thus, despite the fact that the FCIU intervened in nearly 1400 family disturbances which occurred in 962 families, the results failed to conclusively show a significant program impact at least in terms of the above criteria.

This may be, however, a function of a poor choice of outcome criteria as well as an insufficient experimental design. For example, the seemingly greater number of family disturbances and reported cases in the demonstration project may simply be a function of the inherently biased reporting of the police officers involved in both the experimental and the control precincts. First, statistics and reporting were left up to police themselves, not to any unbiased record keepers. The subjective impressions of the police might have inflated or deflated the reported numbers accordingly. The FCIU personnel had an emotional investment in the performance of their experimental team and consequently may have been particularly diligent (even overzealous) in reporting their intervention figures. In contrast, the control group may have actually had contact with just as many family crises but simply not have been motivated to keep such precise records.

Another possible factor affecting the differences in the incidence of these variables in the two precincts may have been the experimental community's response to the unit. Specifically, having become more aware of, or directly involved with, the FCIU, community residents may have been more likely to contact the police department. The control group precinct community may have had just as many crises but no obvious recourse for getting help. The unexpected increase in the demonstration precinct's incidence of family disturbances may have been more a function of biased police and community resident reporting than an actual rise in these statistics.

Another issue in the design is its very use of rather gross crime statistics. Such figures are generally considered rather unreliable measures of law enforcement effectiveness. It appears unfair to expect 18 police officers to have a significant impact on the major crime statistics (i.e., homicide and assault) in a community of over 85,000 residents. Assessment probably would have been more productive if it had focused on the changes occurring within the families with whom the FCIU personnel had direct contact as well as on particular personality and behavioral changes in the police officers themselves.

An additional methodological issue concerns whether the demonstration and control precincts were indeed comparative communities. Both these precincts were relatively large areas, and despite demographic and sociocultural similarities they may have differed during the demonstration period (two years) in the nature of reported and unreported crime.

The Bard (1970) program, despite its highly creative structure and laudible goals, remains insufficiently researched. Further systematic research is certainly warranted on the basis of impressionistic data suggesting the highly favorable response of the FCIU personnel in terms of improved self-confidence, newly acquired skills, and overall police functioning, and the apparently positive acceptance by the community of the unit's presence.

A program developed by Driscoll, Meyer, and Schanie (1973) in Louisville, Kentucky, has attempted to build on the Bard (1970) model while employing more appropriate evaluative criteria. This training program was quite similar but differed somewhat in its more behavioral orientation and its greater emphasis on simulation, videotaping, and fieldwork practice. The most important difference, however, was the Louisville program's use of a variety of "psychosocial criteria" as opposed to crime statistics for assessment purposes. The assumption here was that the best measures of a police officer's crisis intervention effectiveness would be on behavioral and attitudinal criteria, specific and relevant to this particular helping role, not on such vague concepts as homicide and assault rates.

Driscoll, Meyer, and Schanie (1973) developed a Client Telephone Questionnaire and a Police Participant Questionnaire. The former measure was rated by community citizens who were dealt with by trained or untrained police officers. The second scale, the Police Participant Questionnaire, was rated by 12 participating police trainees 4 months after the formal operation of the crisis intervention program had begun. The focus of the questionnaire was the assessment of the police officer's own perceived change on several intervention dimensions following, as compared to prior to, training.

The program results based on the data from both questionnaires suggested that the trained police officers resolved crisis situations more adequately than the untrained police personnel. However, it is not proper to draw definitive conclusions about this program. Among the design problems were faulty scale construction, biased ratings, asystematic assignment of crisis cases to the trained and untrained police groups, and failure to utilize control groups effectively. Despite these methodological problems, this program is important in further pointing the way to a model for properly developing and assessing police crisis intervention programs. The Driscoll, Meyer, and Schanie (1973) program indicates that investigators can be sensitive to the particular demands and limitations of nonprofessional mental health programs while at the same time being relatively attuned to the necessary evaluation issues and, particularly, the need for meaningful outcome criteria.

The four police crisis intervention programs reviewed are quite similar in the training format they employed as well as in generally reporting favorable outcome results. While almost identical in format, the above four programs ran the gamut in evaluative effort, ranging from basically descriptive (e.g., Katz 1973) to suggestive empirical attempts (Driscoll, Meyer, and Schanie 1973). Overall, the small number of such studies, as well as their lack or insufficient use of research, makes final judgments of the effectiveness of police as crisis interveners somewhat premature. More and improved studies of the Driscoll, Meyer, and Schanie (1973) variety are needed. However, these programs strongly suggest the viability of such training interventions, and the seeming enthusiasm on the part of both the police and the community resident participants makes it very likely that police are indeed serving in meaningful mental health helping roles.

Primarily utilizing a didactic-experiential framework, these programs particularly seem to emphasize a "learning-by-doing" approach. Specific features generally incorporated include lectures, small group exercises and discussions, simulated family crises (usually by actors), practiced role play by participants, videotape and live feedback, human relations training, and often some period of ongoing individual and/or group supervisory meetings. Of note is the fact that this reportedly effective training model is quite consistent with the more viable training approaches used with paraprofessionals and teachers.

Further support for this model was suggested by a program carried out by Zacker and Bard (1973a) in which various police training approaches were compared and contrasted. The objective in this project was to ascertain any differential effects of the didactic-experiential format utilized in the earlier study (Bard 1970) and the more typical cognitive (i.e., lecture) approach. The performance of policemen in three matched housing projects was compared on various outcome criteria, with the first group receiving the didactic-experiential training, the second group receiving a series of lectures, and the third group (a nontreatment control group) receiving no special training. The subsequent results of this program indicated that the didactic-experientially trained police officers performed in a generally superior manner to that of the officers in the other two groups.

Additional Issues in Police Crisis Intervention Training

Among the issues explored in police training programs have been the necessity of rapport and trust building and the need for practical and relevant programming. A related concern faced in most of these programs is the initial strong, sometimes even hostile, resistance on the part of the participants. In their discussion of this problem Zacker (1974) and Zacker and Bard (1973b) suggest that professional trainers beginning consultative relationships with police departments are generally ill equipped for such a role. Generally from middle-class backgrounds (or at least espousing such values), these mental health personnel have typically dealt only with people of a similar background or orientation. All too frequently the trainers lack knowledge of actual police demands, the dangers involved, and the feelings engendered.

It is imperative that trainers understand the resistance often displayed by trainees as their felt frustration in translating idealistic program goals into meaningful alternatives in dealing with the life-and-death realities they frequently have to face. Programs must be highly relevant, practical, and quite consistent with actual police functioning. It may mean reassuring police trainees that they are in no way being asked to become miniature social workers who must always talk their way out of dangerous situations. The intervention techniques must be seen as an added alternative tool with which to enhance their usual police duties.

Understanding of the police officer's world may be acquired in a number of ways. Some of the programs described earlier have included professional trainers with actual prior police experience, liaison or previously trained police personnel who could help program needs fit police demands, or actual involvement by the professional in various fieldwork experiences (e.g., traveling in patrol cars) to get a firsthand view of police life. Whatever resource is utilized, it is important for professionals to have a clear understanding of, and empathy for, police trainee apprehensions about the program and for professionals not to readily reduce resistances to formula psychodynamic explanations (Zacker 1974).

Another issue in police crisis intervention training is broader in scope, and this concerns the implications of family crisis intervention training for other areas of police work. Bard (1973) notes that family crises are but one of many intense situations to which police are exposed in their work. He sees family disturbances and the considerable emotional difficulties stemming from crime victimization (e.g., assault, rape) as but two possible crisis intervention roles police may provide.

Police officers are potentially ideal helpers for numerous crisis situations. Their ability to be on the scene of disturbance almost immediately provides them with possible direct remedial and preventive opportunities which professional mental health workers are often unable to achieve. There are a number of training implications stemming from potential police participation in such crisis situations. For example, perhaps the typical family crisis intervention training module instills attitudes and skills which can be applied to these various other crisis events. A research suggestion, then, would be to evaluate not only trainees' subsequent family intervention performance, but also their helping efficacy in other crisis situations. Perhaps certain training modules would be appropriate (with some modification) to help police officers become generalists in crisis intervention rather than specialists in family intervention. While the general principles and format of the Bard (1970) model might be adopted, more focused training packages specifically tailored to the type of crisis situation would need to be developed.

These are developmental and research issues worthy of further exploration. It does mean, however, that professionals would have to further widen their scope and acceptance of police personnel as nonprofessional helpers. It was difficult enough to sell the idea of police as front-line family intervention specialists. What we are talking about here is a much broader mental health helping capacity on the part of law enforcement officers, and possibly the need for some relinquishing of territoriality on the part of professionals.

Results of Police Mental Health Helping Programs

This section will integrate the results of the previous discussions of police mental health activities in general training programs, human relations experiences, and family crisis intervention work. Most of the police helping activity is directed more at community groups than at individuals. This is not surprising since a good deal of the urban difficulties over the last few years have involved conflicts between specific community populations and the police force. Many programs are being developed to improve channels of communication between these two interest groups. The prime purpose for such interactions is preventive in nature, with the goal being to lessen growing tension so as to avoid future conflicts. The concomitant goal is to improve the general image of the police by projecting a new supportive and sensitive role. Various mental health educational experiences and a good many human relations training programs have been developed to provide police with new attitudes and skills with which to achieve these goals. The particular skills taught at this level may involve some direct service work, but generally they focus more on supportive kinds of counseling, referral resources, and liaison activity.

Even more specific direct service work has been done, however, with helping police deal with individual family groups. This level of intervention is quite similar to the thrust of crisis work being provided by professional and paraprofessional mental health workers in various settings. The goal is primarily remedial, but when this intervention appears insufficient, helping recipients may either receive some follow-up from their new police contacts or be referred to other helping agencies.

Consistent with descriptions of other mental health helpers, police are hailed as being capable of providing counseling, supportive, or public relations services similar to those offered by professional personnel. While they do indeed appear to be providing such services, the research offered in support of their effectiveness leaves much to be desired. Out of the eighteen studies reviewed here, three were of a suggestive quality (Bard 1970; Driscoll, Meyer, and Schanie 1973; Lipsitt and Steinbruner 1969) and only one was empirically adequate (Kroeker, Forsyth, and Haase 1974).

At this time it appears that the better research efforts are being directed toward the more intensive types of training programs, such as those dealing with family crisis intervention. This is not surprising for these programs are fairly well structured with specific tasks and operationalized goals. As such, they are more manageable from a research standpoint. In contrast, human relations training is a more nebulous type of experience with often vague, hard-to-operationalize objectives such as "greater respect" or "more open communication." Nevertheless, studies such as that conducted by Lipsitt and Steinbruner (1969) indicate that reasonable research can also be conducted with this particular kind of educational mode.

As has been indicated throughout this review, the ultimate effectiveness of a program will be determined by the actual effects on the recipients. Such outcome measures have typically been absent with the exception of the Bard (1970) and Driscoll, Meyer, and Schanie (1973) crisis intervention programs. These programs have already been reviewed and their strengths and weaknesses discussed. The conclusion drawn was that the positive results achieved by these relatively more sophisticated empirical studies should still be considered suggestive until more definitive research is conducted.

Finally, it is not surprising to find that the particular training modalities described in most of these articles have incorporated some combination of experiential and didactic features. Traditional police academy training has generally involved lecture presentations—an approach often faulted as being boring and unresponsive to trainee needs. The assumption made in the above programs is that training must deemphasize the cognitive approach and instead provide experiences facilitating active participation by police officers.

Summary

This extensive chapter has described and examined the actual and potential mental health roles provided by the following professional community leaders: lawyers, clergy, teachers, and police. It was shown that these natural caregivers are providing a varied array of direct and indirect helping services similar to those offered by professional mental health personnel. Services provided by these "nonprofessionals" have ranged from direct counseling skills (e.g., client-centered therapy, behavior modification) to indirect supportive and developmental services (e.g., human relations) to preventive work (e.g., psychological curricula).

Despite the generally glowing appraisal contained in published reports, a critique of these programs tended to reveal numerous methodological shortcomings, suggesting caution in interpreting the reported outcomes. The better researched programs were highlighted throughout this chapter, and discussion of their implications underscored their promising developmental and research directions. Interestingly, it appears that the caregivers discussed in this chapter may be most effective in client-centered, behavior modification, and crisis intervention roles. While seemingly quite different helping services, they are really similar in being rather specific and focused interventions, each capable of being taught by concrete training approaches. This approach has tended to blend both cognitive and practical features and has also had the advantage of lending itself most readily to evaluative research.

Overall, while future research is needed to clarify various developmental, training, and research issues, the present studies certainly exemplify the numerous helping roles being assumed by clergy, teachers, and police as well as at least suggesting the potential impact of their work.

5 The Medical and Allied Health Professionals

Whereas the previous chapter focused on professional groups of community caretakers, the present chapter continues this examination but focuses now on those medical and science-related students and professionals who are also serving in mental health helping roles. Surveys have indicated that the general practitioner is the key resource person initially contacted by people needing professional psychiatric help. Physicians have estimated that anywhere from 20 to 60 percent of their caseload consists of people with transitional, moderate, or severe emotional problems (Cumming 1962; Gardner 1970; Gurin, Veroff, and Feld 1960; Hartog 1967; Liberman 1967; Locke and Gardner 1969; Rosen et al. 1972).

For example, in a study of 4200 patients of general practitioners over a period of 7 years, Gardner (1970) found 17 percent of the women and 6 percent of the men were diagnosed as neurotic in any one year, and 53 percent of the women and 24 percent of the men were so diagnosed one or more times. Furthermore, about 10 percent of the patients evidenced formal psychiatric problems, an additional 5 percent showed some emotional disorder, and including all psychosomatic difficulties, the total rate of emotional disorders ranged from 15 to 50 percent.

Aside from statistical surveys, numerous articles have described the significant mental health services which may be provided by health personnel such as pediatricians (Belkin et al. 1965; Edelstein 1965; Gabriel and Danilowicz 1969; Stocking et al. 1972), nursing home physicians (Stotsky 1972), internists (Castelnuovo-Tedesco 1970), anesthesiologists and surgeons (Baudry and Wiener 1969; Egbert 1967), obstetricians (Addelson 1973), industrial medical consultants (Laufer 1968), family physicians in the ghetto (Karno, Ross, and Caper 1969), geneticists in a neuropsychiatric counseling center (Kivowitz and Keirn 1973), staff pharmacists on inpatient psychiatric wards (Kohan, Chung, and Stone 1973; Sandusky 1973), and even veterinarians (Levinson 1965).

Mental Health Training for Medical Students and Graduate Personnel

Given these reports, it is not surprising that many wide-ranging educational experiences are being provided to nonpsychiatric medical and related personnel. The physician, particularly, is seen as the natural caregiver because of his unique

63

community role (e.g., Hirschowitz 1972; Kaufman 1971; Krakowski 1970; Perkins and Thompson 1974; Stepansky and Stepansky 1974).

A difficulty confronting prospective trainers is that most physicians have rather strong negative attitudes regarding psychiatric thinking and practice and hence frequently do not avail themselves of mental health educational opportunities. Various surveys, for example, have indicated that medical personnel tend to view psychiatry in a disparaging way. They rarely see psychiatrists as career models, question such ideological tenets as the new community psychiatry movement, and, from an educational standpoint, consider psychiatry one of the poorest taught and learned subject areas in their medical training (Bruhn and Parsons 1965; Castelnuovo-Tedesco 1967; Mathis 1965; Perkins and Thompson 1974; Sabshin 1969; Tucker and Reinhardt 1968).

A major issue in program development relates to overcoming the various resistances physicians might have regarding mental health training. Available evidence suggests that once medical personnel do, in fact, become involved in these educational programs, more positive perceptions develop with greater training exposure (Bruhn and Parsons 1965; Tucker and Reinhardt 1969; Werkman, Landau, and Wakefield 1973).

The particular training programs reviewed in this chapter are quite diverse, ranging from ongoing comprehensive experiences to small weekend workshops. The quality of training tends to be varied as are the efforts, if attempted, to assess the programs. As with the training of other nonprofessional mental health agents, the project reports here tend to espouse a halo effect of "optimism and success."

Mental health training has tended to focus on either medical students or postgraduate physicians. The emphasis on students appears to have two goals in mind: the hopeful recruitment of possible psychiatric residents from the medical school ranks or at least the development of appropriate basic mental health skills so as to enhance these students' subsequent medical practice. Training with postgraduate physicians is not geared so much for recruitment into psychiatry, but rather for developing helping skills which might serve as an adjunct to other professional services. Mental health training for nonpsychiatric medical personnel is available to the novice as well as to the experienced physician. Ideally, it would seem that more emphasis should be placed on the medical school curriculum as the best place to provide mental health skills since the early acquisition of this knowledge would hopefully enable the physician to maximize his effectiveness.

Medical School Mental Health Training

A primary function of psychiatry departments in medical schools is to educate physicians in training, most of whom will not specialize in psychiatry. Nevertheless, there has been a considerable struggle, as reported by various writers, to develop a meaningful and effective method for educating medical students about psychiatry and mental health principles (e.g., Becker et al. 1973; Branch 1965a; Hirschowitz 1972; Kaufman 1970; Reiser 1973; Romano 1973).

While programs often differ widely with respect to goals and format, there appears to be a consensus that the curriculum should bridge the wide theoretical, empirical, and philosophical gaps that too often exist between nonpsychiatric physicians and their professional educators (Becker et al. 1973; Bowden and Barton 1975; Reiser 1973).

Before particular programs are examined, a basic issue arises as to whether medical students should in fact be trained to handle their own psychiatric patients or rather simply refer them to appropriate resources. Although there have been some differences of opinion regarding this matter, the majority of medical educators are in agreement with Branch (1965b) who suggests that medical students be encouraged to take responsibility for directly or indirectly managing the numerous kinds of psychiatric cases confronting them in their practice while at the same time knowing clearly when it is appropriate to seek outside consultation.

There were five articles reviewed and found to be typical of the kinds of psychiatric training programs being offered in medical school (Cline and Garrard 1973; Davanzo 1965; Knopp et al. 1970; Mendel, Wexler, and Brotman 1964; Roeske 1972; Ware, Strassman, and Naftulin 1971). The major thrust in these programs has been on altering knowledge and attitudes about mental health problems and resources, teaching diagnostic and interviewing skills, and developing basic supportive counseling abilities. An underlying goal is that of enabling the medical student to feel more confident about his or her skills, ability to work with difficult psychiatric patients, and the mental health role.

The size and structure of these psychiatry courses have varied and included such teaching tools as lectures, training films, case demonstrations, site visits, intensive small group discussion, group therapy, individual tutorial or apprenticeship experiences, demonstrations and modeling, and supervised practice. For the most part, medical school psychiatric training has moved away from a traditional lecture format to a more learning-by-doing approach combining cognitive and practical elements.

All these studies reported positive changes, but with the exception of the Ware, Strassman, and Naftulin (1971) investigation most were of inadequate to suggestive research value. Typically absent were appropriate designs, control groups, unbiased ratings, and reliable personality and attitudinal measures. While some attempts were made at follow-up (e.g., Knopp et al. 1970; Ware, Strassman, and Naftulin 1971), they appeared to have little to do with actual helpee outcome but rather were concerned with the durability of attitudinal and cognitive changes achieved by trainees during the course.

In a review of this situation, Romano (1973) stressed that the numerous changes occurring in medical school psychiatric training demand the development of valid and reliable assessment procedures. It is difficult to understand why reasonable evaluative steps have not been undertaken in such programs. A frequent explanation for improper assessment in programs dealing with other kinds of nonprofessional workers has been that these programs spring out of real, immediate needs with little time for adequate program development and appraisal. This argument is itself questionable, but even if it had merit, it would seem to be inapplicable to medical school psychiatric training. Here we are dealing with preplanned coursework and curriculum and a captive population, where the educators should have ample time to plan programs, design reasonable research, compare various training modalities, and examine both process and outcome issues. Nevertheless, this has generally not been done. It is very unfortunate as the psychiatric training of medical students would seem to be an excellent vehicle for developing and assessing nonprofessional mental health training packages.

A report by Uhlenhuth and Duncan (1968a, 1968b) illustrates an attempt to systematically evaluate the effects of medical students' helping intervention on a large sample of outpatients at a psychiatric clinic. This study took place during the academic years 1963 to 1966 at the Henry Phipps Psychiatric Clinic, where senior medical students from Johns Hopkins University have traditionally served a clinical clerkship of 9 to 10 weeks. Prior to the beginning of this training experience, students are generally assigned previously screened outpatients whom they meet for a series of weekly hour-long interviews. In this study 128 outpatients with a primary diagnosis of neurosis were randomly assigned to student therapists for a series of approximately six sessions.

Evaluation focused on the subjective changes occurring in the patients as assessed by various measures. Included was a 65-item checklist scored weekly by the patient that involved such symptom clusters as anxiety, depression, anger, compulsive behaviors, and other problems. In addition, three measures were taken at the beginning and end of the series of interviews: severity of chief complaint on a 5-point scale, a condensed version of the Taylor Manifest Anxiety Scale, and the Barron Ego Strength Scale. Results indicated a 22 percent decrease in symptomatic distress, particularly around symptoms of anxiety, depression, and anger; a small but reliable decrease in anxiety; and no change in the Barron Ego Strength Scale. Overall, 72 percent of the patients felt improved, 2 percent felt the same, and 26 percent felt worse.

Compared to the other programs noted above, the work of Uhlenhuth and Duncan (1968a, 1968b) is a more reasonable assessment effort, particularly in its specific focus on patient outcome. The positive results must, however, be judged as tentative in view of the basic design problems; had these problems been properly accounted for, a much stronger study would have resulted. Among the methodological issues were the lack of control groups, inclusion of psychotic along with neurotic patients, biased subjective patient ratings, and inconsistent quantitative and qualitative therapist contact. The conclusions, then, are suspect, but the study is important in pointing out that evaluation of the outcome effects of nonprofessional medical student intervention is empirically possible and, in fact, essential.

Postgraduate Physicians and Mental Health Training

As was the case in undergraduate psychiatric training, postgraduate education has similarly made a transition from a lecture to an experiential format. In recent years there has been a focus on a process model of education emphasizing intensive trainee participation, flexible models, and practical application (Hirschowitz 1972; Kaufman 1971; Miller 1967; Sheeley 1965; Stepansky and Stepansky 1974).

The need for effective nonpsychiatric physician training has been attended to largely by medical schools, professional societies, and hospital departments of psychiatry. Perhaps the largest sponsor of such educational efforts, either via the above channels or independently, has been the National Institute of Mental Health. For example, since 1959 NIMH has awarded grants to institutions for a variety of mental health training projects, such as collaborative programs to offer psychiatric instruction to nonpsychiatric residents and interns, intensive psychiatric training for residents, and specialized training for general practitioners (Gabriel and Danilowicz 1969).

An example of a rather extensive NIMH project has been the General Practitioner Training Program (Robertson and Shriver 1964). Reports describing such NIMH-sponsored programs have dealt more with the figures and statistics involved (i.e., amount of funds, number of grants awarded) than with evaluating the effectiveness of these programs (e.g., Gabriel and Danilowicz 1969; Robertson and Shriver 1964). Nevertheless, these programs are important in encouraging the continued growth and development of physicians with regard to mental health knowledge and skills.

A sample of studies was also reviewed which reflect the more typical, less extensive seminars or courses being offered to physicians, either sponsored independently or through NIMH (Brody, Golden, and Lichtman 1965; Mayer and Myerson 1972; Nicholas and Ransohoff 1965; Rittelmeyer 1972; Zabarenko, Merenstein, and Zabarenko 1971). As was the case with undergraduate psychiatric training, the primary focus in these programs is on increasing knowledge, changing attitudes, and developing basic diagnostic, referral, and supportive counseling skills. Teaching techniques employed have included lectures, visits to psychiatric facilities, small group discussion and exercises, and much practice. Again the emphasis is more on doing than on listening. Also similar is the primarily anecdotal nature of these program reports. Again there has tended to be more of a focus on participant process variables than on actual helpee outcome effects.

Research and Attempts at Sound Application

Much thought has been given to the issues of effective program development and appropriate evaluation (e.g., Sheeley 1965). In particular, Zabarenko (1965) raised the question: given the time, money, and energy devoted to nonpsychiatric physician training, why has there been so little effective evaluation? Some possible answers suggested are as follows. (1) One cause may be the pragmatic orientations of both teachers and trainers where goals are concrete and often urgent. (2) Unlike medical students, graduate physicians are not a captive audience eagerly willing to fill out rating forms and questionnaire data. (3) Perhaps because they are not too sophisticated in research, psychiatric educators may feel the task to be too time-consuming and impractical. (4) Another factor may be the issue of the perceived difficulty of operationalizing the subject matter of psychiatry into researchable data. Nevertheless, Zabarenko (1965) urges that research is both necessary and possible once a reasonable attempt is made at formulating concrete goals, dealing with basic experimental design issues, and creatively utilizing instrumentation and measures which are practical and geared to the specific knowledge and skills being taught.

An intensive ongoing project that has attempted to incorporate such principles is the nonpsychiatric physician training program sponsored by the University of Southern California School of Medicine (Naftulin, Donnelly, and Wolkon 1974). The continually self-evaluating USC program has over the years offered a wide array of educational experiences including time-limited courses, intensive supervised training packages, and weekend workshops. All the typical didactic-experiential teaching tools have been utilized, but particular emphasis has been on small group work and videotape training. Content areas covered have been flexible and modified according to feedback from the physician trainees.

There have been various types of program evaluation such as postprogram satisfaction questionnaires, measures of attitude change and cognitive learning (Donnelly et al. 1972), behavioral ratings of actual doctor-patient contact (Adler and Enelow 1966), and assessment of possible program effects on the availability and utilization of mental health services in a trainee's home community. Overall, results have been in a positive direction. The specific work of Enelow and his associates perhaps best demonstrates the thinking, goals, training methods, instrumentation, and evaluative research inherent in the USC program (Adler and Enelow 1966; Adler, Ware, and Enelow 1970; Enelow and Adler 1964; Enelow, Adler, and Manning 1964; Enelow, Adler, and Wexler 1970; Enelow and Myers 1968; Enelow and Wexler 1966).

Enelow and Adler (1964) described the continuous evaluation of various introductory, intermediate and advanced programs offered over the years, assessing such variables as the personality and demographic characteristics of the physician trainees, the cognitive and attitudinal gains achieved by program participants, and the actual behavioral changes in physician-patient contact before and after the training program. One fairly innovative measure of cognitive change consisted of the prepresentation and postpresentation of films of female patients with various referral symptoms. Trainees were asked to imagine interviewing the patients in their own offices and then to respond to four open-ended questions determining diagnostic, interviewing, and treatment-planning ability. Trainee responses were subsequently subjected to a content analysis which measured the extent to which responses were consistent with the goals of the course and specifically the instructors' own modeled diagnostic and planning skills.

Research programs employing this instrument suggested it was sensitive to the introductory-level course work, but not particularly to advanced-level training. Greater emphasis is now going toward direct behavioral observation of pre-post-physician-patient contact using such measures as the Bales Interaction Scales. As evaluation of the program has become more concrete and behavior-specific, so too has the format for skill training. Much work has been aimed at developing a series of videotapes for teaching interviewing skills (Adler, Ware, and Enelow 1970).

Overall results of these programs appear to be impressive, although the various investigators in the projects recognize some of the methodological limitations in their work as well as the inherent difficulties in developing and promoting such training programs (e.g., Enelow and Myers 1968). To their credit the USC program developers seem quite concerned with the developmental and research issues, with much apparent attention being devoted to further refining methodology and generating more valid training programs. Whether for research or training purposes, these writers have generally adopted a highly didactic-experiential model. Of note is the similarity of this training mode with the particular format often used in the more effective training of paraprofessionals, clergy, teachers, and police. Here again the emphasis has been on breaking down target skills into concrete behavioral goals; modeling, practicing, and refining the skill; and then repeating the cycle with additional target objectives. The USC program appears to be one of the most promising approaches for training and evaluating nonpsychiatric physicians in a variety of mental health helping skills.

Additional Issues in Training Postgraduate Physicians

It is often difficult to interest physicians in simply pursuing postgraduate psychiatric education. This issue was mentioned earlier when it was noted that despite (or maybe because of) physicians' poor prior academic preparation in handling emotional problems in their patients, they tended to look critically at psychiatry as a viable medical career model. Program developers must thus overcome ideological and philosophical differences which physicians apparently feel exist between themselves and mental health professionals (e.g., Borus 1971). An additional underlying factor might be the physician's felt vulnerability about possibly exposing his own personal problems if involved in psychiatric educa- tion. Physicians, in fact, are a high-risk professional group whose involvement in mental health training might also enable them to gain self-understanding and deal more constructively with their own personal development (Waring 1974).

Once physicians have actually participated in psychiatric training, other problems may arise such as the doctors' difficulty in integrating these new skills into their actual practices (Brodsky 1970; Stepansky and Stepansky 1974). A related problem is the basic one of professional identity. Even if the physician works out all the environmental mechanics, he is still left with the problem of how to occasionally assume a mental health identity, one which he has to sell to both his patients and himself. Even if he succeeds, patients may not be comfortable with his new role. The physician may simply not be able to implement new skills even if he would like to do so.

It thus appears that postgraduate psychiatric training is a complex matter. Aside from developing meaningful training packages, it appears that educators must also be particularly sensitive to ways of attracting doctors into these programs as well as enabling them to pragmatically incorporate their newly acquired skills into their practices.

Nursing Personnel

This section will examine mental health roles assumed by nonpsychiatric nurses. The focus is on those individuals who have not received formalized psychiatric training, who may nevertheless be providing helping services in both psychiatric and nonpsychiatric hospitals or community facilities. Also included in this category are student nurses who may happen to be going through training rotations in such settings.

A review of the literature suggests that nonpsychiatric nurses, by virtue of their role variety, experience, education, numbers, and positive public image, are in an advantageous position to provide corrective, preventive, and follow-up mental health services for persons of all ages (Caplan 1974b; Huntington 1968; Kriegman, Harris, and Rosinski 1968).

Training and Evaluation of Nonpsychiatric Nurses

Various formal and informal training programs aimed at capitalizing on this potential have involved nurses as indigenous rural and urban outreach workers (Henderson 1973; Looff 1969), crisis counselors and interveners (Huessy et al. 1969; Mackay and Serrano 1968; Robinson 1971), play therapists for preschoolers (Barnes, Wootton, and Wood 1972), general hospital bedside counselors (Rushing 1966), mental health consultants in local health departments (Maholick 1972), school counselors for adolescent groups (Daniels 1966), community liaisons for antipoverty programs (Hitchcock 1971), and volunteers for providing educational, consultative, and supportive services to inpatient and outpatient patients and their families (Ahmed and Young 1974; Cole and Cole 1969; Leonard and King 1968).

These programs tend to vary a good deal in terms of the extent of training and quality of evaluation. Too often it appears that courses and workshops are one-shot affairs lacking overall planning and follow-up, thus preventing adequate appraisal of the effects of the program (Kriegman, Harris, and Rosinski 1968).

Exceptions to this are the more extensive training opportunities seen in the programs described by Maholick (1972) and Ahmed and Young (1974), both of which deal with the public health nurse's mental health role. In fact, the majority of the studies specifically focused on public health nursing as the key potential helping area since usually more than half of their workload normally involves providing assistance to patients with some emotional difficulty (Henderson 1973). Looff (1969) adds that public health nurses may serve such an important mental health role because of their flexibility, mobility, and proximity to people with various types of problems. Also, their shared cultural background may even facilitate more empathy and rapport than can possibly be established by "professional" mental health personnel.

The Maholick (1972) project is an extension of the Bradley Center training program for community caretakers (e.g., clergy) that was described in Chapter 4. The present program incorporated a similar training format, but this time focusing on nursing personnel in a local health department as the needed workforce resource for the delivery of helping services. The project specifically consisted of the following four phases: intake (phase 1), evaluation (phase 2), actual counseling (phase 3), and follow-up (phase 4). The public health nurse served as the key therapeutic agent in this four-step approach to outpatient client care and carried the major responsibility for patients from their first to last contacts. Professional mental health workers provided strictly backup and consultative support to primary nursing personnel.

Evaluation of this program has been more descriptive than substantive, perhaps because of the newness of the project and the apparent field testing of the method that is currently being conducted. What data are provided suggest both a powerful training model and the viable use of public health nurses as helpers. For example, figures show that in 1967 six nurses devoted 25 percent of their time to mental health work by conducting 7800 counseling sessions while seeing a total of 245 new and reopened cases and carrying an average monthly caseload of 303 patients. Hopefully, future research will further clarify the results of this training approach on both the attitudes and skills of the nursing participants as well as the actual specific effects on the patients themselves. In general the Maholick (1972) program appears to be a heuristic, innovative mental health training approach for public health nurses, but with the same strengths and weaknesses as the overall Bradley Center program, which were noted in Chapter 4.

Another fairly comprehensive program was developed by Ahmed and Young (1974) in which a collaborative relationship was established between outpatient and inpatient hospital psychiatric units and public health nurses. The general goal for this joint partnership was to develop a complement of trained nurses who would deal appropriately with the problems they encountered in families as well as comfortably accept their role in an interdisciplinary treatment team dealing with discharged psychiatric patients.

The training format included twenty sessions; ten consisted of didactic lectures and ten involved experiential group meetings. Further training in milieu therapy was provided via hospital observation and actual participation in patient meetings. Following training, on-the-job nursing intervention consisted of an assessment of the about-to-be-discharged inpatient's family, home, and community situation and subsequent supportive outpatient care and ongoing communication with the hospital staff regarding patient progress.

As with Maholick's (1972) work, the Ahmed and Young (1974) project has not been adequately researched. Impressions have apparently been quite favorable from both participating agencies. Statistics were provided for one 9-month period during which time 66 patients were referred to the trained nurses who made 220 home visits and generally helped avoid rehospitalization. In addition, the public health nurses were considered to have provided a key preventive service in both diagnosing and referring to staff a considerable number of potential psychiatric patients. Although the relative newness of this program might have precluded adequate evaluation, such basic research is essential to delineate program effects on both nursing trainees and patients. Thus, both the Ahmed and Young (1974) and Maholick (1972) programs stand out as examples of intensive program development, training, and application; but they, like many of the other programs noted above, nevertheless failed to empirically substantiate their seemingly positive effects.

Even when these programs do consider evaluation, they seem to be more concerned with process variables relating to nursing training than with actual patient outcome. While nearly all certainly discuss apparent benefits to patients, little work has been done examining specific patient outcome effects. Two exceptions to this are the programs of Hartlage (1970) and Korson and Hayes (1966), both of which dealt with the intervention of nonpsychiatric student nurses working with severely disturbed inpatients.

Hartlage (1970) gave 22 student nurses 10 hours of therapy skills, 5 hours devoted to basic reinforcement approaches (e.g., social and material reinforcers), and 5 hours of simple supportive traditional counseling (e.g., empathy, encouraging self-acceptance). Forty-four diagnosed chronic schizophrenic patients were involved in this program, with each student nurse seeing two patients 1 hour per day for 7 weeks while using one or the other therapeutic approach. Before assignment to the two respective counseling groups patients had previously completed a self-concept scale and had been rated and matched by attendants on hospital adjustment.

At the end of the 7-week intervention period, patients again completed the self-concept measure, and they were rated on hospital adjustment. Also, student therapists evaluated their patients in terms of a variety of improvement criteria. Both posttreatment hospital adjustment scores and therapist improvement ratings showed significant change for behavioral but not for traditional counseling. Improvement in patients' self-concept was suggested by both techniques. Hartlage (1970) concluded that relatively untrained therapists, particularly when utilizing reinforcement principles, might facilitate positive changes in hospitalized schizophrenics' self-concept and hospital adjustment following a period of brief therapy.

Korson and Hayes (1966) developed a somewhat more intensive training and therapy program for student nurses working with a variety of severely regressed hospitalized patients. Prior intervention training focused on building general interpersonal supportive helping skills with an emphasis on personal awareness, nursing-patient transactions, and basic listening and communication skills. Specific training included 5 hours in occupational therapy, 3 hours of recreational therapy, 4 hours in music therapy, 1 hour in bibliotherapy, 4 hours in communication skills (e.g., role playing), 6 hours in remotivation and hospital milieu techniques, and a 4-hour practicum experience with individual patients followed by feedback and critique.

After they finished this training, 33 student nurses assumed responsibility for a total of 126 patients. Usually nurses worked in tandem teams, two nurses being assigned a group of about eight patients to work with throughout their entire psychiatric rotation. Each student spent approximately 6 hours daily (30 hours per week) taking part in the above activities, receiving consultation and supervision from professional staff when needed.

There was a focus on the benefits that both students and patients derived from this interaction, specifically in the patients' hospital adjustment and the student nurses' acquisition of helping skills and knowledge. Results of this pilot program were reported as successful with a 5-year follow-up revealing 60 percent of the 126 patients discharged from the hospital, 25 percent of whom were considered greatly improved and returned to their homes and 33 percent somewhat improved but needing appropriate aftercare community facilities. Of the patients remaining in the hospital program, 2 percent of the 126 made a better institutional adjustment, with 11 percent still in the program. Korson and Hayes (1966) concluded that their program had merit for both patients and nurses.

Both the Hartlage (1970) and the Korson and Hayes (1966) programs suffer from numerous methodological problems and thus fail to deal with important training and outcome issues. Hartlage's (1970) program evidenced basic design flaws, particularly the absence of no-treatment or attention-placebo control groups, possible contamination of treatment approaches, and lack of follow-up. The Korson and Hayes (1966) project presents an additional difficulty in interpreting results. Besides the lack of control groups and of a systematic research design, this program *did not have* clear, matched patient groups, uncontaminated therapeutic approaches, precise outcome criteria, objective and valid means for assessment, or unbiased judges.

For example, nurses were asked to intervene with quite a variety of psychiatric patients, and it seems fallacious to presume manic-depressive and brain-damaged patients would necessarily be at the same baseline in terms of hospital adjustment and responsiveness to intervention. It is essential that screening, matching, and random assignment be instituted as a basic requirement in a program such as this. Also, although patients are reported to have improved and been subsequently discharged, no criteria of improvement, either behavioral or attitudinal, was specified. In addition, since student nurses were trained in a range of approaches, it is difficult to determine whether the intervention was the salient factor or whether the general hospital milieu facilitated change. Finally, the criterion for nursing performance was solely the students' scores on standardized psychiatric nursing tests. Nowhere during actual fieldwork are the nurses' particular helping behaviors systematically appraised and modified.

The failure to include appropriate control groups in both the Hartlage (1970) and Korson and Hayes (1966) programs is a fundamental drawback. The addition of appropriate control groups might have effectively dealt with some of the concerns cited above and might also have helped to address another essential issue. If student nurses are indeed helpful to psychiatric inpatients, one must consider whether their effectiveness is a function of their particular skills or merely the result of who they are.

The typical negative features of the psychiatric hospital regimen have been noted time and again. It is too frequently described as a milieu where even the most enthusiastic professional and supportive staff eventually become jaded in their outlook and behavior; consequently hospital life too readily takes on a dull routine and custodial nature. Now thrust into such an environment are young, refreshing, enthusiastic, and energetic nursing students who then begin spending considerable time with patients, essentially abandoned as suitable treatment candidates years before. The speculations are interesting, for quite possibly these patients are now exposed to a dose of intensive interest, concern, and tender loving care, the quality of which they may never have had. The strong implication is that it might be this basic attention and caring quality rather than a particular therapeutic approach that facilitates productive patient change. It appears necessary, then, to include an attention-placebo control group in such programs to clarify what exactly is producing reported positive outcomes. Similarly, follow-up measures would be essential to see how durable patient changes are once these student helpers terminate their program involvement.

Additional Program Issues in Nonpsychiatric Nurse Training

In many of the previously reviewed programs, a number of points were frequently mentioned as being critical for the effective training of nonpsychiatric nurses. Of note is that these issues are consistent with the concerns most often grappled with by program developers offering training for many of the other types of nonprofessional helpers.

The first issue concerns continuing education. Effective skill building is dependent not only on preintervention training but also on some ongoing process of training and supervision to which nurses can turn for further refinement of skills, additional knowledge, and particularly backup support for difficult situations. A second point relates to building features into programs which facilitate the personal growth and awareness of the nurses themselves. Often accomplished through small group work and intensive supervision, such a process is particularly important as these nurses are repeatedly exposed, both in and out of psychiatric facilities, to a good deal of emotional crisis and pain. An awareness of their own reactions and feelings will enable them to have a clearer picture of their own helping style and impact as well as greater sensitivity to the experiences of their patients.

A third area pertains to the nurses' comfort with their new mental health role. At issue here is the new helping identity the nonpsychiatric nurses are being asked to assume or at least recognize. Nonpsychiatric nurses must feel capable and confident in their new mental health roles and be accepted by their professional colleagues if they are to capitalize on the great potential their work offers. Such comfort is needed if these nurses are to demonstrate both initiative and effectiveness as change agents (Hitchcock 1971).

Summary

Medical personnel are primarily dealing with individuals and their families and are providing a variety of supportive and direct helping services. These generally consist of information about emotional problems, diagnostic and referral procedures, and supportive counseling. Overall, medical personnel have received a wide range of educational experiences in mental health, varying from rather informal apprentice work to highly structured comprehensive programs. The general thrust appears to be in the direction of more practical training and experiences emphasizing greater participant involvement. Evaluation of these programs has tended to be rather poor, with only 6 of the 28 programs achieving at least a suggestive level of research adequacy. The following specific conclusions may be drawn from the results:

(1) It appears that physicians, nurses, and related medical personnel have always functioned in various mental health roles because of such factors as their status and accessibility to the communities they serve. Current undergraduate and postgraduate mental health education, despite wide differences in goals and format, is essentially aimed at fostering this helping identity, enhancing existing skills, and actually encouraging medical personnel to provide many of the same direct and indirect services traditionally offered by professional mental health workers.

(2) A good deal of conceptualizing and program development is occurring in the psychiatry departments within medical schools. The thrust here has been either to interest medical students in subsequent psychiatric careers or to at least provide them with sufficient knowledge and effective basic helping techniques so that they can deal appropriately with patients who have emotional problems. Training courses and seminars have been quite diverse and generally poorly researched. Conclusions regarding training effects on both students and patients are premature. Nevertheless, adequate research should be quite possible because training programs are structured and evaluation can be easily built into the curriculum. Hopefully, future researchers will capitalize on the potential of medical schools to be excellent settings for nonprofessional programs.

(3) Considerable effort is being directed at developing mental health training for postgraduate physicians. More and more of these individuals have been drawn to such educational experiences because of the perceived lack in their medical school psychiatric training as well as the extensive number of patients they encounter who have emotionally related problems. As noted earlier, physicians estimate that anywhere from 20 to 60 percent of their caseload involves patients with mild to severe emotional problems.

Mental health education has run the gamut from weekend workshops to year-long intensive training programs. Unfortunately despite the growing abundance of these highly needed programs, basic assessment of their actual merit has been neglected. Better controlled research is badly needed to determine the best mental health training and ultimate effectiveness of postgraduate physicians.

Fortunately, some very promising work has emerged from the intensive programs being developed at the University of California School of Medicine. This group of investigators has struggled for over a decade with the important issues of recruitment, effective training, and program evaluation. Out of their work has evolved highly practical didactic and experiential training packages, a strong concern for process and research methodology, and a commitment to balance the very real practical needs with systematic evaluation. Results so far have been fairly impressive, suggesting that postgraduate physicians can be effectively trained in various mental health capacities.

(4) Nonpsychiatric nurses have also been functioning and trained in various helping roles. Public health nurses in particular were seen to be key caregivers. In reviewing typical training programs in this area, it was noted that the quality of training and research has been rather varied, hence producing generally inconclusive program results. Projects developed by Maholick (1972) and Ahmed and Young (1974) were highlighted as demonstrating that comprehensive training was possible in preparing nonpsychiatric nurses for helping roles. In general, more research is needed to explore specific program effects on both trainees and patients. A particular issue raised in discussing the few nursing studies which were concerned with patient outcome (Hartlage 1970; Korson and Hayes 1966) was whether training or specific interventions had anything to do with reported patient improvement or whether changes were simply a response to the stimulation and interest provided by nurses.

(5) An essential criterion in evaluating the merits programs reviewed in this chapter is the actual intervention effects on patients. In those studies where research had at least been considered, the focus was more on changes in trainees than on actual helpee effects. These projects have been previously critiqued, and the point was made that various design flaws (e.g., lack of control groups) rendered the reported positive outcomes questionable. Of note is that these programs utilized students either in medical school (e.g., Uhlenhuth 1968a) or in psychiatric nursing rotations (Hartlage 1970; Korson and Hayes 1966). It is striking that no helpee outcome research efforts were found in any of the postgraduate physician and nursing programs, as these were considerably more numerous in the literature. The implication here is that further research is necessary at both the postgraduate and the student levels, specifically focusing on patient outcome effects. Only as such work is done will more conclusive statements regarding the training and effectiveness of medical and allied nonpsychiatric personnel be possible.

(6) The following additional issues were repeatedly cited as important ingredients for successful program development: the need for strong public relations to overcome the suspicions and fears of medical personnel regarding psychiatric training; active recruitment efforts to attract these people to mental health educational experiences; a didactic-experiential training approach particularly geared to practical suggestions and techniques which can easily be translated into practice following training; some provision for ongoing supervision, some type of backup support, or additional programs; and some built-in program feature (e.g., group process) which would promote group support, the personal expression of feelings, and overall comfort with this particular helping identity.

6   The Urban Agents

Urban agents include those nonprofessionals who are involved in less formal helping relationships than the caretakers described in the previous two chapters. Their roles within the community put them in key positions to offer direct help to troubled people or at least to serve a liaison function to appropriate professional agencies. Potential urban agents are such people as shopkeepers, foremen, taxicab drivers, bartenders, and beauticians (Caplan 1974a).

"Natural Neighbors"

The primary goal of a project described by Collins (1972) was to identify, recruit, and support those particular individuals who seemed to possess natural helping skills. These were the type of people that others turned to for aid during both mild and severe crises. A specific aim, was to locate those individuals engaged in some kind of child care activity and improve their skills through professional consultation. It was hoped that there would be an increase in the number of families to whom these individuals could be supportive. If one of these "natural neighbors" is involved with 50 to 75 families and the consultant has contact with 15 such individuals, then professional input can in effect be influencing, to some degree, over 750 families. "Natural neighbors" can be viewed as an important preventive mental health resource, particularly in their contact with populations often inaccessible to professionals.

Industry-Labor Personnel

As labor unions have begun to provide comprehensive medical programs, there has been a growing awareness that mental health services should be included to help ensure productive functioning both at home and on the job (Sommer 1969; Stone and Crowthers 1972). O'Connell (1968) has made several suggestions for improving the mental health services provided to industrial workers: (1) collective bargaining to see that adequate insurance coverage is available for diagnosis, psychotherapy, and other needed rehabilitative services; (2) legislative efforts at the local, state, and national levels to promote awareness of the latest mental health developments; (3) support of community efforts to develop mental health resources whose services would be available to union members; and (4) development of mental health services within the industry structure by contracting for outside professional help and/or training actual indigenous union members in specific helping roles. It is in this last area that organized labor's efforts are beginning to generate particularly creative mental health services.

Initial consultative attempts in industry were directed more at managerial and executive personnel than at lower-echelon workers such as foremen (e.g., Balinsky 1964). Recent programs have, however, been geared toward lower-echelon workers. Shop stewards and foremen have been trained to function in a front-line preventive role and to identify any peers in emotional crisis or manifesting psychological problems (e.g., O'Connell 1968; Tureen and Wortman 1965). In addition such workers might be trained to intervene in some more direct helping capacity after consulting with professionals as well as serving as referral links to other community resources. Since these programs have tended to be anecdotal, there are not much data to assess how well these individuals function in their new roles or the short- and long-run effects of their services.

Stoudenmire, Clark and Fleming (1974) suggest that the essentially supportive skills taught in these programs are undoubtedly quite useful, but they fault these training efforts for not going beyond such limited services and providing education in more direct, basic counseling skills. These writers strongly feel that the extensive mental health needs in industry require such an approach, and they have conducted two programs that have suggested that such training is indeed feasible and beneficial.

One moderately successful effort was conducted at a local garment factory (Stoudenmire 1972). Mental health consultation was initiated because of the difficulties the supervisors of the line operators were having in handling the variety of problems presented to them. Since these supervisors were essentially functioning as "counselors," it was decided, after a few planning meetings, to conduct a six-session seminar with the goal of providing them with some theory and background information as well as basic helping techniques. A particular aim was to make the supervisors more comfortable in their counseling role.

The training format was set for twice-a-week, 45-minute sessions that would extend over a 3-week period. The particular outline of the meetings was to include a 30-minute lecture followed by a 15-minute discussion. Lecture tapes focused on the meaning and significance of work, an understanding of why people behave as they do, employee and company morale, management of tensions and frustrations, and a discussion of the causes and effects of absenteeism. However, by the third session the structure of the seminar had to be modified as supervisors began to air personal problems regarding management, feelings of being overworked and not appreciated, and an overall sense of frustration with their numerous roles. Much of the lecture material had to be scrapped in favor of what was essentially supportive group meetings devoted to ventilation and discussion of feelings.

Postseminar results failed to show consistently positive changes in such variables as amount of counseling contact, types of problems handled, and perceived effectiveness. In general, there did appear to be a subjectively felt positive response on the part of participating supervisors, the majority of whom indicated that the meetings had been helpful and that they were desirous of future seminars. Stoudenmire (1972) suggested that insufficient planning of the seminar, and perhaps some lack of sensitivity regarding actual participant needs, may have prevented this program from fully achieving its intended goals. A particular problem he noted was the too theoretical, impractical nature of the lectures themselves, with an insufficient amount of time built into the program for supervisor participation and discussion. It appeared that once the focus did change to more of a discussion orientation, a greater amount of positive participation was evoked from the group members. There was a need for relatively concrete and specific suggestions that supervisors could subsequently utilize in their work.

The problems encountered in this program could be dealt with by the type of didactic-experiential training model highlighted throughout this book—an approach where skills can be practically learned and employed along with some format whereby participants can cope with their own feelings and personal growth. Stoudenmire made some relevant recommendations for future programs. For example, he emphasized the necessity for more planning both among the actual program participants and among all levels of the particular target group (e.g., managers, supervisors, and operators). Also, he stressed that experiential features should be programmed into training to generate more active and personal involvement by the participants. In addition, with the goal of greater precision in training and evaluation, it would be important to develop specific goals that are both objective and measurable.

A subsequent program developed by Stoudenmire, Clark, and Fleming (1974) capitalized on the strengths and weaknesses of the earlier project and incorporated the above suggestions into its planning and development. The participants in this program were twenty-one male foremen at a chemical plant. These individuals were experiencing some of the same difficulties facing the supervisors in the earlier program. After a series of preliminary planning meetings a program was developed consisting of ten weekly 1-hour sessions. During the first session the foremen were administered various questionnaires, adjective checklist measures, and, a personality inventory. The second through fifth meetings were specifically devoted to group process whereby foremen had an opportunity to ventilate and explore their personal and vocational problems. The sixth through ninth sessions focused on interpersonal relations, alcoholism, and other emotional problems. Various audiovisual aids were used to concretize how problems developed, were expressed at work, and therapeutic means for dealing with them. The last meeting of the program involved readministration of the tests.

Pretest and posttest results indicated moderate program success. Overall, foremen were better able to recognize emotional problems, assist workers with their difficulties, and feel more comfortable in their helping role. While this study appeared conceptually and methodologically sounder than the earlier program, it was still similarly empirically weak as seen in the failure, for example, to employ basic control groups, to deal with actual helpee outcome effects, and to follow up results. Despite these flaws the program did explicitly employ more practical and meaningful training approaches and underscored the need for operationalized behavioral training and research goals.

The work of Stoudenmire, Clark, and Fleming (1974) may perhaps serve as a model for future programs concerned with the training of lower-level industrial leaders. Their work points to the numerous issues inherent in preproject planning, actual program development and administration, posttraining follow-up, and evaluation. Only as these concerns are systematically dealt with will we be in a better position to clearly ascertain the most viable mental health training approaches to foremen and the subsequent impact of their intervention. Of merit in this program was its broader perspective to the foreman's helping role, seeking to acknowledge and embellish his counseling skills and not simply his referral capabilities. This is important because ultimately the professional workforce shortage will be alleviated by the development of new helping resources for much of the actual front-line work.

In summary, foremen, supervisors, and shop stewards have already been functioning in a supportive mental health capacity. The few programs reviewed here suggest that their existing skills can be sharpened and expanded. These individuals may be better trained to recognize problems, refer to other resources, or even provide supportive counseling when suitable. It is important that these workers accept and feel comfortable with such helping roles. Probably the most effective training of foremen is one that deemphasizes formal lectures, instead providing practical experiences, suggestions, and practice. Also apparently essential is the opportunity for group participants to explore their own frustrations and feelings about their new helping identity. At this point training programs are sparse and the research rudimentary. The results are nevertheless promising, and the conceptual and methodological issues raised point to reasonable leads for future substantive work in this area of nonprofessional training.

Bartenders

Because of the tendency of many persons to talk about their problems to bartenders and barbers, the mental health potential of these kinds of community agents is currently being explored (e.g., Snyder 1971). Dumont (1967), for example, has closely studied tavern culture and observed that bartenders are providing for the needs of numerous homeless and disturbed individuals untouched by available health and welfare agencies.

One rather innovative program sponsored by the Milwaukee County Mental Health Association clearly exemplifies the issues involved in training bartenders (Hunt 1972; Malcolm 1974). This program was initially spurred on during the late 1960s by the dearth of organized mental health programs in Milwaukee's inner city, an area saturated with many economic and social problems. Considerable doubt was initially expressed, however, about using bartenders in mental health roles. It seemed that bartenders making referrals would have to adversely affect a tavern's business and that patrons would resent intervention into their personal lives. Finally, even if these were not real drawbacks, the strongest issue concerned the all too frequent attitude that bartenders are primarily concerned with selling drinks and not helping people.

Despite such concerns, an attempt was made to recruit bartenders interested in participating in a mental health training course. Nine bartenders (three females and six males) from Milwaukee's central city comprised the training group. Of the participants, five were tavern owners, two were full-time employed bartenders, and two were part-time. The program consisted of ten sessions providing lecture and discussion around the following areas: problem customers for bartenders, identification of deviant behavior, ways of handling drunken patrons, the techniques of reflective listening skills, depression and suicide, mutual help techniques, and facts about alcohol abuse and treatment. Presentations were buttressed by field visits to alcohol rehabilitation centers, outpatient mental health centers, and day hospital and adolescent treatment units. Some excellent public relations and pragmatic steps facilitated attendance at the sessions. Inducements included paying bartenders $10 a session to offset possible loss of income for participating, providing taxi fares for those individuals with no means of transportation, and conducting the sessions at some convenient tavern within the inner city.

As this was a preliminary pilot project, little hard data were obtained regarding the impact of the program on the bartenders and their subsequent interactions with patrons. Hunt (1972) indicates that the assumption was made that traditional evaluative instruments (e.g., pretests and posttests) might have threatened the bartenders and inhibited their program participation. Instead, evaluation relied on (1) process notes of each session, which were systematically kept by observers; (2) structured interviews 2 months after the end of the program, focusing on such items as participants' impressions about the project, the extent to which they made referrals, and whether they perceived their understanding of and communication with patrons to have improved; and (3) informal follow-up contact with the bartender for additional feedback.

Results, then, were relatively informal and subjective. Overall impressions were favorable with bartenders increasingly utilizing information-giving and counseling techniques, feeling better able to recognize emotional problems, and making more use of referral resources for their own families and friends as well as patrons. Most important, it became readily apparent that bartenders demonstrated a great deal of interest and concern for their troubled customers and were not just interested in selling drinks.

Despite its basically descriptive nature, this program has been presented in some detail, because it highlights various features important to nonprofessional training. It is possible to negotiate a professional relationship with this important, but traditionally inaccessible caregiving group. The program described here was imaginative in its approach, planning, and actual program development. Particular sensitivity was paid to the existing skills and concerns of bartenders with the thrust being directed at meeting trainee needs. The project was also important in dispelling some myths and prejudices about bartenders, thus underscoring their considerable helping function.

Other creative work like this is being developed under the auspices of the North Dakota Mental Health Association (Miller 1973). This work is more expansive than the above bartender program. The aim here is to offer a mental health education course for all those individuals involved in selling alcoholic beverages to the general public. Included here would be bartenders, cocktail waitresses, club managers and owners, liquor store salespersons, and distributors. As yet no results of this program have been published, but the implications for recruiting and training such individuals are challenging.

Summary

Relatively few articles were available regarding the mental health work of this type of nonprofessional caregiver. Nevertheless, they appear to be highly important helping agents with a variety of natural "counseling" skills already available to them, as evidenced by the numerous people seeking their guidance and friendship. Snyder (1971), having surveyed the influence of both nonpsychiatric professionals and nonprofessional caregivers in the urban community, found that more people turned to family and friends than to physicians, lawyers, and clergy. This is consistent with the large number of troubled people seeking help from such diverse individuals as "natural neighbors," foremen, and bartenders. One overriding commonality appears to be strong perceptions of these people as friendly and sensitive individuals with whom others can share and talk about problems.

Too few articles were available regarding training and outcome to permit an extensive empirical discussion about the role and impact of these change agents. What work has been done seems to avoid "contaminating" the natural skills of these people so as not to make them over into miniature psychiatrists. Rather, training is designed to enhance and not replace existing capabilities. Such a cautious approach would seem to preclude structured training and systematic assessment. However, the work of Stoudenmire, Clark, and Fleming (1974) with foremen, and Hunt (1972) with bartenders, suggests that meaningful and researchable training programs can indeed be developed.

7

Self-Help Programs

Self-help programs include those subgroups of individuals either too often neglected or not sufficiently provided for by mental health professionals. Under this rubric are many diverse groups including the aged, addicted, impoverished, and liberated women—all evidencing considerable dissatisfaction with the inability of traditional mental health to provide them adequate services. Such individuals have increasingly attempted to sensitize professionals to their needs and/or have become involved in rather innovative self-help programs.

As will be demonstrated in this chapter, these people appear to be quite capable of serving in effective helping roles and producing positive changes both in themselves and in others being helped. This is quite consistent with Riessman's (1965) "helper-therapy principle," which contends that a person giving help to another will himself benefit from such a role. This helper-therapy principle is at the core of the self-help programs and also probably has an important function in the success of most other types of nonprofessional helpers. This reciprocal helping process has similarly been referred to as the "double change" phenomenon (Guerney 1969). The reader is urged to examine articles by Dumont (1974), Grob (1970), and Hurvitz (1970) for more detailed analyses of the background and theoretical underpinnings of the self-help movement.

Retired and Aged

The plight of the aged in our society is increasingly receiving attention, as this group may very well be the fastest growing, disenfranchised minority (Brotman 1974). The lack of appropriate physical and mental health services for the aged has been amply documented (e.g., Eisdorfer 1972; Hammerman 1974; Ozarin, Taube, and Spaner 1972). Lawton (1974) poignantly suggests that the numerous problems facing elderly people may be, in part, an artifact of the environmental strains society places on these people and not simply a reflection of the natural developmental loss of physical and mental capacity.

Fortunately this trend is beginning to change as attention is now being paid to retired people as a potential workforce resource. There is increasing recognition of the productive lives so many retirees have led as well as the interpersonal skills and "wisdom in living" they may have achieved (Cowen, Leibowitz, and Leibowitz 1968). Rather than continuing to delegate our elder citizens to years

85

of inactivity, more emphasis is now focused on recruiting and training these people for a variety of community service programs (Cowen 1970; Randall 1971; Rosenblatt 1966; Thune, Tine, and Booth 1964).

With respect to mental health work, retirees have served as companions to mental health center patients (Featherman and Welling 1971), aides for problem school children (Cowen, Leibowitz, and Leibowitz 1968), and as foster grandparents for emotionally disturbed children (Johnson 1967) and for institutionalized retarded children (e.g., Gray and Kasteler 1969; Hirschowitz 1973; Ryback, Sadnavitch, and Mason 1968).

With few exceptions, these reports present a sensitive account of constructive interactions between retirees and those they are helping, particularly when they are dealing with troubled children. These programs have tended to be informal with little training per se beyond some orientation, lectures, and on-the-job experience. Instead, the emphasis has been on capitalizing on the inherent experiences and feelings of the elderly as they begin to help their new "grandchildren."

Little research has been conducted on such programs aside from the collection of basic questionnaire and observational data. Overall impressions suggest much benefit for both retirees and those they are supposed to be helping. In this process two somewhat neglected groups of people (i.e., retirees and institutionalized children), when suddenly thrust upon each other, are able to establish a meaningful, loving relationship which provides for mutual needs in ways sorely lacking in their present lives. Among the particular gains of the "grandparents" are the satisfaction of simply doing productive work, the gratification of having helped a child in need of individualized attention, the feeling of competence in having worked collaboratively with professional staff, the sense of group support and identity from working with peers in an important endeavor, and an increased awareness of the potential political power and personal impact they, as elderly citizens, can still have on the system (Hirschowitz 1973).

Out of the above sample of programs, the project described by Cowen, Leibowitz, and Leibowitz (1968) is the most sophisticated in terms of structured training, research, and outcome. This particular program was actually part of a more extensive research project at the University of Rochester which was concerned with the development of techniques for the early detection and prevention of emotional problems in school settings. One focus in the program was on recruiting, training, and supervising a group of retirees to work as aides with young children manifesting adjustment problems in school.

After some preliminary inquiries to various relevant community agencies and "golden age clubs," twelve potential participants were interviewed and screened. Eventually six retired men and women, ranging in age from 65 to 80, were accepted as aides into this program. Following selection, trainees participated in a 2-month training program involving eleven 1½-hour sessions. The format of the meetings included the following: lecturettes on such areas as parent-child interactions and behavioral problems in children, discussion of issues related to intervention with children, film presentations depicting various relevant mental health situations, visits to schools to become familiar with personnel and existing programs, classroom observation, and various group supportive meetings to engender cohesiveness and confidence among participants.

Toward the end of the training period, participants were committed to a program involving 3 half-days a week for which they received payment of $15. Teachers from grades 1 to 3 referred any students to the program whom they felt might benefit from contact with the aides. The children evidenced problems such as academic underachievement and acting-out behavior. The amount of contact between children and adults varied, the average being two meetings per week for 30- to 45-minute sessions. The actual activities engaged in also differed depending upon the needs of the child. Some students might be engaged mostly in play activities, others in reading and writing, while still others in just talking and discussion. The aides apparently had some leeway to initiate activities they considered reasonable. Formal and informal ongoing supervision was provided on a weekly basis, either individually or in groups. The entire intervention phase of the program lasted for approximately 2 months subsequent to the initial training period. During this time a total of twenty-five children were seen by the six retired aides for anywhere from four to fifteen sessions per child.

Much of the evaluation was generally impressionistic, based on data obtained during the course of the program and the supervisory meetings. Those observations generally indicate that the schools were pleased with the effects of the program on the children. It appeared that program participants were highly committed to their work and both responsible and helpful in their dealings with the children. Somewhat more objective information was obtained by having aides fill out postprogram rating scales measuring their general attitudes toward the program as well as the gains they felt that the children had made during the project. Teachers were also asked to independently rate the progress of any children whom they referred to the program. Additional data were gathered by having teachers provide summary reports as well as from individual structured interviews with each of the aides. The results from the rating scales, summary reports, and interviews indicated that both the children and their helpers profited from their interactions—the former by making improved vocational and behavioral adjustments, the latter in feeling they had learned a good deal and provided a very useful service.

Cowen, Leibowitz, and Leibowitz (1968) recognized the limitations of this research (i.e., poor design, no controls, biased ratings, small sample size) and the inadvisability of generalizing from the reported positive findings. Nevertheless, both the limited objective and the clinically impressionistic data strongly suggest the viability of using retirees in this helping capacity as well as other related activities. Their high motivation, considerable free time, and minimal absentee-ism seen in this and other programs, indicate that they are a readily available and useful nonprofessional resource. It is not surprising that by 1970 more than 4000 retired adults were already participating in foster grandparent programs throughout the country and dealing with children in more than 180 different settings (Hirschowitz 1973).

Mentally Retarded

As there has been insufficient mental health services for the elderly, so too has there been a lack of adequate comprehensive care for retardates, particularly in settings such as community mental health centers (Dupont 1967). Among the problems impeding the provision of services through community settings have been attitudes and training deficits of professional personnel, community-held myths and taboos about retardation, and the lack of agreement between the public and mental health officials as to what kinds of help should be provided (Savino et al. 1973). For example, too often professional mental health workers have viewed retardation as a basically incurable and untreatable syndrome (Robinson and Robinson 1965). Such pessimism generally has often led to inadequate, half-hearted rehabilitative programs. Fortunately, as noted, the trend is now beginning to change with apparently productive treatment pro-grams being available through various community settings, such as special education classes within schools, clinics, agency-sponsored workshops, halfway houses, and other transitional living arrangements.

Developments in recent years have led to programs utilizing specially selected and trained retardates capable of providing supportive care to some of their peers. The helper-therapy principle is very much operative here, with the expressed hope that the helpers will gain as much as the helpees.

McKinney and Keele (1963) utilized 12 mildly retarded mother surrogates (with IQs of 40 to 80) to care for 48 profoundly retarded young boys (of IQ less or equal to 30). Pretreatment levels of helpee functioning were based on extensive staff ratings and direct behavioral observations. Subjects were assigned to either an experimental treatment group or a nontreatment control group. The subjects were matched on variables such as IQ, feeding, and toilet habits. The two groups were placed in different housing units.

Surrogate helpers were chosen for expressed interest, demonstrated nur-turance, and the desire to mother two chosen boys in the experimental group. These "mothers" played with the boys, taught them new words, skills, and interests, and initiated much physical contact such as touching and hugging. This intervention phase with the experimental group boys lasted 1 month, with the surrogate helpers providing care for at least 4 hours a day, 5 days per week. Throughout the treatment period, constant supervision of the helpers was provided. Results indicated significant differences between groups, with the experimental boys demonstrating increased adaptive and goal-directed behavior, social interaction, and verbal and nonverbal communication. These changes were attributed by McKinney and Keele (1963) to the "increased sensory aspects" provided by the surrogate mothering.

There are, of course, empirical problems with this study such as the vagueness of the "mothering behavior" and just what types of supervisory help were provided. The available data do not allow one to differentiate whether a particular type of nurturance or simply increased stimulation accounted for the changes observed for the experimental group. The results may also be interpreted as due to unspecific modeling effects, and the positive reinforcement the mothers may have provided for adaptive behavior (Craighead and Mercatoris 1973). Greater precision in defining the independent variables (e.g., operationalized behaviors) and use of attention-placebo or alternative treatment control groups would have allowed a clearer understanding of the effects of this promising program.

In recent years there have, in fact, been a plethora of such programs for retardates, all aimed at concretizing intervention and research goals in terms of behavioral and learning principles (see Kazdin 1973 for discussion of issues). Yates (1970) hailed behavior modification technology as the necessary antidote to the presumed uneducable and unrehabilitative nature of most mentally deficient individuals. He particularly underscored the advantages of a behavioral approach in both defining the nature of deficits and developing systematic techniques for effectively dealing with them. It is not surprising to note the emergence of programs describing retardates helping other retardates, utilizing behavior modification approaches with appropriate positive reinforcement for both helper and helpee. For example, feelings of self-esteem and competency have been enhanced in retarded individuals trained in modeling and reinforcement techniques aimed at teaching adaptive behavior to younger children (Whalen and Henker 1969, 1971a, 1971b) and eliminating disruptive classroom behavior (Drabman and Spitalnik 1973).

Helper training in such programs usually consists of very concrete explanations, modeling, practice, and ongoing feedback and supervision from a staff person experienced in behavior modification approaches. The specific interventions of these peer helpers typically involve developing imitative motor and verbal behavior, establishing eye contact and attention behaviors, and eliminating disruptive actions. It should also be emphasized that the ability of retarded helpers to perform such tasks appears to be contingent on the concurrent ongoing verbal (praise) and nonverbal (e.g., tokens) reinforcement they themselves receive from staff for success in their work. The implication here is that once positive reinforcement from staff is withdrawn, there might be a concomitant drop in effective helping behavior by the retarded aides.

Craighead and Mercatoris (1973) have critically reviewed some of the available literature on retardates as peer helpers, particularly those residential programs focusing on the use of behavior modification techniques. They make the following pertinent points:

(1) Mentally retarded individuals appear to have successfully served in limited mental health roles. While the data are promising, they are still somewhat meager and thus further research is strongly encouraged to buttress this conclusion.

(2) They have effectively functioned primarily as reinforcing agents for particular target behaviors in specific experimental situations.

(3) Attempts at broader field research and at generalizing both the helper and helpee gains to other situations have been inconclusive.

(4) A major goal in utilizing paraprofessional manpower is to conserve staff time for other kinds of services. As helping performance of retarded aides seems so linked to staff involvement, it would be important to develop further programs whereby these helpers could function in a more independent fashion.

(5) There is a need for research efforts aimed at developing peer helpers capable of functioning in broader, more extensive roles than those noted above. For example a peer helper might serve as a milieu change agent rather than in more typical one-to-one interactions. The greater the range of service the helper could provide, the greater the increase in available professional time.

(6) Finally, despite the fact that retarded helpees may benefit from contact with their peer helpers, just as important gains are achieved by the helpers themselves. The amount of time spent with the training staff and the clear expectations and reinforcements given by the staff to them may be the major factors in gains manifested by the peer helpers.

Psychiatric Patients

In Chapter 1 it was pointed out that extensive rethinking was occurring regarding psychiatric care whether in or out of the hospital. The community mental health movement, in particular, was seen as a revolutionary attempt to offer better-quality services to more members of the general population (Hobbs 1964). Changes in theory and philosophy, requisite skills and possible programs, and types of service providers have all been evident in the community mental health movement. Legislators, various consumer groups, and patients themselves have all joined ranks in calling for effective, readily available, and accountable mental health services (e.g., Ginsberg 1974). This broad trend may be seen as a strong reaction to the general failure of traditional psychiatric practices to provide adequate services as well as to the deplorable and archaic conditions too often existing in private and state institutions (Bloom 1973).

Inpatient Programs

With regard to increasing the effectiveness of current hospital settings, changes have been directed at the physical, environmental, and program levels. Critics have been most concerned with understanding and counteracting those particular institutional conditions reinforcing chronicity and the dehumanization of patients (e.g., Braginsky, Braginsky, and Ring 1969; Cumming and Cumming 1969; Goffman 1961).

The use of patients in self-help or mutually supportive ways is a particularly important development as it challenges traditional stereotypes of patients, namely, that they are basically passive, withdrawn individuals, unable to responsibly care for themselves, let alone others. Instead, the new assumption is that patients are indeed capable of initiative and responsible action provided that there are clear expectations for such behavior and that emotional strengths are emphasized as opposed to disabilities (Wolkon, Karmen, and Tanaka 1971). Psychiatric inpatients have served therapeutic functions as individual counselors (Pfeiffer 1967), ward assistants (Kent 1969), psychiatric interviewers (Shiloh 1969), and mutually supportive participants in milieu therapy (Kale, Zlutnik, and Hopkins 1970; Pomerleau, Bobrove, and Harris 1972).

Typically these programs are characterized by minimal research and training. Some exceptions have emerged in the literature describing somewhat better-researched, innovative efforts, all attempting to deal more with methodology, training, and outcome issues (e.g., Hanson et al. 1969, 1970; Ludwig and Marx 1969; Magaro and Staples 1972; Orlando 1974). For example, Ludwig and Marx (1969) developed a structured "buddy treatment" model whereby teams of paired patients became responsible for one another's functioning on a psychiatric ward. Privileges and rewards were made contingent only upon the team's joint behavioral progress and not just the gains evidenced by one patient or another. Each team member had to be just as concerned about his "buddy's" as his own performance level if added privileges were to be accrued.

Whereas in the Ludwig and Marx (1969) program participants helped one another in various ward work and activity situations, another inpatient program described by Hanson et al. (1969) focused on human relations training and mutual support through intensive group interaction. It is a self-help, self-governed, program. As of 1970 over 1500 patients had participated in this program. There have been several studies investigating the short- and long-term impact of this program. Results suggest improvement in hospital adjustment, interpersonal skills, and increased self-esteem and competency (Johnson et al. 1965; Rothaus and Hanson 1965; Rothaus et al. 1966; Rothaus et al. 1963).

This program and some of the other projects noted above, such as those described by Ludwig and Marx (1969) and Orlando (1974), while relatively better developed and researched than earlier programs, are still somewhat limited empirically (e.g., occasional absence of controls, vague and gross criteria, and lack of follow-up). Nevertheless the general results suggest the viability of using inpatients in a variety of self-help roles. Such programs also demonstrate that better research is indeed possible, and hopefully more sound investigations of this nature will be forthcoming. Perhaps, most important, they highlight the fact that chronic patients are not simply regressed, ineffective subhumans, but rather often quite responsible individuals capable of therapeutically caring for themselves and for others—if they are involved in an environment reinforcing such behaviors.

Therapeutic Communities

The articles cited in the previous section involved various inpatient projects specifically aimed at promoting individual (e.g., Pfeiffer 1967) or small group (e.g., Hanson et al. 1969) self-help. Other programs, more intensive in nature, also facilitate mutual self-help, but in a less structured manner. The focus now is on a more global mode involving the whole ward milieu. Overall, this "therapeutic community" approach has attempted to incorporate the latest progressive thinking and programming in psychiatric hospitals, with particular emphasis on total community involvement (i.e., all patients and personnel on a ward) and highly active rehabilitation programs.

Jones (1953, 1968), particularly, has been a prime developer of therapeutic communities and views such milieus as comprehensive healing environments characterized by continual analysis of all ward events, community meetings, role examination and blurring, and flattening of the typical hierarchical boundaries between patients and professional workers. Such diffusion of roles has promoted considerable patient initiative and responsibility. For example, decision making processes have been established whereby patients themselves have considerable leverage in determining policies and programs for individuals and groups, monitor progress or problems, and help determine sanctions (positive or negative).

Despite the popularity of this approach to hospital rehabilitation, there has been little adequate research examining the effectiveness of such programs. This may be a function, in part, of the seemingly impossible task of quantifying and assessing a therapeutic social climate in which programs and helpers may be quite intertwined and forever changing. So much is going on in these wards in a given day that it is quite difficult to distinguish exactly who or what is having an impact. A program by Myers and Clark (1972) did attempt to empirically assess a typical therapeutic milieu in terms of its own value as well as in comparison to a more traditional ward program. In this study two matched psychiatric wards were compared, one traditional, the other a therapeutic milieu. These wards were at two different hospitals, both of which were the only psychiatric inpatient facilities for medium- or long-stay patients in their respective catchment areas. The general goal of the program was to examine periodically the progress of every man taken into either ward in a particular year and to specifically compare the effects of the two regimes. The specific variables under investigation were how these wards compared on the acceptance and containments of patients.

The therapeutic community ward was actually integrated into a mixed male and female patient milieu, in which most of the patients were involved daily in hospital workshops, occupational therapy, and paid work in the community for some. A particular program emphasis on the unit consisted of frequent meetings constantly examining everyday events on the unit. Aside from these group meetings, traditional treatments were utilized such as tranquilizers, ECT, and anticonvulsive medication.

The general atmosphere on this ward appeared to be quite flexible with much interaction between male and female patients and patients and staff. Ward meetings involved everyone on the ward as well as other interested hospital staff members and relatives. Open contact with the rest of the hospital and the outside community was strongly encouraged, as evidenced by a series of outings and parties throughout the year.

The traditional psychiatric ward was in marked contrast to the therapeutic milieu. Although it was an open ward, patients were essentially isolated from the outside community. While ECT use was similar to the therapeutic ward, all patients were on major tranquilizers. Professional staff had minimal involvement on this ward, seeing their major ward function as maintaining "discipline." Significantly absent were any organized meetings for evaluating ward events, discussion of mutual feelings, development of programs, and exploration of policies. Instead sanctions tended to be punitive and exclusively staff-imposed.

Compared to the traditional ward, the patients in the therapeutic community unit made significantly more positive changes with respect to clinical symptoms, overall adjustment, discharge from the hospital, and interaction with both staff and fellow patients. Myers and Clark (1972) concluded that the therapeutic community model is far superior to traditional psychiatric hospital treatment and thus well worth the time and effort spent in utilizing professional personnel. While this may be so, it is a conclusion not strongly supported by the results of their program.

Too many empirical irregularities mute positive findings reported by Myers and Clark (1972). These deficiencies include not carefully matching and randomly assigning patients to wards, poor measures and biased ratings. Even if these shortcomings were corrected, the question would still remain as to whether there can be a valid comparison of two such differing and frequently changing ward programs. The units differed on such variables as male and female patient ratios and interactions, use of medication, number and methods of staff involvement, types of programs on and off the ward, contact with hospital personnel and visitors, and community participation. Each of these variables could possibly play a major or minor role in facilitating positive patient change, but these factors were not held constant or controlled. It thus seems invalid to make comparisons between two such wards. In this study it is not clear what factors were being compared and contrasted.

It is very likely that therapeutic communities are quite beneficial to patients' hospital and subsequent community adjustment. The staff investment in time and energy, the strong reinforcement of growth and responsibility, and the overall stimulation and attention program participants receive in such milieus are all variables which undoubtedly promote patient gains. While it would seem that patient mutual self-help would be an important ingredient in a therapeutic community, it is difficult to sift out just how important an influence the process is by itself or in interaction with the various other factors.

Effective research would have to more clearly operationalize the numerous elements involved in the therapeutic community. However, concretizing and controlling these factors may be rather difficult as the therapeutic concept is as much a philosophical attitude and emotional commitment as it is a specific program. The Myers and Clark (1972) program is commendable, but obviously further research is needed to grapple with the above issues.

Critique of Hospital-Based Programs

Regardless of the reported efficacy of any psychiatric hospital-based inpatient programs, there still continues to be an avalanche of criticism regarding this approach and a concomitant push for alternative treatment programs (e.g., Clayton 1974; Miller 1966; Polak and Jones 1973). Psychiatric hospitalization, regardless of the program, is still seen as a debilitating and stigmatizing intervention with little consistent relationship to modern mental health thinking and helping techniques.

Polak and Jones (1973), for example, view the hospital as a potentially irrational social system. They critically question a number of basic assumptions such as that hospitalized patients and therapists work toward the same treatment goals, that the main problem to be treated is the patient, that the patient's deviant behavior can be assessed and diagnosed in the hospital better than in his own natural home environment, and that problems patients exhibit outside the hospital will necessarily be repeated inside the hospital. Polak and Jones (1973) conclude that all these assumptions are fallacious, and thus most hospital programs could profit from a thorough review of their inherent values and treatment techniques.

In contrast to the previous trend of criticism are the conclusions reached by Atkinson (1975) in a recent sobering review of the literature on current and emerging models of residential psychiatric treatment. He suggested that the challenge to the utility of traditional psychiatric hospitalization is based more on impressions and rhetoric than on adequate empirical, generalizable data. He emphasized the lack of consideration of variations among the populations and communities served by different hospitals.

Partial Hospitalization—Community Self-Help Programs

One finding that does appear quite tenable is that even the most effective hospital-based inpatient programs do not seem able to reduce readmission rates. Miller (1966), for example, cited figures indicating that while more and more patients are exiting from hospitals, their rehospitalization rate is also steadily increasing to the point where readmission is becoming a major public health problem.

It would seem that the success of patients' subsequent community adjustment may not necessarily be related to their previous hospital involvement, but rather to the relative availability of posthospital follow-up care (Weiss, Roberts, and Wolford 1969). It is with this in mind that programs have been developed to provide transitional and aftercare experiences to buttress the effects of the hospital program. Such efforts offer rehabilitative experiences which can more concretely affect a successful reentry into community life (e.g., Daniels 1969; Daniels, Zelman, and Campbell 1967; Fairweather 1964; Fairweather et al. 1969; Lurie and Ron 1971; Sanders, Smith, and Weinman 1967; Weinman et al. 1970, 1974).

Fairweather and his associates described an experimental hospital ward where patients became involved in problem-solving groups (Fairweather 1964; Fairweather et al. 1969). The emphasis was on self-help as group members worked their way through a four-stage program terminating in hospital release. A key element in the process was in group feedback regarding correct behavior and future plans. A behavior modification feature complemented the autonomous small group work such that the patient's progress during each of the stages was reinforced with increased spending money and hospital passes. Evaluation over a three-year period compared experimental treatment patients with a matched group of traditional ward patients on a variety of criterion measures (e.g., patient attitudes and behavior ratings, length of hospital stay, discharge follow-up). Results indicated significantly superior changes for the experimental treatment patients.

However, a 6-month follow-up failed to show significant differences in the readmission rates for both wards, forcing Fairweather and his associates to conclude that further community training and practical experiences were needed to translate any of the newly acquired hospital skills into subsequent successful community adjustment. A new feature was added to the program: released patients were sent to live in a community lodge, run and operated by the patients themselves. Essential to the community living experience was the development of employment opportunities for the ex-patients. Patients were trained in janitorial and gardening skills and subsequently placed with interested community customers. A central aspect in the development of the lodge was its highly autonomous nature; both professional and nonprofessional contact were minimal. This part of the program was assessed by comparing lodge program patients with a matched control group of patients who were directly released into the community without specific training opportunities. Results over a 40-month period (i.e., measures taken every 6 months) indicated that lodge participants had a significantly higher rate of employment and remained longer in the community than the control group patients (Fairweather et al. 1969).

A similar combined hospital-community program has been described by Daniels and his associates (Daniels 1969; Daniels, Zelman, and Campbell 1967). In this program, the overall goal was again to promote patient responsibility, initiative, and mutual self-help. To achieve these goals, a house painting company was formed consisting of eight VA-hospitalized patients who themselves had the primary responsibility for working out their interpersonal relationships, discussing their goals and upcoming community painting projects, and overseeing most of their own outside-the-hospital experiences. Of note is the fact that over a 10-month period, 20 painting projects were completed, grossing over $24,000. Other results indicated a favorable reception by customers, as well as a good improvement in the vocational and behavioral adjustment of the patients.

Another feature incorporated into this program was the creation on one of the hospital wards of the Dann Services Program (DSP), a project in which patients have the responsibility for giving other patients vocational training in a sheltered workshop and, if possible, finding them outside employment. An evaluation comparing DSP patients with another ward control group suggested more behavioral improvement and better work adjustment for the DSP patients as well as continued community adaptation at an 18-month follow-up during the first year of discharge (Daniels, Zelman, and Campbell 1967).

However, this program failed to positively affect rehospitalization rates. Daniels and his associates saw a need to develop community living experiences to ensure better adjustment upon release. This was accomplished through the development of a special housing division which was similar to Fairweather's lodges in that it was a community arrangement operated and maintained by the ex-patients themselves. Unfortunately, sufficient data are not available to adequately assess the impact of this phase of the program.

Weinman and his colleagues have developed a series of rehabilitative projects quite similar to the above programs in terms of conceptualization, goals, program developments, successes and failures, and the essential necessity of community living experiences (Sanders, Smith, and Weinman 1967; Weinman et al. 1970, 1974). This program tends to differ, however, in its somewhat lesser emphasis on patient self-help and greater reliance on community volunteers and professional support.

The combined hospital-community projects discussed in this section are of a suggestive to adequate research quality. There has generally been a concern with objectively assessing the merits of the programs as well as paying particular attention to the short- and long-term outcome effects on the patient participants. There have been adequate controls including nontreatment and/or alternative treatment control groups. Multiple outcome criteria have been measured in these programs such as inpatient and outpatient attitudinal and behavioral ratings, length of hospital and/or community stay, follow-up after discharge, reports from significant others, and readmission rates.

The results tend to support the effectiveness of this kind of combined transitional rehabilitative program. Successful posthospital adjustment (in terms of work, interpersonal skills, and daily living ability) seems to be linked to participation in community-based programs emphasizing concrete training, application, and feedback. While the concept of individual and group self-help is a paramount feature in these programs, there is some variation in the degree to which nonpatient support (e.g., professionals) is included in some or all aspects of the programs.

Despite the better research quality of these programs, some caution should still be noted in generalizing the results. For example, such interventions were really quite complex treatment approaches (e.g., multiple programs, variety of staff, etc.) which makes it difficult to tease out the impact of particular variables such as the role played by patient self-help. While the community experience appears essential to effective posthospital rehabilitation, it is sometimes not apparent what specific program factors are contributing to the success.

Is it the type of task group, the development of group cohesiveness, the extensive autonomy promoted, the nature of the particular living arrangements, the involvement or uninvolvement of professionals and paraprofessionals, or the relationship of family, friends, or other external support systems that contribute to an effective program? All these variables may either individually or in combination play an important role in such programs, but their actual contribution is not yet clear. The work of Weinman et al. (1974) has, however, attempted to examine such issues. In their study, they included a variety of comparative control groups such as patients working with professionals, patients working with nonprofessionals, patients living in apartments with peers and receiving visits from such helpers, and patients actually living in the helpers' homes. Such research can be important in clarifying the essential or superfluous elements in these programs.

Another line of caution is suggested from Atkinson's (1975) comments concerning the inconclusive nature of much of the research evaluating the effectiveness of inpatient psychiatric programs. He noted that the failure to control for a number of patient and hospital variables made some of the conclusions tenuous. Since not all these variables were stringently accounted for in the combined transitional programs, definitive statements about these projects may also be somewhat premature.

The very nature of the patient groups selected for the hospital-community programs raises questions in appraising the results. Although the patient participants in these programs are usually quite disturbed (e.g., diagnosed chronic shizophrenics), they may nevertheless be in better emotional condition than the patients either excluded from the programs or comprising other no-treatment or alternative treatment control groups. These patients tend to be described as volunteers, having somewhat stable outside community resources (family and friends), and are apparently generally cooperative in the treatment programs. Patients who are either excluded from or fail to complete these programs are usually in a higher risk category (e.g., assaultive, suicidal, physically ill, socially isolated). The patients included in these programs may be a biased sample in terms of already being favorably predisposed to treatment effects while excluded patients possess characteristics often unamenable to most interventions. One implication is that if these programs are indeed effective, they may be so with only a limited kind of patient population. Also, as the patients comprising both experimental and control groups are not really matched, one wonders whether any reported significant outcome effects are a function of the actual program or simply a reflection of important pre-treatment patient differences.

Another implication is that numerous individuals desperately in need of adequate services are simply not receiving them. It is little wonder that readmission rates are so high. As these programs point out, even better adjusted patients must have intensive community work to increase their chances of making an adjustment outside of the hospital. It is no surprise, then, that the more difficult patient, not involved in any transitional community work, is very quickly rehospitalized. The more seriously disturbed patients, perhaps most in need of services, are generally not even exposed to sound rehabilitation techniques. This is not necessarily a fault of such programs, as they might be quite effective when tailored to specific types of patients meeting their particular criteria. It does mean, however, that more expansive rehabilitative projects are needed to meet this deficit in chronic patient care. Fortunately, recent programs have begun to be described in the literature which attempt to offer vital and effective services to a truly broad sample of psychiatric patients (e.g., Stein, Test, and Marx 1975).

A third area needing consideration is that of the very criteria measures gauged in these programs, such as the length of hospital stay, readmission rates, degree of adequate social conformity, manifest symptoms and maladaptive behavior, and reemployment (e.g., Erickson 1972). The problem here is that such measures may have little to do with actual treatment success or failure.

Length of stay or lack of readmission may be primarily a reflection of the cost accounting of the funding agency rather than an indication of the individual's ability to function (Atkinson 1975). Such "payoff variables" may accordingly become the major barometer of program selection as funding agencies may be concerned only with favorable statistics in these particular areas. Simply measuring rehospitalization and considering it as a unidimensional concept is highly questionable. The complexity of readmission rates must be systematically taken into account.

This line of reasoning may be equally applicable to the other types of criteria typically measured in these programs. For example, community, family, and work adaptation typically seem to be a function of the subjective evaluations of relatives, friends, and employers rather than a more objective appraisal according to unbiased yardsticks. It often appears that "coping" is more a reflection of others' particular value expectations than a precise definition of the functioning of patients' real limits and capabilities. Similarly, inpatient rating measures of hospital adjustment (e.g., manifest symptoms) also seem vulnerable to the pitfalls of biased and inferential judgment.

The suggestion is made that, along with these more global, "payoff" kinds of criteria, greater precision should be achieved in operationalizing specific criteria which fit more consistently with the actual program training and experience. More concrete and behavioral criteria could be developed directly from the program itself. For example, many of these programs are concerned with developing specific instrumental and problem-solving behaviors to meet the goals and demands of life (e.g., laundry upkeep, cooking, shopping, going to restaurants, grooming, budgeting, use of transportation, working). Training and assessment should thus focus on specific skills and not on some more complex criterion such as discharge rates which may be a function of influences external to the program. Such specific behavioral criteria would probably better reflect actual program effects. This issue is similar to the one raised in the earlier discussion on police crisis work (Chapter 4), where it was suggested that crime rates were not a particularly sensitive measure of the training and subsequent intervention effects of police personnel.

Aftercare Facilities and Programs

Mention should also be made of other transitional community living arrangements for patients newly released from the hospital, but who are in no condition to return home. These programs differ from those in the previous section in not being specifically connected with a particular inpatient program. Rather, these are more independent aftercare programs which also attempt to respond to the ex-patient's need to develop appropriate self-help and problem-solving skills. Currently, the facilities utilized by hospitals to meet such needs include sheltered workshops, halfway houses, boarding homes, family-care homes, nursing homes, hotels, and independent or cooperative apartments (e.g., Beard et al. 1964; Blumberg 1970; Brook 1973; Chien and Cole 1973; Rausch and Rausch 1968; Richmond 1970).

These programs tend to vary in terms of quality, program development, emphasis on self-help, degree of external support, and continuity with other hospital or community resources. For example, the nursing home care often sounds little better than traditional custodial ward care, while the more in-depth programs (e.g., Chien and Cole 1973) encourage the kind of self-help and skill building found in the comprehensive hospital-community programs. It is difficult to evaluate these programs as they tend to be descriptive or of minimal research value. The empirical and conceptual questions raised in previous sections are largely left unanswered.

A particularly exciting idea for an aftercare type of facility was developed by Miller (1966). This program would consist of an "aftercare supermarket" and adult education center. There would be possibilities for various types of transitional aftercare programming. Furthermore, Miller envisions building into the program delivery services as a means for getting to the less ambulatory ex-patient as well as 24-hour services to provide comprehensive coverage for evening and weekend crisis periods. Perhaps most important is the emphasis on self-help. She suggests that, as much as possible, all departments in the supermarket be manned by ex-patients themselves.

Despite its somewhat idealistic and fanciful nature, Miller's (1966) proposed program is consistent with the best ideas in comprehensive mental health care, concrete skill-building development, and patient self-help. If even only a small portion of this "supermarket" notion came into being, it might very well provide the essential continuity in care needed not simply for some marginal patient reentry into the community, but rather for a higher adequate aftercare adjustment. What also is suggested is that such a program has preventive as well as remedial possibilities. Many ex-patients undoubtedly lack basic instrumental and problem-solving skills prior to their hospitalization. It is possible that if these individuals had had such a facility available to them earlier in their development, institutionalization might have been avoided. This type of program also has implications for the other kinds of undeserved, often disenfranchised groups noted earlier in this chapter. In any case, such an aftercare service would probably help ex-mental patients make a satisfactory adjustment within the community and avoid repeated returns to the psychiatric hospital. Hopefully, programs of this nature will be developed in the future and their effectiveness appropriately assessed.

Ex-patient Self-Help Groups and Social Clubs

Perhaps the most striking example of the helper therapy principle in action is the tremendous growth of nonprofessionally led self-help clubs or groups. The persistent increase of these organizations in the face of great difficulties in financing, staffing, and managing is very impressive. Psychiatric social clubs may be seen as the furthest extension of transitional care into the community. Individuals involved in such programs may be making a somewhat better community adjustment and thus may not require the more protective environment of boarding homes or halfway houses. Or they may be people for whom other aftercare modalities have simply not been effective. These clubs have also attempted to provide comprehensive programs for individuals who have been either underserviced or ineffectively provided for. Despite their variety, these groups are similar in their essential goals of establishing peer-run therapeutic communities aimed at fostering self-help skills and personal and vocational development (e.g., Dean 1970, 1971; Grob 1970; Hawxhurst and Walzer 1970; Lee 1971; Wagner 1965).

Typical of these programs is an intensive and supportive group system filled with purpose and mission and the strongly held belief that such "clubs" are essential, either as an adjunct to or in place of traditional services. Particular criticism has been directed at psychiatric services where the therapeutic roles, definitions of healthy and disturbed behavior, and intervention approaches are seen as counterproductive to true patient growth and development. These clubs attempt to counteract such traditional helping models by instead promoting new definitions, roles, and interventions—the basic ingredient being self-help by individuals who have been through similar experiences.

The common elements in these programs include intense emotional identification with a peer group; an emphasis on action and experience; communication with individuals of similar education, social and cultural background, and psychological problems; free and open group work and discussion; and much peer modeling, social learning, and feedback/confrontation (Steele 1974). Overall, there appears to be a degree of caring and involvement in these mutual help groups essentially absent in most professional treatment approaches. Although they have common underpinnings, these self-help programs may differ in size and structure, intensity of interventions, cultural and locale influences, and degree of commitment to mutual help and outside community or professional support.

Evaluation of Psychiatric Self-Help Clubs

Despite the growth and fervor surrounding these programs, it is difficult to objectively appraise their actual effectiveness. Certainly on an impressionistic basis they must be providing viable services, given the increasing number of individuals joining these organizations as well as the expansion of such groups throughout the country.

However, hard data to empirically evaluate these programs are not available. This is not surprising given the essentially "lay" nature of these organizations and the usual absence of individuals sophisticated in research skills. But also contributing to the lack of evaluation are anti-intellectual, antiprofessional attitudes often held by program participants who may strongly mistrust professionals and their methods.

Given these factors, it is little wonder that these programs lack the most basic empirical data to support their claims. Aside from this lack of evaluation, other criticisms have been aimed at these programs, particularly at their intensive encounter approach, common failure to recognize individual differences, lack of organization, occasional inspirational and religious flavor, and somewhat middle-class orientation.

It also needs to be emphasized that too often the professional mental health worker is patronizing and condescending in his attitudes toward self-help clubs, at best viewing them benignly as mild supportive resources lacking real therapeutic clout. However, if research began to support the effectiveness of self-help clubs, and particularly if solid data indicated that these groups were equal to, if not better than, professional interventions, then professionals would be compelled to reexamine both their thinking and their services. For example, long-held views regarding the nature of therapy time, legitimate types of help, and professional-patient roles may turn out merely to reflect values espoused in theory and graduate school—without particular relevance to effective patient care. Of course such a proposition may be a threat to professional workers and hence may relate to their ambivalence regarding self-help clubs (e.g., Mabel 1971). But if legitimate research is forthcoming, there might be more impetus for professionals to recognize the merits of these groups and examine their own intervention repertoire. Ultimately, if this crucially needed interface is to occur between professional caregivers and self-help clubs, the members of both camps will have to shelve their mutual antipathy and biases about each other's motives and skills.

It appears that self-help clubs may be providing an important service to numerous types of outpatients; but not enough empirical data are available to objectively support this assertion and particularly to identify exactly *who* is being helped, by *what* means, and for *how long*. As indicated above, such information would have important ramifications for both nonprofessional and professional helpers. Very likely, based on conclusions drawn in previous chapters, the key ingredients in these clubs are their specific skill-building emphasis, peer modeling, feedback and confrontation, and continual refinement of skills—all in a mutually supportive group atmosphere.

Summary

The previous sections have examined the self-help role played by psychiatric patients in a variety of settings. There was an evaluation of services relating to patient hospital wards, combined hospital-community transitional programs, community aftercare projects, and patient-run self-help clubs and groups. It was usually difficult to assess the extent to which the self-help principle was operative. For example, while it was a seemingly key element in all the above programs, mutual help was easy to pinpoint as a major process in the psychiatric clubs, but was generally buried within the context of the many services offered in some of the more comprehensive transitional programs. There was also much variety in the actual helping services provided, some programs clearly offering individual and group counseling, with other projects essentially providing strong supportive care. While all these programs fit under the broad rubric of psychiatric self-help, there is actually considerable variety in the nature of this help and the degree to which it is provided by the patients themselves.

Given these broader generalizations, the following specific points may be noted:

(1) While psychiatric inpatients have reportedly functioned well in self-help roles, the quality of research supporting such claims has been limited. The conceptual and methodological issues in the majority of these studies are much in need of clarification (Atkinson 1975).

(2) Relatively effective examples of patient mutual self-help seem to be embedded in some of the comprehensive hospital-community transitional programs. Research has suggested that structured aftercare programs are essential to successful posthospital adjustment and to reduction in readmission. While these programs have tended to be reasonably researched, issues were raised regarding imprecisely controlled patient and program variables as well as vague and irrelevant criterion measures. Caution is indicated in interpreting the reported findings. Suggestions were offered for adding better controls and operationalizing concrete, behavioral criteria more consistent with actual program format and goals.

(3) Other more community-based aftercare facilities (e.g., nursing homes, halfway houses, etc.) were also discussed. These programs tended to vary in breadth and quality, and their primarily anecdotal nature prevented objective evaluation of their merits. One particular program described by Miller (1966) was focused on as a potentially heuristic working model for both developing and evaluating true self-help aftercare programs.

(4) Outpatient self-help clubs and organizations were similarly examined, and they appeared to be the clearest examples of mutual caring and the helping process. Both the philosophy and actual application of these groups were noted as well as their apparent drawing power and impact on individuals who have so often become disenchanted with traditional services. The additional role of such organizations as either a follow-up or an adjunct resource to other professional work was also cited.

Despite much enthusiasm as to the need for and effectiveness of these groups, little systematic research is available to specify just how helpful these clubs really are and, if so, what factors are contributing to their success. One of the problems blocking such assessment is the antiprofessional attitudes of the club participants on the one hand and the negativism and condescension evidenced by professionals on the other. As was pointed out, such mutual antagonism has often inhibited objective appraisals which might have important implications for the functioning of both the clubs and the professionals.

In addition, the helping group process inherent in these organizations was seen in terms of behavioral and social learning principles. Such elements as concrete behavioral skills, peer modeling, and group feedback may be viewed as being consistent with the didactic-experiential nonprofessional training model noted throughout this book. While this type of training is most apparent in psychiatric clubs, they are probably equally operative in many of the other types of self-help programs for patients and ex-patients.

(5) Various empirical and conceptual issues warrant the continued examination of the nature of patient self-help as well as the further substantiation of the actual impact of such a process. The findings, though scanty, are promising and encourage the development of future programs aimed at capitalizing on psychiatric patients' own assets and capabilities as part of the rehabilitative process. Utilizing patients in this manner actually constitutes the creation of another nonprofessional resource pool—a development which hopefully helps to fill the large service void.

Addictions and Self-Help Services

This section will examine those particular self-help programs focusing on individuals evidencing a variety of repetitive, seemingly uncontrollable self-defeating behaviors. The self-help programs to be discussed include those that relate to those individuals who are obese, alcoholic, and drug-addicted. Certainly these are not necessarily discrete categories, and as such these groups may often overlap. However, the individuals within these groups do seem to manifest some similar physical and emotional difficulties and to respond positively to self-help interventions. Of course, such individuals are likely to demonstrate many of the same psychiatric problems as the patients described in the previous sections. However, they are grouped here because of their primary involvement in addictive behaviors.

The point must also be made that the term *addiction* is itself a vague, ill-defined concept which at various times reflects legal, moralistic, lay, and professional perceptions. Without belaboring the definitional issue, the commonly used terms *obesity, problem drinking,* and *drug addition* will be referred to here with the awareness that they are imprecise and often mean different things to different people.

While many books and articles have been written concerning these topics, the particular projects reviewed in this section were limited to only those special programs fitting the description of the self-help clubs and groups described in the previous sections. The focus is on those particular self-help, nonprofessionally run community organizations grappling with many of the same philosophical principles, organizational problems, and methodological and research issues noted earlier.

Obesity

Numerous studies concerning obesity have continued to appear in both the lay and the professional literature. Much "evidence" abounds purporting the fact that overweight people may be helped through the use of all kinds of psychotherapy, medical management, and drugs. The problem is that on careful inspection most of these approaches appear to be unsuccessful, particularly over time (Payne, Rasmussen, and Shinedling 1971). Much of the work seems rather piecemeal and poorly substantiated and contributes little to coherent data or therapy (an exception is Schachter 1971).

Because of the frequent failure of professional help and the wide array of commercial gimmicks, it is not surprising that overweight individuals have been turning to their own resources for assistance. Perhaps the greatest thrust has been in the direction of self-help groups as epitomized in the clubs sponsored by the famous Weight Watchers organization. Another large, though somewhat less well-known group, is TOPS (Take Off Pounds Sensibly), a 25-year-old self-help organization comprising roughly 320,000 members in more than 12,000 chapters nationwide. This organization is reportedly treating more individuals with weight problems than any other mental or allied health resource (Levitz and Stunkard 1974; Stunkard, Levine, and Fox 1970; Wagonfeld and Wolowitz 1968).

A typical TOPS 1½- to 2-hour meeting emphasizes group cohesiveness and support. There are individual "weigh-ins" and a public announcement of each member's success or failure during the previous week. Accompanying such announcements are group reactions such as applause or booing. Two additional features of the TOPS program are the use of a "buddy system" for members experiencing anxiety and loss of control between meetings and the special added membership to KOPS (Keep Off Pounds Sensibly), a seemingly elite group consisting of those people who have achieved and maintained weight loss. The important ingredients in the TOPS experience include concrete behavioral change, strong group identification, ongoing support, and positive and negative feedback. These elements may be seen to be readily consistent with the ex-patient psychiatric club helping process.

Research investigating the effectiveness of TOPS has been inadequate. Despite the reported positive impact of this growing national program, articles have tended to examine more the helping process itself, the demographic and personality characteristics of TOPS participants, and short-term program effects rather than its actual long-range influence (e.g., Wagonfeld and Wolowitz 1968). Frequently lacking are basic experimental designs, appropriate control groups, adequate premeasures and postmeasures, and attention to the durability of any reported weight losses. This last item is quite important in assessing the merits of TOPS, for numerous other weight reduction approaches have also achieved temporary weight loss—but members revert to obesity at follow-up.

Also lacking in these studies has been an in-depth appraisal of the individuals dropping out of TOPS. The important question here is why these individuals leave. If they have left without achieving weight loss, it is important to know what variables might have contributed to their exit. Or if the goals have in fact been achieved, at what point is termination decided and what, if any, steps have been taken for subsequent maintenance? TOPS members are quite variable along numerous personality and behavioral dimensions despite their similar superficial overweight appearance (Stunkard, Levine, and Fox 1970).

An awareness of such differences and answers to the above questions might explain why some people do achieve significant, durable weight loss while others do not. Perhaps TOPS might be particularly effective for a certain kind of individual, but not for other types of overweight people. If this is the case, then TOPS programs should screen and be selective about their participants, tailoring their activities toward certain individuals. Such speculations first require empirical efforts involving appropriate matched experimental and control groups.

The very issue of weight reduction versus weight maintenance is one also requiring further research attention. For example, even if an organization like TOPS is effective in achieving weight loss, it may or may not be providing a program capable of maintaining this goal. Added services or intervention strategies may be required for support during the maintenance phase of the program. The problem in many of the professional programs reviewed is that more attention has been paid to weight reduction than weight control, with the whole maintenance issue being of seemingly secondary importance (Payne, Rasmussen, and Shinedling 1971). There is a tremendous need for systematic, controlled research where different approaches and techniques may be compared during both the weight loss and the maintenance phases.

That these kinds of investigations are imperative is indicated in the recent findings reported by Levitz and Stunkard (1974). These writers described the results of an extensive 2-year study of 485 TOPS members which revealed the following: attrition rates were 47 percent the first year and 70 percent the second; terminating members were those individuals losing no or little weight rather than successful weight reducers; and although a small percentage of people are effectively able to achieve and maintain significant weight loss while participating in TOPS, the majority of members are not substantially helped. These findings underscore the need for research to determine exactly who is or is not being helped by TOPS, both during and after the program, and what specific intervention approaches are beneficial within the process.

Recent work suggests that behavioral modification techniques may be an effective means for dealing with overweight individuals (e.g., Stuart 1967; Stuart and Davis 1972; Stunkard 1972). In fact, TOPS members have been shown to increase weight loss and evidence lower attrition rates when involved in behavior modification programs (e.g., Hall 1972). Similarly, Levitz and Stunkard (1974), in a controlled study combining TOPS self-help principles with behavioral management techniques, found significantly greater weight loss, lower dropout rates, and continued maintenance of these losses at a 9-month follow-up.

In conclusion, TOPS fits very well the self-help group model in terms of philosophy, organization, goals, and format. It is a mutual, self-help organization in the fullest sense, usually having an independent, cordial relationship with professional resources. Its membership is growing vastly and attracting numerous overweight people who have found little success with traditional and "gimmicky" services. This growth attests to the strongly felt enthusiasm and sense of success espoused by the participant members of TOPS.

However, close scrutiny of the articles describing TOPS revealed little adequate research, and the available data were at the least equivocal. As indicated above, investigators need to be more concerned with basic experimental design and particular methodological issues such as appropriate controls and follow-up. In addition, suggestions were offered regarding possibly greater screening and selectivity of program participants coupled with other intervention techniques to buttress the basic TOPS self-help approach. Behavior modification tools may provide leads in this direction. In conclusion, the current optimism regarding the effects of TOPS may be premature. Additional research and program modifications are still needed to determine if this particular self-help model can indeed make a durable impact on obesity.

Alcoholism and Problem Drinking

The self-help approaches to be considered here will be most concerned with severe drinking problems, frequently referred to as *alcoholism*. This term presents many definitional problems as both professionals and the public may differ widely in their attitudes toward drinking. The severe drinking problems under discussion here will be loosely defined as characterized by (1) an increasing need for alcohol to function in certain situations, (2) the ability to drink increasing amounts of alcohol to achieve the same effects that once took place after just a few drinks, (3) eventual loss of control over drinking, and (4) specific physical and emotional reactions to the sudden withdrawal of alcohol. Alcoholism as described here covers but one area of alcohol-related problems. The broader term *problem drinking* refers to any controversy or disagreement about beverage alcohol use or nonuse, and to any drinking behavior that is defined or experienced as a problem.

There is a lack of clearly and consistently defined standards about the use of alcoholic beverages. Definitions aside, it has been estimated that over 80 million people in the United States drink alcoholic beverages and that over 5 to 8 million (one out of twenty Americans) may by some definitions be defined as alcoholics (Chafetz 1967; National Institute on Alcohol Abuse and Alcoholism 1972).

The serious nature of alcoholism is increasingly being recognized as perhaps the most significant drug problem and among the top three or four prevalent "diseases" in the United States (Burgess 1971; Plaut 1972). Given the enormity of drinking problems in this country, more effort must go into clarifying all the issues, increasing public and professional awareness, and continuing support for new programming in the areas of research, prevention, rehabilitation, and treatment.

Numerous approaches have been utilized in the treatment of alcoholism including social control, medication, hypnotherapy, behavior modification, individual and group psychotherapy, preventive educational programs, and self-help groups such as Alcoholics Anonymous (AA). A long-term study in which a random sample of 400 patients from state-supported alcoholic clinics were studied and followed over a number of years suggested that traditional intervention services have not been particularly effective in dealing with this problem (Gerard, Saenger, and Wile 1962). Follow-up results indicated that 18 percent were still abstaining, 14 percent still used alcohol but did not consider themselves as having drinking problems, 41 percent used alcohol and were unchanged, and 17 percent were dead.

In general, the services provided by traditional helping agencies for alcoholic and related drinking problems—whether via emergency intervention, inpatient care, outpatient care, or transitional facilities—have tended to be ineffective, haphazard operations, often lacking coordination and planning. In fact, it appears that professional mental health caregivers have traditionally had very negative feelings and attitudes toward alcoholics, are not very willing to treat these individuals, and tend to feel pessimistic about intervention effects (e.g., Knox 1969, 1971; Robinson and Podnos 1966; Plaut 1967; Schulberg 1966).

It is little wonder, given the dearth in the quantity and quality of alcoholism treatment services, that people with severe drinking problems have often turned to mutual help organizations such as AA. Being the most visible, durable, and best known self-help organization, AA, which was founded in 1935, has increasingly had an immense impact on public attitudes and on professional programs for problem drinking.

AA attempts to be all-encompassing with its heavy spiritual and religious orientation. This emphasis on moral values and personal reform is most apparent in the "twelve steps" which are essentially guidelines dealing directly or indirectly with God. Apparently, full commitment to the program and the strong chance for achieving sobriety are contingent upon program participants accepting and following these twelve tenets. Basically, they entail the acceptance of God and of one's own wrongdoings and a commitment to helping others. In addition to these steps are "twelve traditions" which members are also expected to follow, upon achieving sobriety, as a means for maintaining individual gains as well as assisting other people with drinking problems. Members are asked to help spread AA philosophy, actively assist others wishing to deal with their drinking problems, and set an uncontroversial, respectable image within the community.

The primary teaching/training tool utilized in promoting the above goals is the large group meeting. These sessions occur frequently and involve the participation of all those present in the discussion. The major focus of these weekly meetings is the welcoming of new members and the public testimony of participants of how their behavior is or is not improving. There is much expression of mutual concern at these sessions, a feeling of brotherhood, and the availability of individual sponsors or tutors to help peers experiencing crises and prevent possible resumption of drinking. Sobriety is rewarded with possible tutor status and with continued success and involvement in the program, possibly meriting a leadership role.

Once again, the helping ingredients noted in the TOPS interactional process are operative in AA. These are an essentially autonomous, nonprofessional climate, intensive group identity and support, a focus on concrete behavioral changes, continued group and individual confrontation and feedback, and continuity through available ongoing helping contact. AA, like TOPS, provides an essentially social learning milieu with the primary focus on reeducating program participants.

Evaluating the effectiveness of AA is difficult. Although relationships with professional caregivers have steadily improved over the years, there nevertheless exists some degree of antiprofessionalism and anti-intellectualism along with little concern for objective appraisal of program outcome. Gross figures are impressive, with AA claiming hundreds of thousands of program participants who have achieved sobriety. More specifically, while many people drop out of the program, of those who stick, AA emphasizes that 75 percent have maintained abstinence. Much subjective support of AA is seen in the lay public and professional community's increased recognition of this organization's growing role as one of the key effective treatment approaches for problem drinkers.

Unfortunately, few investigations are available that have systematically examined both the process features and outcome effects of AA. The numerous articles and books describing AA have been primarily favorable and descriptive with occasional statistics regarding the numbers and characteristics of its membership. Lacking are the same features missing in TOPS, namely, basic experimental design, control groups, valid and reliable measures, comparison to other treatment methods, and follow-up. Research regarding alcohol-related problems is relatively sparse. Data specifically regarding the effectiveness of AA might add considerably to our knowledge. Among the areas which should be carefully researched are the demographic and personality characteristics of those remaining or leaving AA, the factors associated with recovery or failure, comparisons between AA and other treatment modalities, and the study of combinations of helping interventions (e.g., AA and behavior modification).

These are but a few of the areas which might be investigated in the AA approach. The enormity of the drinking problem as well as the increasing professional regard for AA underscore the need for systematic research. Not only would the AA approach itself benefit from such data but so would professionals utilizing other alcoholic treatment modalities. In fact, more and more traditional hospital and community alcoholism intervention approaches are incorporating AA features within or as adjuncts to their own programs. There is a need to clarify just how useful the principles and format of AA are before they so readily adopted into other programs. These combined traditional-AA programs deserve systematic evaluation in their own right as it is often unclear if the multiprogram elements are singularly or additively of help. As more and more of these programs are being funded, increasing accountability should be required.

Implications of the AA Approach

At any rate, AA has obviously been a crucial force in the treatment of alcoholism and most probably the key approach in the social reeducation of problem drinkers. Very likely it has had the most impact in effectively treating drinking problems either under its own auspices or through influencing most other current treatment approaches. It should be reemphasized that quality research is essential to clarify the degree to which AA is of help and, if so, what features most facilitate this process. Such data would be important to the field at large, to AA programs themselves, and to professionals and nonprofessionals involved in any other related treatment programs. Perhaps the most important contribution of AA has been its ability to begin dispelling time-honored myths depicting problem drinkers as second-class citizens incapable of responsibly overcoming their difficulties.

Despite these contributions, there are some controversial issues which have led to difficulties among AA members themselves and between AA and the professional community. For example, AA's highly inspirational, religious, and middle-class nature has been viewed as a real deterrent to the successful involvement of some problem drinkers. Similarly, its confessional aspect has turned away various people fearful of this type of public exposure. Thus, AA may not be attending to individual needs, but instead promoting a very particular approach helpful for some individuals and barring successful participation by others. Careful research investigations might be able to ascertain just what types of individuals current AA practices are best suited for. Such information might then be utilized for selective screening of the more amenable program applicants, or related programs might be developed, tailored more to the needs of problem drinkers who were previously not helped by AA.

In addition, many in AA have come to feel that professional involvement should be kept minimal. In like fashion, community caregivers themselves have adopted this attitude, frequently looking toward AA to assume major rehabilitative responsibility in treating problem drinkers. Plaut (1967) criticizes this mutually held attitude and suggests more of an interface between AA and other community resources. He suggests that although AA has been an outstanding influence in the rehabilitation of problem drinkers, it has only reached a small percentage of such individuals. AA thus needs to be seen in perspective, with an appreciation of its unique contributions tempered with the recognition of the limits of its applicability and also the necessity for including, when appropriate, professional input.

Two other alcohol-related mutual aid groups also deserve mention. These are Al-Anon and Alateen, which are organizations for the families and friends of problem drinkers who may or may not be involved in AA (Alcohol and Health Notes 1973; Bailey 1965). Both groups are quite similar in philosophy and format to AA, generating mutually supportive fellowships. Al-Anon, a direct outgrowth of AA, was incorporated in 1954 as an independent organization. Alateen was established in 1957 to meet the needs of 12- to 20-year-olds facing alcohol problems in their families. That the need for such groups is warranted is suggested by figures estimating that over 36 million persons are affected in some way by the drinking problems of others.

Meeting informally and weekly, both Al-Anon and Alateen are closely modeled after AA's principles and guidelines for living. Typical sessions involve group discussion of these guidelines, the sharing of personal alcohol-related experiences, and periodic visits of guest speakers such as professional personnel. These essentially autonomous, self-supporting groups have grown over the years with current estimates suggesting over 120,000 members spread over 8000 Al-Anon and Alateen groups in 50 countries. Some of the same conceptual and methodological issues raised in evaluating the impact of AA would also be applicable in appraising these two organizations.

Drug Addiction, Dependency, and Abuse

As was the case in defining alcoholism and problem drinking, so too is it difficult to reach a clear definition of drug-related problems. Numerous chemical substances, other than alcohol, may be ingested and possibly lead to addiction, dependency, or abuse. Included here are the opiates, barbiturates, amphetamines, sedatives and tranquilizers, cocaine, cannabis derivatives (e.g., marijuana), and hallucinogens. Problems in definition stem from the wide variety of drugs, the range of physical and personality effects, and the inconsistent cultural, legal, medical, and pharmacological views of drug use.

Of particular concern here are the opiates and their natural and synthetic derivatives such as morphine, heroin, Demerol, methodone, and codeine. Most narcotic addicts have utilized these drugs, particularly heroin because of its availability and potency. Certainly these individuals may be simultaneously ingesting any of the other chemicals noted above, but opiate addiction has tended, until recently, to be most often in the public and professional limelight, receiving the major share of legal, preventive, educational, treatment, and research action.

Despite the extensive lay and professional literature, accurate estimates of heroin addiction are difficult to determine. For example, even law enforcement estimates may only reflect convictions, not arrests. Similarly, numerous addicts may have contact with a variety of lay and professional community caregivers who may or may not be reporting statistics regarding addiction incidence. Finally, there are those addicts who may simply be unknown to any formal or informal caretaking resources. And this includes not only the stereotypic ghetto addicts, but also middle-class and other people taking narcotic drugs regularly to relieve pain and doctors and nurses who may also be narcotic addicts. Given these limitations in accurate addiction estimates, studies by the National Institute of Mental Health have generally found heroin addiction to be spreading among people with varying backgrounds, ages, socioeconomic levels, and occupations. Nationally, estimates by the end of 1971 indicated over 560,000 narcotic addicts, a figure that is 10 times higher than a decade ago (Scott and Goldenberg 1973).

Treatment for drug addiction has varied, but traditionally it has focused most on medical problems associated with physical addiction and withdrawal sickness. Results of such approaches have not been particularly impressive. For example, Duvall, Locke, and Brill (1963), found that of a sample of 453 patients released from Lexington, 97 percent were readdicted during a 5-year follow-up period. Similar statistics have been obtained by others (Hunt and Odoroff 1962; O'Donnell 1965; Levy 1972; Vaillant 1973). Such findings suggest that effective drug addiction treatment must be more multifaceted, dealing extensively with personality and social variables as well as with factors related to actual physical addiction. The most important phase of intervention is after the addict has overcome his habit, when he often returns to the same old emotional stresses and too frequently has no effective treatment resource (Myers et al. 1972).

As was the case with most problem-drinking treatment approaches, many addiction programs appear to be irrelevant and ineffectual. Current addicts and ex-addicts have sought assistance by helping to develop their own brand of mutual self-help residential programs such as Odyssey House (Edmondson 1972), Daytop Village (Romond, Forrest, and Kleber 1975; Shelly and Bassin

1965), Phoenix House (Rosenthal and Biase 1969), and, perhaps the most famous and influential, Synanon (Cherkas 1965; Yablonsky 1965). The disenchantment with professional services is extremely apparent in such programs.

The basic assumption underlying all these therapeutic communities, regardless of format, is that the first step in the rehabilitative process is participation in an environment drastically different in values and interpersonal relationships from the addict's previous life-style. Essential factors include honesty and mutual concern and conditions facilitative of growth, maturity, trust, and self-acceptance. An additional premise in such programs is that to achieve such personal growth, rather intense confrontational steps are necessary to break through the addict's entrenched defenses and self-destructive attitudes and behaviors.

Perhaps the most important assumptions in the functioning of these residential communities concern the major therapeutic role of the ex-addicts themselvs. Specifically, as these individuals know first-hand the severe problems and defenses of the addict subculture, they may be the only members of the treatment team with whom the addict can communicate, particularly at the onset of treatment (Kadushin and Kadushin 1969). Needless to say, such a view has often led to mutual antagonism between self-help communities and professional groups. These residential treatment programs see themselves as the key helping agents with professionals at best playing a minimal and secondary role. This blanket rejection of professionalism has unfortunately inhibited honest, objective criticism and accountability.

Synanon

This organization was the first such drug self-help program to attract national attention, and it has served as the working model for most subsequent residential treatment programs. Founded in 1958 by an ex-alcoholic, Synanon initially evolved from a spin-off of Alcoholics Anonymous to a mutual help group comprised of addicts living together. Among the key features included in this program are: an autocratic family setting; a 9-to-30-month training program aimed at changing inappropriate attitudes and behaviors; an intense screening procedure; and a gradual process whereby privileges and status are earned contingent upon improved work and peer relationships (Scott and Goldenberg 1973). Two particularly major ingredients in this approach are the "synanon" meeting and the "haircut," both of which are techniques for releasing emotions, confronting inappropriate behaviors, reinforcing desirable actions, and providing modeling and feedback (Zax and Cowen 1972).

Most striking about the whole Synanon approach is its consistency with the social learning, skill-building model noted in the discussions on the TOPS and AA programs. However, the behavioral model seems even more apparent here as addicts are clearly regarded as rational and not sick, with their inappropriate behavior continually being assaulted and modified. Required vocational and emotional skills are defined early, and these two areas are refined and shaped throughout the addict's involvement with Synanon. By means of a systematic combination of punishment and positive reinforcement residents gradually begin to create new and different roles for themselves that are characterized by greater complexity, responsibility, status, and material and social rewards. The group is perhaps the most powerful element in fostering social identity, solidarity, and, most important, a variety of sanctions for stopping one behavior and substituting it with another more personally and socially desirable.

Despite Synanon's own increasing growth and prototype influence on other residential programs, insufficient objective research is available to document its effectiveness. Descriptive investigations have examined the demographic, personality, and criminal/drug-abuse histories of program members who stay in, or drop out of, Synanon. The research suggests a very high initial dropout rate (Cherkas 1965), with those members who are able to stick it out evidencing significant treatment gains and drug abstinence (Volkman and Cressey 1963).

In fact, a rather high attrition rate of program participants tend to characterize most residential drug programs, and of those remaining addicts completing the program, over half tend to remain as staff members or become coordinators of newer programs. Scott and Goldenberg (1973) suggest that this phenomenon may account for the success the programs do have. An implication here is that even if individuals control their addictions, continued abstinence may be dependent on forever being tied to some kind of drug program. The definition of *cure* may have to be expanded as ex-addicts may not be able to adequately function in the community independent of peer culture of drug programs.

These speculations are suggested by available statistics and research, but little systematic evaluation has been conducted in these areas. Also lacking are basic empirical studies including control groups, reliable measures, and follow-up, which could objectively focus on the basic question of program effectiveness. Who remains in, and who leaves, these programs and why? What happens to these people after completion or premature termination? Exactly what about the program is effective in facilitating change? Is it the vocational training and work assignment, the "synanon," the "haircut," and/or the overall sense of group identity and caring? How appropriately are the criteria for vocational adjustment, emotional progress, and readiness for graduation defined and measured? These are but a few of the issues which have *not* been carefully investigated in the Synanon program. Until systematic studies are conducted, it will be impossible to establish cause-and-effect relationships between graduating, or dropping out, and posttreatment outcome.

All these conceptual and methodological issues are just as critical in evaluating other prominent drug rehabilitation organizations. Among the best known and fastest expanding is Phoenix House, which, like Synanon, has grown from a single facility to multiple facilities. By 1971 Phoenix House had over fifteen separate facilities including residences, outpatient centers, and storefronts (Rosenthal and Biase 1969). The level of research on the effects of the Phoenix House programs has been limited in both scope and quality. What data are available suggest that those residents remaining in this program evidence less criminality (De Leon, Holland, and Rosenthal 1972), fewer psychopathological signs (De Leon, Skodol, and Rosenthal 1973), and more positive changes in emotionality (De Leon, Rosenthal, and Brodney 1971). Again, the available studies have given little attention to follow-up and the fate of the numerous dropouts from the program.

Some general conclusions may now be drawn regarding the nature and impact of these intensive self-help approaches to drug problems. First, these programs tend to be quite similar in philosophy, structure, functioning, and goals. The primary emphasis is on mutual self-caring, creation of a strong group subculture, and the development of healthy vocational, emotional, and interpersonal skills. Particular skill building tends to be concrete and specific, accomplished with much group modeling, practice, and strong feedback blending supportive care with intense confrontation.

A recurrent problem is the high attrition rate with little concern regarding dropouts and an apparent attitude that these individuals just do not have what it takes to make a successful adjustment. These programs do not consider the possibility that drug addicts (like obese individuals and problem drinkers) are really a diverse group of people perhaps manifesting a common behavior but nevertheless differing in personality, and degree of emotional problems. Although dropouts from these drug programs indeed may not be amenable to the Synanon type of process, they may be quite reachable through other approaches. It too often appears that these programs expect addicts to fit the needs of the program rather than having the program fit the needs of the addict.

Another important issue, touched on earlier, concerns the role of the ex-addict. As indicated above, a good many of the graduates tend to join the treatment community, and the implication is that these individuals may not be able to effectively function independently. This trend is also seen in the difficulty some TOPS and AA members have when similarly attempting to terminate their group participation. Very possibly the warmth, sense of caring, and group identity that permeate such organizations (and which are markedly different from members' everyday "civilian lives") become so much a part of the member's existence that to leave creates new emotional voids and problems. Graduates seem to face an extremely ambivalent situation nearing the time of program completion. They have the fulfillment of successfully finishing a rigorous, demanding process, but this is coupled with the pain of then having to terminate from a very accepting and reinforcing environment. Quite possibly the high continuance of people in TOPS, for example, who never achieve desirable weight reduction may be explained by their avoidance of expected termination once "goal" is reached. In other words, losing weight may be punished by its loss of friends and a safe, accepting climate while being overweight allows continuance with the group.

It is not surprising that over half the graduates of the drug programs tend to stay on in some capacity. Perhaps in order to successfully join the ranks of the greater community, more transitional experiences are needed to gradually wean the member away from the organization. Another problem, aside from reentry into the community, may also arise due to the retention of drug program graduates within the organization. Unless some positive steps can be taken, there will be a continuous need for new programs to develop and existing ones to expand so that there will be an increase in the number of prestigious and responsible positions for new graduates (Scott and Goldenberg 1973).

These are but a few of the issues inherent in an objective assessment of the self-help drug programs (as well as other mutual support addiction organizations). It is very likely that these drug programs are having beneficial effects for at least a particular type of addict. Systematic research is required to differentiate which addicts are being helped by existing programs and under what posttreatment conditions successful results are durable.

As a group, the addiction programs of TOPS, AA, and Synanon are fairly similar in their goals, mission, structure, and problems. They perhaps embody the clearest example of the "self-help" principle in action, and their increasing popularity and remarkable growth clearly suggest that they may be effectively meeting the needs of some of their membership. Unfortunately, there has been little objective data to support their reported success. There are no clear answers to questions relating to who is helped, by what means, how well, and for how long.

Self-Help and the Single, Divorced, and Widowed

Whereas the previous sections have considered self-help programs for individuals experiencing long-standing difficulties, the programs to be reviewed now are more crisis-oriented. Specifically, the focus here is on organizations catering to people who have suffered a major loss or deprivation. Caplan (1974a) views groups such as Parents Without Partners as providing new helping communities in which members can quickly immerse themselves.

Parents Without Partners (PWP) is an international self-help group that was started in 1957. Since that time its membership has grown at a phenomenal rate, with well over 200 chapters in the United States alone. PWP was developed to take care of the practical and emotional needs of single parents and their children. Regardless of the extent of the problem and the single parent's coping capacity, there is apparently an increasing need for support and guidance. Often friends and relatives are simply not enough, and most of these parents do not want to seek professional help. Instead, PWP provides a more acceptable resource for meeting their needs (Harris 1966).

The actual programs available to both parents and children are quite varied, ranging from group counselinglike experiences to guest lectures to movies and recreation. There is no specific program format that members must follow, but rather considerable flexibility in terms of the types and number of functions individuals wish to pursue. The overall goal of PWP is educational rather than strictly rehabilitative or therapeutic. Members tend to be relatively sophisticated about psychological issues and are thus responsive to a variety of informal or formal groups. The groups themselves may be led by professionals or untrained members and, as opposed to being viewed as group therapy, may instead more accurately be seen as family life education workshops.

While it obviously meets important needs, the impact of this organization, in the short and the long run, has not been systematically assessed. Data have been gathered more by word of mouth and subjective appraisal, with the reported results generally being highly favorable. PWP appears to be a fun as well as educational resource which helps to meet the emotional and interpersonal needs of both parents and children.

Harris (1966) has examined the organization in terms of the makeup of its membership, types of programming, impact on participants, and utility as a professional referral source. She found that members varied widely in terms of the extent to which they viewed themselves as having emotional problems. Many, for example, considered their difficulties situation-related, but more sophisticated parents recognized that their own reactions and coping skills were just as important in dealing with stress as the problem itself. In addition, PWP tended to be comprised of generally younger, white, middle-class individuals with women outnumbering men and those who were separated or divorced outnumbering those who were widowed.

Harris suggested that professionals considering referral to PWP be aware of the characteristics of its membership although technically all single parents are eligible. For example, it would probably not be productive to refer unmarried, poor, and older single parents to the group as they might have difficulty fitting into the program. PWP suffers from the same drawback as other previously described self-help groups in that it responds to the needs of a rather limited subgroup of its potential constituency. Overall, Harris views Parents Without Partners as a useful supplement to professional help for particular individuals, but not as a counseling substitute for people experiencing severe emotional problems. As was the case with the other self-help groups, a more systematic evaluation of PWP would buttress Harris' suggestions and clarify the type of helping role PWP might have for its membership.

In contrast to the basically supportive nature of PWP is the much more intensive, crisis intervention-oriented Widow-to-Widow program. Silverman

(1967, 1969, 1970, 1972) developed this program after she found that existing community agencies and professional caregivers were not adequately helping the recently widowed. In fact, whereas increasing attention is being paid to the problems of separated and divorced people, widowhood has, until recently, hardly been noticed.

Silverman (1967) has observed that most community caretakers, including professional mental health workers, may not be equipped to adequately deal with the crises of widowhood. Certainly friends, relatives, and clergy are available at the initial phase of mourning. However, these support systems tend to diminish just when widowed people lose their initial numbness and begin to feel all the pain, soul searching, facing of the past, and grappling with the future that comprise the later phases of the grieving process.

Silverman (1967) suggests that professionals are not suited for assisting these people because of their own felt vulnerability; their discomfort in handling intense grief feelings; their too frequent tendency to quickly label the mourning reaction in emotional and mental illness terms rather than as a natural transitional life situation; and their general inability to respond to the multiple needs of the widowed throughout all phases of the grief process.

The best caregiver for the recently widowed person may be another widowed person who has already been through the grieving process and knows firsthand about the difficulties the individual is experiencing. Silverman (1969) observed that widows found talking to experienced peers particularly helpful. Experienced peers were not apt to tell them, as most others did, to "keep a stiff upper lip" during a time when they felt that life was over and the future gone. Instead, these widow aides seemed to know grief was temporary but necessary, a process that had to run its course if equilibrium was to be achieved again.

The Widow-to-Widow program was initiated as a pilot project in 1967 in a socially heterogeneous section of Boston. The initial target population consisted of all new widows under the age of 60. Specific individuals were located from data supplied from the Bureau of Vital Statistics and from funeral directors. A beginning cadre of five widow aides was recruited from major racial and religious community groups. These women had met the criteria of successfully coping with their own widowhood, a local community acceptance as informal helpers, and competency in basic interpersonal skills (e.g., empathy). They had no special education or training, but were seen as natural caregivers.

Beginning in June 1967, aides began contacting widows, most of whom were receptive. First, letters were sent out to the newly widowed offering condolences, describing the program, and requesting possible contact. Advertisement for the program was also accomplished via newspaper, radio, and television advertisements. By 1970, over 400 new widows had been contacted by the five aides, with some being seen personally, while others were repeatedly spoken to by phone.

The actual intervention tended to vary, but regardless of its nature it was always available. Perhaps most important, aides provided friendship, support, and empathy. On another level aides provided highly concrete guidance in finding jobs, sorting out finances and budgets, handling children, and meeting new people. Since these contacts were generally on an individual basis, caseloads increased rapidly. A variety of groups were developed to more effectively handle the growing number of participants and to offer a vehicle to best answer questions and meet the special-interest needs of the members.

The Widow-to-Widow program was expanded from an initial crisis intervention orientation to a much more comprehensive self-help support system meeting a variety of needs at multiple levels. The ultimate development has been the creation of a network of mutual help groups for widows and widowers throughout the Greater Boston area. This has been accomplished by developing a 24-hour-a-day "hot line" counseling service staffed by additional volunteers who are in turn educated and supervised by the original core group of widow aides.

The Widowed Service Line (WSL) has turned out to be a rather inexpensive way to cover a wide geographical area and reach out to a large number of widows and widowers who might not be receptive to the individual/group outreach approach. Abrahams (1972) reported that during the first 8 months of operation WSL received over 760 calls from all over the greater metropolitan Boston area. The "hot line team" comprised 18 volunteers (13 widows and 5 widowers) backed up by two of the original aides who spent time in training, supervision, and public relations.

Abrahams (1972) analyzed a sample of 570 telephone contacts with the information being recorded, coded, and processed immediately following each conversation. The coded information covered such areas as demographic data, types of problems, employment and financial needs, present living arrangements, and the volunteers' plan of action. General impressions suggested that a wide age range of widows and widowers was being reached at all stages of bereavement and adjustment. Specific help was particularly requested during the early grieving stages, but also at subsequent times when callers were struggling with coming to terms with their new life-styles and changing roles. Unlike typical hot line counseling services, these volunteers went beyond the more usual one-call kinds of contact and on the average called back three to five times.

Aside from gross statistics and the type of analyses conducted by Abrahams (1972), this program has not been objectively evaluated. One reason for this, as was pointed out in the Silverman articles, may have been the aides' strong desire to provide an important service and not simply be part of a research project. Also, Silverman's essentially hands-off policy would preclude a tight empirical study. Finally, it would seem that the very intense emotional nature of the intervention, for both the helper and helpee, would make evaluation difficult.

Nevertheless, even on a subjective basis it seems very likely that this program is providing a highly viable means for effectively dealing with the many problems of widows and widowers. Caplan (1974a) noted that the program has expanded and its reputation grown to the point where Silverman and her aides have participated in national conferences, have been requested to help develop similar projects in other states, and have been contacted by other national mutual help groups. Thus, the Widow-to-Widow program, like many of the other self-help programs reviewed in this chapter, lacks objective validation but has received much support from its staff, membership, and the public.

Consciousness-Raising Groups and Self-Help

The final group of articles to be discussed in this chapter concerns the intensive self-help groups deriving from the women's liberation movement. Recent years have seen the concerted effort by women to reexamine and redefine their personal, social, and sexual roles. Such analysis has particularly focused on the historical and current roles of women as defined by the major institutions of society. According to the "movement," women have been treated as second-class citizens and systematically have been discriminated against and penalized in all areas of our culture. This scathing attack of our society by the women's movement is not unlike the views of most of the disenfranchised minority groups. The women's liberation movement has been especially critical of the professional mental health field (e.g., Barrett et al. 1974; Broverman et al. 1970; Carlson 1972; Chesler 1972; Rice and Rice 1973; Smith 1972; Weisstein 1971).

Traditional counseling approaches are viewed as inherently antifeminine and conducive to promoting the status quo. Specific aspects of psychotherapy called into question are the pervasive explicit and implicit Freudian position, the predominance of male therapists, the tendency to conceptualize female role unhappiness as psychopathological, and the felt threat by male therapists to their increasingly assertive female patients. There is also an emphasis on the male therapists' typical ignorance of the real significance to women of such life-cycle experiences as marriage, career conflict, abortion, menopause, the "empty nest syndrome," and widowhood (Barrett et al. 1974; Rice and Rice 1973).

What particularly alarms advocates of women's liberation is that given all the negative stereotypes and ignorance evidenced by professionals, the majority of psychotherapy patients in hospitals, outpatient facilities, and private practice continue to be women (Chesler 1972). There is the fear that clinicians will inadvertently reinforce the myth of female inadequacy and second-class citizenship, rather than promote true growth and independence.

Consistent with the self-help process, women have increasingly banded together to find mutual support and a means by which to creatively deal with the new issues they are struggling with. Of particular relevance to counseling has been the development of the consciousness-raising (CR) group. Women meet regularly to develop a new sense of themselves, examine male-female relationships and destructive sex roles, develop a strong group identity where diverse "problems" are intimately shared, and participate in a therapeutic type of experience quite different from those already available (Brodsky 1973; Gardner 1971).

The similarity between CR groups and most of the other self-help organizations described earlier should be apparent, particularly in terms of explicit philosophy and goals, supportive roles, helping processes, and negative feelings toward traditional caregiving services. The development of CR groups has had important mental health implications. Many women who either were uncomfortable about seeking traditional help or had become disappointed with such services have found CR groups very supportive. The growing popularity of this helping approach is seen by the recent emergence of CR groups for men (Barrett et al. 1974) and school children (Gerson 1974).

However, consistent with the dearth of research on other types of self-help programs, there has been little objective examination of the nature and effects of CR groups. Most of the articles have been basically descriptive, presenting findings in glowing, somewhat militant terms. Quality assessment would add considerably to our understanding and evaluation of this quickly expanding self-help approach. If it is indeed as effective a helping mode as its advocates claim, then it would be important to answer some basic questions. For whom is it (or is it not) effective? What particular attitudes and behaviors are modified? What helping processes have greatest impact? How durable are the results? And what are the treatment effects compared to those of traditional services? Answers to these questions would have implications for utilizing CR groups as an adjunct or alternative intervention to professional services. Relevant data might also provide new directions for professionals in terms of helping approaches for both men and women.

The women's movement is increasingly meeting strong emotinoal and growth needs that the mental health field has either inadequately dealt with or avoided. Some writers have begun to address themselves to the issue of how traditional counseling might best incorporate some of the principles and techniques of the liberation movement and CR groups (Barrett et al. 1974; Rice and Rice 1973). The assumption underlying this trend is that even if CR groups are highly effective, there are nevertheless going to be many people who will still need additional professional help.

Among the suggestions for modifying and expanding professional approaches are the following: greater consideration of research concerning sex differences and the psychology of women, increased awareness of alternative life-styles, openness with clients about one's own personal value system, more trained women therapists, further use of female-male cotherapist teams, and consciousness-raising groups for therapists of both sexes. Hopefully, these suggestions, coupled with use of CR types of groups as a legitimate alternative, will lead to psychotherapeutic approaches which are more responsive to the needs of many women.

Summary

This chapter has reviewed articles describing nonprofessionally led, mutually supportive programs for a variety of populations. These programs have tended to emerge as a result of an insufficient professional workforce, the felt inadequacy and ineffectiveness of traditional services, and the growing conviction that lay people with similar problems can best help one another. The populations sampled in this chapter included the aged and retired, psychiatric inpatients and outpatients, alcoholics, drug addicts, single parents, widows, and members of the women's liberation movement. These varied groups are similar in their feeling of being disenfranchised from traditional mental health services and in their banding together to take care of their own needs. The particular self-help services are frequently similar in goals, structure, program format, reported outcome, and the issues and problems facing them.

Since the results of the specific self-help programs have already been summarized in the body of the chapter, it would be fruitful to take an overall look at the general findings. The various helping interventions evident in the 38 programs reviewed were mainly supportive in nature or combined with some direct service features. With the exception of some of the crisis intervention work with widows, addict encounter groups, or the behavior modification programs of peer retardates, most programs placed more emphasis on concrete emotional and vocational skill building while dealing with a variety of practical concerns.

Peer training is either nonexistent or rather informal. This is to be expected since many of the self-help programs reviewed place a great emphasis on members' own life experiences and "natural" helping skills. This reluctance for structured training is further reinforced by the members' frequent antiprofessional attitudes and antagonism toward traditional intervention. Where more formalized training is built into the program, it may include classes, lectures, study groups, and ongoing structured experiential group meetings. While most of the programs were inadequately researched, nine of the articles were of a suggestive quality, with three approximating an adequate empirical level (Fairweather 1964; Fairweather et al. 1969; Magaro and Staples 1972).

Most of the better research was seen in those studies specifically examining psychiatric inpatient, outpatient, and transitional programs, with the remaining relatively adequate research being done with programs dealing with retardates and drug addicts. Overall, the research analyses are not sophisticated enough to warrant uncritical, favorable impressions regarding self-help programs. Even in the areas where some relatively adequate studies have been carried out, there is still not enough quality research to warrant definitive conclusions.

There were four programs which were at least of methodologically suggestive quality and which dealt specifically with outcome questions (Fairweather 1964; Fairweather et al. 1969; Ludwig and Marx 1966; Myers and Clark 1972).

These four programs were all concerned with psychiatric inpatient and transitional programs. These studies have already been reviewed and their strengths and defects noted. Glaringly absent are any good outcome studies dealing with program effects of self-help programs for other types of populations. This is unfortunate since the ultimate empirical test of their success or failure will rest on objective outcome data.

Perhaps it is the very nature of self-help programs, in terms of their conceptual and program complexity, anti-intellectualism, and often emotionally charged atmosphere, that makes systematic evaluation so difficult. What makes careful assessment perhaps most problematic may be the basic helper-therapy process itself. If everyone is apparently being benefited in a given program, it is not so much a matter of who is the helper and who is the helpee, but how much each is helping one another—and by what means. Thus, the dependent and independent variables in these programs become rather complex and diffuse, necessitating much greater precision in operationalizing definitions and concretizing variables and criteria.

Regardless of the reasons for inadequate research, even the most vociferous advocates of self-help organizations call for systematic evaluation of these programs (Grob 1970; Hurvitz 1970). Empirical support seems particularly needed if professionals are to increasingly recognize and utilize these groups either as adjunct helping resources or as possible models for their own interventions. As has been noted throughout this chapter, there is often much mistrust between professional and nonprofessional helpers, and the lack of hard data would seem to provide professionals with another excuse for ignoring these kinds of programs. Self-help organizations will probably continue to flourish whether or not professionals accept them. Dumont (1974) sees the self-help movement as a growing force which has tremendous implications for the planning of mental health care, anticipated workforce needs, and the funding of human services—irrespective of professional input.

While perhaps overstating the case, Dumont's (1974) observations do point out the too frequent distance between professional and nonprofessional caregivers and the strong need for collaborative interaction between both parties. Very possibly, traditional mental health may be left behind whether or not the effectiveness of new helping services is validated according to professional criteria. The urgency here is for professionals to reexamine their relationship to self-help organizations not only to protect their own position and relevancy but for the sake of the self-help programs as well. Self-help programs often suffer from as much prejudice and insulation as they claim their professional counterparts evidence. Their very self-aggrandizement may in fact rigidly delimit much needed input which professional colleagues could provide. Both professionals and nonprofessionals can gain from effectively working with each other.

Caplan (1974a) predicts that the next decade will see much systematic research concerning self-help support systems as well as a variety of other ways in which professionals can make important contributions to such organizations. First, professionals can help to organize new support systems within existing *community institutions*, such as in religious organizations (e.g., Caplan 1972). Second, they can organize new support systems in the *general community*. An example of such an endeavor is Silverman's (1969) Widow-to-Widow program. Third, they can offer consultation and education to the organizers and other key members of *existing support systems* such as AA and Synanon. They can also provide consultation to members of *unorganized supportive networks* within the community. As described in Chapter 6, Collins (1972) identified, recruited, and successfully utilized "natural neighbors."

Caplan's (1974a) four-step model offers a range of possibilities by which professionals can have an impact on self-help systems. These types of professional interventions may be quite heuristic, having meaningful benefits for both professionals and nonprofessionals. Perhaps, then, interaction between traditional and lay caregivers may develop into a particularly clear expression of the helper-therapy principle of mutual growth.

8

The Indigenous Poor and "Exotic" Helpers: Further Examples of Self-Help

This chapter continues the examination of types of self-help programs, but specifically focuses on particular individuals indigenous to their community who are serving in formal or informal nonprofessional roles. Such individuals tend to be community residents, often poor, from working-class backgrounds who have had experiences similar to their clients (Grosser 1968; Reiff and Riessman 1965). Often they are also in some paid position, so they are thus similar in status and function to the paraprofessionals described in Chapter 3.

The failure of professionals to meaningfully provide for the mental health needs of the poor was discussed earlier. Both traditional and new counseling approaches have been strongly criticized, particularly in terms of the explicit or inadvertent exclusion of impoverished clients, the offering of irrelevant and impersonalized services, the overemphasis on personality dynamics, and the fostering of the political and economic status quo (e.g., Carter 1973; Garfield 1971; Graff, Kenig, and Radoff 1971; Rusalem 1973; Tolson 1972; Vontress 1969; Ward 1970; Wilson and Calhoun 1974).

Jones (1974) described the issue as a rather complex one which is not simply a function of class differences. He noted that the expectations that the poor have regarding therapy and the counselor's own attitudes toward lower-class clients need to be considered. Even where services are available, they tend to be little used by the poorer community residents (Rosenblatt and Mayer 1972; Hart and Bassett 1972). There may exist a mutual reluctance on the part of both professional mental health workers and low-income clients to seek out one another.

These issues have been noted in articles detailing the mental health needs of blacks (e.g., Brooks 1974; Comer 1973; Gilbert 1974; Jackson 1973; Kincaid 1969; Mayo 1974; Waite 1968), Mexican-Americans (e.g., Koegler and Williamson 1973; Padilla and Ruiz 1973), Puerto Ricans (Callan 1973; Cohen 1972), Asian-Americans (Kim 1973; Sue and Sue 1972), and various groups of American Indians (Dinges, Yazzie, and Tollefson 1974; Kahn and Delk 1973).

All these articles forcefully critique present programming and point out the need for new mental health resources. Perhaps the most unfortunate aspect of such inadequate programming is that the people who suffer the most are the minority group individuals who are at the highest risk of being defined as psychiatrically ill (Selig 1973). To help meet this large gap in mental health delivery, various programs have been developed utilizing indigenous paraprofessionals. Through their ability to do things professionals have difficulty doing,

125

such as identifying with the client's life situation, language, values, and attitudes, indigenous paraprofessionals may serve important advocacy and liaison functions (Grosser 1968; Ozarin and Thomas 1972; Reiff 1966; Rusalem 1973; Ward 1970).

Among the activities that have been engaged in by indigenous workers are casework and supportive counseling (Berman 1970; Lockwood and Dingman 1971; Wolcott 1969), crisis intervention (Budner, Chazin, and Young 1973), outreach work (Fabian and Tanner 1971), community action and development (Birnbaum and Jones 1967; Brager 1965), behavior modification (Staats, Minke, and Butts 1970), and family life education (Halpern 1969). As a group, the articles describing the work of indigenous workers are more anecdotal than empirical, vividly describing program needs, possible directions, and various conceptual issues.

Lincoln and Harlem Hospital Programs

The Lincoln and Harlem Hospital neighborhood service centers have multiservice programs which tend to be walk-in, storefront facilities in low-income neighborhoods, providing residents with quick, immediate counseling, a range of related services and information, and referral resources. They are important long-term projects which exemplify the philosophy, training, and activities of indigenous paraprofessionals (Christmas 1966, 1969; Hallowitz and Riessman 1967; Lehmann 1970; Peck 1969; Richards and Daniels 1969; Riessman and Hallowitz 1967; Kaplan and Roman 1973; Ruiz 1973; Ruiz and Behrens 1973; Ruiz, Vazquez, and Vazquez 1973; Shaw and Eagle 1971; Wade, Jordan, and Myers 1969).

The Lincoln Hospital Mental Health Services, initially begun in 1963, was an attempt to create comprehensive services in one of the most impoverished areas in New York City. After a beginning period, it soon became apparent that the crisis intervention outpatient clinic was simply not reaching a considerable number of needy individuals in the catchment area. In 1965 the hospital established three neighborhood service centers, which were conceived as "psychosocial first-aid stations" where people could bring virtually any type of concern. In an attempt to move out further into the community, the hospital has been developing a mobile unit for direct outreach work to deal firsthand with any emerging crises (Ruiz, Vazquez, and Vazquez 1973).

Probably the most significant feature of the entire Lincoln Hospital program is the heavy involvement of community residents at the governing, planning and policy setting, and direct helping levels. For example, staffing figures indicated that the Lincoln programs employed a total of 203 staff, consisting of 71 professionals, 74 indigenous paraprofessionals, and 58 clerical workers (Ruiz, Vazquez, and Vazquez 1973). Thus, over one-third of the staff consists of paraprofessionals.

Recruitment and selection of nonprofessional staff were intensive, with active public soliciting followed by carefully screened large and small group applicant meetings. Particular criteria scrutinized included the candidates' attitudes toward the neighborhood, people on welfare, minority groups, discrimination, and disturbed people. In addition, applicants were rated by judges according to empathic skills, group comfort, ability to communicate feelings and ideas, trainability and flexibility, degree of self-awareness, and relevant work experiences (Hallowitz and Riessman 1967). Acceptable candidates typically lack formal education, have resided within the community at some point in their lives, and have usually been poor and gone through very similar life experiences as the center's clients.

Preparation of trainees is extensive and highly action-oriented. The typical 6-week training period generally involves three phases. The first phase is a prejob, 3-week period in which trainees get a taste of the range of supportive services (e.g., helping the intake team). During this period formal coursework is minimal, the emphasis being on practical experience with role playing and simulations being used as training vehicles. The second phase is a 3-week placement where trainees fill a variety of assignments for half their time, providing direct help to actual clients. The remaining time during this second phase is devoted to on-the-job training. Following this formal training, during the third phase, workers continue to receive a variety of ongoing training experiences. There are individual and group supervisory sessions, continuing seminars, and weekly staff meetings. There are also specific sessions to further improve skills in individual and group interviewing techniques, community organization, and family intervention.

Staff jobs are quite varied, including such diverse services as helping clients to fill out applications, obtain financial aid, find employment and housing, seek legal advice, organize community projects, and provide supportive counseling skills (Lehmann 1970). The indigenous worker's multirole assumes an ombudsman status whereby he or she is both an advocate and counselor for the client.

As was the case with the studies noted earlier, the articles describing the Lincoln Hospital (as well as the Harlem Hospital program) are more descriptive than empirically substantive. Most of the authors vividly retell the issues in counseling the poor, the beginnings of their respective programs, the numerous pitfalls they have had to deal with, and the strengths and weaknesses of their numerous projects. What data are available relate to who actually comes to the neighborhood service centers, why they come, and in what numbers. For example, Lehmann (1970) found that the people in the community with the most problems extensively used the centers. There was the expected range of problems typical of residents living in such an impoverished neighborhood. Also, it is estimated that when the neighborhood centers were operating at peak efficiency, they could make contact with over 6000 families per year per center (Hallowitz and Riessman 1967).

While most reports offer highly positive accounts of the effective services provided by the nonprofessionals both in and out of the center, they are mostly in the form of subjective impressions. These programs have emerged out of desperately felt needs with little time allocated for deliberate planning and assessment. If their constituents are in severe psychological crises, the last thing these workers have on their minds are empirical studies. However, some kind of accountability must be built into these programs. If not, they may become guilty of the very thing traditional mental health services have been criticized for, namely the provision of inefficient, unresponsive, and possibly ineffective services.

Other matters which must be dealt with include developing appropriate training procedures (Riessman 1967b), clearly defining the role and status of the indigenous nonprofessional (Morrill 1968), working out supervisory relationships and support systems (Lynch and Gardner 1970), clarifying the relationship between nonprofessional and professional staff (Grosser 1968), and opening up career ladders (Collins 1971). It is this last point, job availability and upward mobility, that is the key to the whole "new careers" movement (Gartner 1971; Riessman and Popper 1968). The major thrust is the provision of services to the disadvantaged by actually employing talented indigenous poor who are hired through attractive career ladders, increased income possibilities, opportunities for advanced educational and personal development, and improved life situations (Boyette et al. 1972; MacLennan 1969; MacLennan et al. 1966; Willcox 1970).

All these programming, training, and status issues are quite similar to the concerns of paraprofessionals (Chapter 3). What is different, however, is the degree of clashing that can occur between professional and indigenous workers around role, supervisory, and interrelationship issues. Perhaps no where else is the potentially high hostility between professional and nonprofessional mental health workers clearer (e.g., Kaplan and Roman 1973; Ruiz 1973; Shaw and Eagle 1971).

The indigenous workers bring with them their fears and anxieties regarding the general power structure. Middle-class professional personnel may be viewed as harboring the same basic prejudices and exploitive attitudes as the community at large. The professional personnel themselves may also feel a range of conflicting emotions. They may have a sincere regard for their nonprofessional colleagues but may too easily become paternalistic, defensive, and overly controlling in their attitudes and behavior.

It is thus not surprising, given the differences in background, training, thinking, and style between professional and indigenous nonprofessional workers, that much intra-agency hostility can develop. This was most dramatic in 1969 when indigenous paraprofessionals at the Lincoln Hospital program went out on strike and shut down the operation of services (Kaplan and Roman 1973). The relative conservatism of, and control by, professionals is quickly perceived by indigenous workers as synonomous with exploitation and racism. Thus, their already preconceived negative set is self-fulfilled. It would seem that professionals walking on such a tightrope have to "fall" and perhaps become even more entrenched in their traditional ways of thinking and acting. Thus, a vicious cycle ensues whereby both indigenous and professional workers feel self-righteously abused and assured that their actions are wholly sincere and well intended, with members of the opposing camp being in the wrong. There is a need for ongoing communication between professionals and nonprofessionals where all these issues and feelings are systematically shared and hopefully resolved (Ward 1970).

Key Issues Concerning Indigenous Paraprofessionals

As indigenous community workers are increasingly utilized at all levels in the delivery system, there are necessary concomitant changes in the role of the professional with respect to the catchment community (e.g., advocate, community organizer, "politician") and in relation to the nonprofessional staff within the agency. As previously indicated among the many issues being grappled with in these programs perhaps the most important is the quality of interpersonal relationships between professional and nonprofessional staff. Ideological and emotional clashes between professionals and nonprofessionals may severely hamper program services.

Certainly mental health programs for the poor, as was the case with other self-help processes, may continue whether or not professionals choose to involve themselves in a meaningful manner. These programs seem to be meeting needs that have been unmet by traditional programs. However, if nonprofessionals and professionals do not work together, the opportunity for mutual learning and growth will be lost. The professional-nonprofessional struggles described in the above programs may be seen as a microcosm of the larger issue of community versus professional control in mental health care. The interested reader may find the hotly debated issues of consumerism versus professionalism adequately explored by the following authors: Darley (1974), Hersch (1972), Peck (1974), Riessman (1967a, 1967b), Rosenblum (1972), and Ruiz and Behrens (1973).

A variety of other problems and issues need to be worked out before indigenous nonprofessional mental health programs can be evaluated. Most of the articles reviewed here were descriptive. Until evaluative research is available, the actual training and subsequent intervention aspects of indigenous helping programs remain innovative and promising, but highly speculative.

Exotic Helpers

While the indigenous paraprofessionals may be quite different in terms of values, life-styles, and helping skills from their professional colleagues, they are actually quite conventional when compared to another group of individuals also indigenous to the community—the exotic healers. These exotic helpers are people found in both Western and "primitive" society who function as mental health healers although they are likely to be regarded by professionals as charlatans or quacks who prey on the fears, hopes, and superstitions of troubled people (Hartog 1967).

With the advent of the cross-cultural and community psychiatry movements, some clinicians have come to recognize the important role played by exotic helpers. They have become aware of the actual overlapping functions served by healers and professionals as well as the similarity of helping processes used in delivering these services (Frank 1971, 1974a, 1974b; Goldstein 1971; Torrey 1969, 1972, 1973). For example, an analysis of faith healing in American Fundamentalist and Pentacostal sects noted the importance of attitudes, personality, sociocultural factors, and belief systems (Pattison, Lapins, and Doerr 1973).

There are many subtypes of exotic healers who together serve a vast constituency. There are indigenous black "root doctors" (herbalists), prophets, and magic venders (Hall and Bourne 1973; Stewart 1971; Tinling 1967), Puerto Rican spiritualists (Fisch 1969; Lubchansky, Egri, and Stokes 1970), Indian gurus (Neki 1973; Watts 1963), Spanish curanderos (Edgerton, Karno, and Fernandez 1970; Gobeil 1973; Kiev 1968, 1972), Asian shamans (Sasaki 1967; Tseng 1972), and American Indian medicine men (Bergman 1973; Boyer 1964; Miller and Schoenfeld 1973; Posinsky 1965).

There is a growing trend by some professionals first to recognize and identify these particular indigenous helpers and then to develop some sort of cooperative relationship with them. Professionals have established collaborative programs with faith healers (Bergman 1973; Singer, Araneta, and Aarons 1967; Ruiz and Langrod 1974), actually incorporated some of their practices within a traditional therapy framework (Casper and Philippus 1975; Kreisman 1975), or at least initiated mutual referral systems. For example, one psychiatric social worker, unable to effectively deal with a woman who believed she was hexed, made a referral to the local herbalist. This healer was able to successfully remove the spell, thus permitting the woman to continue more productively with her therapy (Hall and Bourne 1973).

If mental health professionals are to adequately help the indigenous poor, they must first inquire about their cultural backgrounds, religious practices, and mystical experiences (Douglas 1974). These data should then be put into a conceptual framework to understand the troubled person's life-style, as well as the meaning and maintenance of his symptoms. The professional's acceptance of such a framework might then suggest the inclusion of an exotic healer as the most appropriate resource person. Such respect for the healer's curative abilities is counter to the notion of trying to transform him into a miniaturized psychiatrist (as has occasionally been attempted). Attempts to completely "professionalize" healers might only jeopardize their unique skills.

A rather exciting example of the growing professional respect for exotic healers is a program sponsored by the National Institute of Mental Health which established an actual school for medicine men on a Navajo reservation (Bergman 1973). "Trainees" are schooled in modern mental health concepts as well as participating in a stringent apprenticeship program under the guidance of experienced medicine men from whom they learn a variety of complete healing rites for physical and emotional problems.

It is not surprising that there is little available systematic data regarding the nature, function, and effectiveness of exotic healing. Since these individuals are often viewed as deviant by both their own culture and the greater community, it becomes difficult to find out exactly who these people are and to get individuals to admit that they have used their services. There tends to be a clandestine network of consumers and healers often cloaked in some degree of secrecy. Even when the existence of these services is acknowledged, an entry into the system by outsiders is not always feasible.

Most of the articles concerning exotic healers tend to be anecdotal or case studies of a particular shaman. Where some element of research has been attempted, it has focused on the incidence of healing in a given community, the number of such helping individuals and people seeking their services, and interviews with either helpers or helpees to assess the attitudes and behavior involved in the healing transaction. In general, these articles describe field or case studies attempting to examine if these types of helpers are effective and how much so.

In recent years there has emerged some research investigating related types of nonconventional healing such as telepathy, laying on of hands, and auras produced by Kirlian photography (Frank 1974b). Hopefully, more systematic efforts will be specifically directed at exotic healing practices. Despite the paucity of hard data, some understanding of the intervention of the exotic healer may be derived from the writings of careful observers of transcultural psychiatry. As noted earlier, various studies have appeared that compare the functions and processes of traditional and exotic mental health helping approaches (e.g., Frank 1971; Kiev 1972; Kleinman 1973; Torrey 1969).

Universal Elements in the Helping Process

Tseng and McDermott (1975) suggest that there are certain universal elements in all psychotherapy: the presence of a healer supposedly possessing a special ability to help others, a client or patient seeking help from the healer to solve problems, and an attempt to influence the troubled individual in the cognitive, emotional, and behavioral areas.

Torrey's (1973) work is one of the most extensive analyses of exotic and traditional helping. After a thorough anthropological and psychiatric study of the indirect and direct evidence of the variety of helping interventions, Torrey, attempted to concretely identify the universal helping elements. Torrey conceptualized the following four ingredients as basic to any helping approach: a shared world view between helper and helpee, the personal qualities of the counselor, the particular expectations of the troubled person, and the actual techniques of intervention. Torrey strongly feels that with few exceptions witch doctors and psychiatrists are basically quite similar along these dimensions.

For example, the ideas of a shared world view between helper and helpee simply refers to the fact that both parties think and speak the same language, share similar value and belief systems, and generally would agree on how the world basically functions. A most important aspect of this common cultural set is the healer's ability to identify what exactly is troubling the person (e.g., childhood experience, violation of a taboo). Essentially, Torrey viewed this process as the "Rumpelstiltskin principle," whereby the ability to communicate and come up with the right name and assessment in itself begins the curative process.

The second major ingredient of the helping process concerns the various personal qualities of the helper, including his actual characteristics as well as those attributed to him by the helpee. Depending upon the culture, these will be particular demographic and personality variables which strongly affect helper-helpee interactions. Status, reputation, accessory paraphernalia, and educational training are all involved in this category. All these elements add to the image of authority that the helper presents.

The third element concerns the helpee's expectations about his problems, the means for getting help, and his view of the helper. The influence of helpee expectations is so important that it often appears that what a person expects to happen will happen. As Frank (1971) observed, the apparent success of healing methods based on all sorts of ideologies and methods compels the conclusion that the healing power of faith resides in the patient's state of mind, not in the validity of its object.

There is support for the influence of expectations, and particularly their relationship to helper characteristics, stemming from the work on the placebo effect in medical and psychiatric intervention (e.g., Adler and Hammett 1973; Shapiro 1971; Shapiro and Struening 1973). Situational, healer, and helpee variables (e.g., suggestability, personality, faith, and hope) all contribute to the impact of the helping process.

Further evidence for the role of expectations and the function of healer and helpee characteristics comes from the social psychology literature (e.g., Goldstein and Simonson 1971). For example, Karlins and Abelson (1970) have reviewed much of the research on factors influencing persuasion in individual and group contexts. They found that persuadability (i.e., changed expectations) appeared to be heightened when the helper provides specific information, both helper and helpee actually participate in the process, there is available group participation and reinforcement for conformity, the helpee has a susceptible personality, the helper has credibility and status, and both helper and helpee view themselves as highly similar. All these factors appear to be operating in exotic healing as well as in most nonprofessional and professional helping. Much of the recent psychotherapy research has itself begun to examine these very same variables, suggesting similar findings. These data will be discussed in Chapter 11.

Another universal element concerns the helping techniques employed by healers of all persuasions. Torrey (1973) suggested that even while skeptics might reluctantly accept the notion that witch doctors and psychotherapists may indeed be similar in terms of the previous dimensions, they draw the line when it comes to the actual tools and services both helpers provide. It is at this level that the superiority of the modern Western mental health worker is assumed, given his utilization of a "scientific" repertoire of skills.

However, Torrey (1973) strongly challenged this contention, suggesting that a careful comparison of professional and exotic interventions reveals rather similar approaches in the use of physical, psychosocial, and group milieu therapies in combination or alone. He points out that witch doctors utilize their own particular variety of psychotropic drugs, shock therapy, and counseling and psychotherapy.

In summary, our current understanding of the nature of exotic helping rests not on systematic empirical study, but on observations of the healer and client interactions, the conceptual speculations of cross-cultural psychiatry, and data emerging from social psychological and psychotherapy research. All these sources strongly suggest that the exotic helper is providing an important service. The effectiveness of the exotic helper is probably determined by the combination of his personal and professional qualities and by the troubled person's expectations of him and his work—and not by his technique per se.

The viability of this notion of underlying universal helping principles is important for understanding all forms of professional and nonprofessional mental health intervention. If personality, expectations, and placebo variables are the essential elements in effective helping, then particular training, educational background, or techniques may not necessarily be that important. Perhaps attention should instead be paid to recognizing, identifying, and embellishing the important ingredients in the helping transaction with less time on specific theory and technique. This idea is explored later in Chapter 11 where there is an analysis of recent psychotherapy research.

A review of the work of the exotic healer suggests a need for professional caregivers to have some humility. They should not too readily assume expertise and innovation in areas where exotic healers may have already paved the way for thousands of years. In addition, the observations on exotic healing have implications for an understanding of nonprofessional as well as professional helping. Throughout this book the work of numerous types of nonprofessional helpers has been examined. The point often has been made that while a lack of solid data prevented adequate appraisal of their work, much indirect evidence pointed to effective helping. If indeed these generally lesser trained and educated individuals are performing appropriately (and sometimes as well as professionals), then some explanation may be found in the ideas suggested in this chapter—namely, the influence of those basic ingredients operative in various types of helping transactions.

9

Parents as Mental Health Helpers

This chapter emphasizes the increasing involvement of professionals in developing preventive and educational programs for parents. The goals of such programs include increasing parents' knowledge of child development, training them (if necessary) to be change agents with their own children, and helping them to learn specific helping skills for working with other parents. These projects may also be seen as further examples of mental health-related self-help programs.

Educational Programs

Whatever their particular format (discussion groups, courses, or workshops) educational programs are generally aimed at providing parents with basic childrearing information, strategies for handling problems, and developing greater self-confidence through a mutually supportive group atmosphere (Greenbank and Cameron 1968; Greenbank and Gilbert 1969; Hollister 1958).

Typical examples of educative projects incorporating such goals have been in drug education programs for parents (Thomas, Frisone, and Lipson 1971); crisis-oriented programs for parents of newly entering kindergarten children (Signell 1972); discussion groups aimed at exploring parental attitudes, values, and feelings regarding children (Beale 1974; Bouska et al. 1974; Dinkmeyer 1973); and focused, time-limited communication workshops for parents of adolescents (Brownstone and Dye 1973). The highly popular Parent Effectiveness Training (PET) program (Gordon 1970; Peterson 1969) is another example of a client-centered approach with its heavy emphasis on total family communication and the development of listening, conflict resolution, and problem solving skills.

Most of these programs tend to be short-term courses, and there has been little built-in assessment of their effectiveness. Available data do suggest that in a viable program the material must be related to the real needs of the participants and not simply to the values of the sponsoring agency (Freeman and George 1972). Additional issues which must also be considered relate to successfully organizing and publicizing these groups and working with appropriate agency administrators. Parent education projects tend to vary greatly in terms of type, goals, intensity of programming, and concern for assessment.

The available objective evaluative attempts (both published and unpublished) often have been concerned with the PET program. For example, Larson

135

(1972) compared the influence of three different small group approaches (Achievement Motivation Program, Parent Effectiveness Training, and Discussion-Encounter Group). Data were gathered in order to assess family communication, behavioral and attitudinal changes in parents, and observed changes in children. Based on self-report data, parent attitude surveys, self-concept inventories, and problem checklists, the Parent Effectiveness Training group made the greatest overall positive gains while the Achievement Motivation Program was particularly effective in changing the self-image of parents. The conclusions of this study can be questioned because of various methodological problems. There was a failure to randomly assign parents to the three experimental groups and a lack of control for group leadership. There was also an inconsistent use of assessment techniques in the various experimental groups and seemingly biased ratings.

Support for the effectiveness of the PET program comes from a variety of nonpublished resources including masters and Ph.D. theses (Cline 1971; Garcia 1971; Haynes 1972; Knowles, unpublished; Lillibridge 1971; Peterson, unpublished; Piercy and Brush 1971; Stearn 1970). These studies tend to be at a suggestive empirical level. They reflect problems inherent in most attempts to evaluate parent education programs—namely, often exclusive reliance on paper-and-pencil tests, too little use of objective behavioral measures, and the lack of follow-up to assess whether children as well as their parents experience positive effects. There is little doubt that parents in these projects can achieve considerable attitudinal and behavioral gains both in terms of themselves and in relation to their children (Cullen 1968). But if program goals are also geared toward subsequent changes in the children, then there should be appropriate follow-up evaluations (e.g. Lillibridge 1971; Peterson, unpublished; Stearn 1970).

The PET program is to date one of the better researched educational training approaches for parents. Despite methodological shortcomings, a generally promising picture of the program's viability emerges from the available data. The program emphasizes the use of the didactic-experiential, step-by-step skill-building approach noted repeatedly throughout this book, and it is consistent with other client-centered training models utilized, for example, with teachers (Chapter 4), and student volunteers (Chapter 10).

Parents as Change Agents for Their Own Children

Although courses and group-centered approaches may be beneficial for either preventing or dealing with relatively mild childrearing concerns, still it is often necessary to work more directly with particular parents around specific concerns regarding their own children. For example, low-income mothers have received training in various childrearing strategies, via home visits and professional role modeling. The goal is to have these mothers serve as the primary agents in developing emotional and cognitive growth in their high-risk children (Gordon 1967; Karnes et al. 1970; Lambie and Weikart 1970; Levenstein 1970).

A recent preventive program for low-income parents engaged families with children as young as 1-year-old (Johnson et al. 1974). This was an intensive 2-year training program involving the whole family. It included home training, several weekend sessions, subsequent mother and child participation in a nursery school, and fathers' involvement at a series of evening meetings. The whole thrust of this program was to emphasize the already existing capabilities of parents. Building upon this foundation, other childrearing skills were taught through discussion and practicum experiences.

This training approach is another example of the didactic-experiential educational model with its emphasis on specific behavioral criteria, skill building, group feedback, and further practice. Most of the other low-income parent programs have not had a solid empirical foundation, and the Johnson et al. (1974) project stands out as a relatively sound research effort. The design of this program included the random assignment of parents to both experimental and control groups, premeasures and postmeasures utilizing both paper-and-pencil tests and behavioral observations, and adequate follow-up. However, the program would have been further strengthened by the use of alternative treatment or attention-placebo control groups and longer-range follow-up of both parents and children.

Mothers as Client-Centered Therapists

Filial play therapy, based on the client-centered approach, has already been cited in the discussions on teacher and student therapist roles (Chapter 4). The key elements of this essentially didactic-experiential model are the examination, observation, and practice of Rogerian-based play therapy (Guerney 1964). In many ways similar to the principles and techniques espoused in the Parent Effectiveness Training model, this training approach is less educative/preventive in nature and more concerned with direct service skill building to ameliorate existing problems. Groups of six to eight parents are trained to conduct play sessions with their own emotionally disturbed children. After this training phase, they conduct play sessions at home while continuing in an ongoing weekly group meeting with professionals (Andronico et al. 1967; Fidler et al. 1969; Guerney 1964; Guerney, Guerney, and Andronico 1966).

The research of Stover and Guerney (1967) was aimed at assessing the effectiveness of training mothers in "reflective" and "empathic" counseling modes of responding as they conducted actual weekly 1/2-hour play sessions with their emotionally disturbed children. Two experimental and two control groups of six to eight mothers were randomly formed from a group applying to a university psychology clinic. Children were similar in terms of diagnosis, age, intelligence level, and socioeconomic status. Background characteristics of the mothers in the different groups were also similar. Assignment of mothers to either training or control groups followed an initial baseline 1/2-hour mother-child play session.

The step-by-step skill-building process was evident in the training approach for the experimental groups. The features inherent in the didactic-experiential model were apparent including the emphasis on formal discussion, repeated observation, practice sessions, individual and group feedback, and continuing group process sessions for personal growth and specific refinement of skills. In contrast, the control group received no formalized training and had minimal contact with the clinic during the study.

Objective measures and observations of both experimental and control group mothers focused on three additional 1/2-hour play sessions which were observed, taped, and rated by independent trained recorders. The experimental group mothers were generally more reflective and empathic than the control group mothers. The experimental group children were generally more verbally and nonverbally responsive than the control group children. This research is important in being one of the empirically more adequate studies so far discussed in this chapter. It also stands out as supporting the viability of using parents in direct service capacity and not simply as supportive helping agents.

There are some problems, however, in generalizing from the results—difficulties similarly noted in discussing the positive findings of the related program for training teachers as filial therapists (Chapter 4). For example, despite the highly favorable results, this is the only reported research utilizing this method for training parents. Further replication studies are vitally needed. Also, it is not really clear, without appropriate attention-placebo or alternative treatment control groups, just what are the effective ingredients involved in this helping process. Certainly, reflective and empathic parental responding may be important. But the key ingredients might be the new hope and optimism that program participation provides for parents and the high level of concern and attention that is given to their troubled children. Thus, while something may indeed be happening to parental behavior that in turn facilitates changes in their children, further variable specificity and control are needed to clarify just what elements are or are not helpful.

In addition, some measures should be taken of parent-child interactions outside of the brief, formalized play therapy sessions to determine whether parents' newly accrued skills, as well as the children's behavioral changes, transfer beyond the clinic situation. What is occurring in the home milieu that may or may not be conducive to a more generalizable client-centered therapeutic process? There are other research possibilities such as long-term follow-up of behavioral changes in both parents and children, comparative studies of parent and professional helpers utilizing a client-centered approach, and an examination

of the application of this process to various types of parent-child interactions.

In summary, the filial therapy approach appears to be a useful model for
training parents as direct service mental health aides as well as for effectively
facilitating positive behavioral changes in their emotionally disturbed children.
However, the firmness of this conclusion awaits further outcome research more
attentive to specifying and controlling the complex variables inherent in this
particular helping process.

Parents as Behavior Modifiers

The burgeoning behavior modification literature perhaps best reflects the use of
training programs to develop parents as change agents (Bornstein 1974; Brown
1972; Cone and Sloop 1971; Lebow 1973). Bornstein (1974) attributes this vast
growth to the fact that behavior modification procedures appear ideally suited
for home management programs because they are simple and direct. In addition,
another advantage of parents as change agents is that they have relatively easy
access to their children and are inexpensive treatment resources (Brown 1972;
Cone and Sloop 1971; Johnson and Katz 1973; Lebow 1973).

In the 1970s there was an outpour of behavior manuals and programs for
parents. The goal of these materials is to help provide parents with various skills
in analyzing and manipulating environmental contingencies so as to better cope
with emotional, academic, or physical problems in their children (e.g., Alvord
1973; Becker 1971; Hall 1971b, 1971c, 1971d; Lundell 1972; McIntyre 1970;
Palumbo and Kurtz 1973; Patterson 1971a; Patterson and Gullion 1968; Rettig
1973; Smith and Smith 1966; Wittes and Radin 1969; Zifferblatt 1970).

Methods of parent training have varied from general educational programs
to acquaint parent groups with the basic principles of effective contingency
management (e.g., Toepfer, Reuter, and Maurer 1972) to more specifically and
intensively focused parent training procedures. There are programs developed for
such problem areas as antisocial and oppositional behavior, speech and reading
dysfunctions, school phobias, enuresis, seizures, and self-injurious behavior (e.g.,
Butterfield 1973; Fodor 1973; Hawkins et al. 1966; Moore and Bailey 1973;
O'Leary, O'Leary, and Becker 1967; Risley 1968; Tahmisian and McReynolds
1971; Wagner 1968; Wahler et al. 1965).

Unfortunately, there are insufficient data to conclude just what are the key
training approaches and variables in successful parent behavior modification
training. While there is some indication that didactic and practical experiences
are essential, the lack of sophisticated controlled comparative research makes
conclusions rather tentative (O'Dell 1974). For example, an analysis of different
training modes should compare such techniques as modeling, lecture, reading
assignments, group discussion, and training in observation skills (Johnson and
Katz 1973).

There have been many critical reviews concerning the development of parents as behavior modifiers (e.g., Berkowitz and Graziano 1972; Johnson and Katz 1973; Lebow 1973; O'Dell 1974; Tavormina 1974, 1975; Tramontana 1971). Most of these reviews have utilized similar empirical yardsticks and found deficiencies in much of the available research. The numerous projects reviewed tend to be quite varied in concept, degree of training, level of parent involvement and responsibility, professional participation, and experimental design. For example, there were simple case studies, single-subject studies employing reversal designs, and group studies utilizing experimental manipulation. The more sophisticated studies are in the minority, and there is a strong need for the greater use of control groups and factorial designs to more clearly determine the effectiveness of parents as behavior modifiers (Mazza and Pumroy 1975).

Despite the various methodological problems found in these studies, there seem to be a sufficient number of empirically sound research projects to at least tentatively conclude that behavioral techniques may be effectively applied to children's problem behaviors through the training of their parents. Further research more attentive to the basic empirical criteria noted by O'Dell (1974) would provide more specific data regarding the most effective training, application, and evaluative approaches. It should also be emphasized that even the best designed behavioral training program must deal with maintaining the motivation and cooperation of the parents themselves with regard to consistent attendance, required record keeping, and carrying out the actual child management program (e.g., Mira 1970; Patterson et al. 1967; Patterson and Reid 1970; Patterson, Shaw, and Ebner 1969; Peine and Munro 1973; Salzinger, Feldman, and Portnoy 1970).

Parents as Peer Helpers

Various programs have been developed to capitalize on the ability of talented, trained parents in helper, advisory functions with other parents (Anderson and Jones 1972). An example of a particularly innovative program was reported by Gluckstern (1973). Parents were intensively trained to be drug counselors, ombudsmen, and community organizers for other families and agencies. A group of fourteen parent trainees received a concentrated 60-hour training program divided into the following three phases. The first phase was a structured weekend encounter focusing on experiential exercises, team building, and goal clarification. The second phase involved counseling and human relations skill development along with detailed drug information. This phase included systematic didactic-experiential training in such areas as attending behavior, reflecting feelings, paraphrasing, and nonverbal behavior. The final phase was aimed at the development of techniques for trainees to actually engage in community action and to initiate programs in cooperation with community agencies. It is this last phase of the program which marks the uniqueness of the Gluckstern project.

This program has utilized such techniques as individual and group practice and supervision, audio and visual taping sessions, continued group support, and ongoing inservice training. The expansive nature of this program apparently resulted in the parent trainees broadening their service base and providing counseling for marital concerns and parent-child conflicts as well as for drug related problems. In addition, a parent-to-parent hot line service was also established.

The evaluation of this program was relatively extensive and consisted of three assessment periods: just prior to the second phase of training, immediately following the second phase of training, and 7 months after the completion of training. Some of the assessments were geared at analyzing the effects of the program on the trainees themselves with respect to attitudes and drug knowledge. There were also analyses of training effects on both the helpers and the helpees in terms of behavioral and attitudinal changes and the role played by trainees within the community. Results indicated significant positive changes in the trainees' knowledge and skills and ability to communicate about their personal feelings and relevant issues. Unfortunately, even though it was reported that trainees made successful contact with over 100 community clients, follow-up revealed insufficient community entry and impact.

The findings strongly suggest that a selected group of nonprofessional parents can be systematically selected, trained, and utilized in a variety of direct and indirect helping roles with peers. However, the data are inconclusive in terms of the subsequent employability of trainees within community settings. In spite of Gluckstern's (1973) rigorous efforts to offer effective training in community entry and organization, there were still unsettled problems in community acceptance and appropriate utilization of trainees.

While reasonably researched, the Gluckstern study did lack some important methodological features which necessitates caution in interpreting the generally favorable reported findings. For example, there were no measures taken immediately prior to or following the sensitivity training experience. A 20-hour structured encounter weekend might very likely involve some introduction and practice in the very same communicative responding processes further explored in the subsequent skill-building training phase. The failure to measure the effects of such an experience makes it difficult to assess whether baseline helper performance was simply a reflection of the specific 60-hour training program or also a measure of the earlier sensitivity training phase of the project. It is not at all clear just what program features were important ingredients in the trainees' attitudinal and behavioral development.

The lack of nontreatment and alternative treatment control groups further clouds the issue of the actual effectiveness of the training program. There are also other apparent methodological and procedural deficiencies in this project.

There was a strong reliance on self-reports and other potentially biased data. The taped "counseling" sessions between trainees and "volunteer" clients seemed rather artificial. There were a relatively small number of trainees, and they varied considerably in terms of their social backgrounds, experiences, and initial level of helping skills.

Despite such problems the Gluckstern project is important in several respects. The project emphasized peer self-help, comprehensive training, and the basic conviction that trained parents can offer an extensive range of services within the community. Greater concern for experimental control and rigor could lead to much stronger support for what seems like a particularly promising training model for parent helpers.

Summary

This chapter on parents as mental health helpers demonstrated the extent to which the nonprofessional movement has been spreading. It seems logical that if emotional problems derive, in part, from early familial experiences, then parents should be trained in both directive and preventive mental health procedures to use with their children. This has been the thrust of the newer family and network intervention counseling approaches as well as the spearhead of the preventive mental health movement.

In addition to the fact that there are not enough professionals to meet the growing mental health demands of families, parents can be viewed as particularly appropriate helpers for several clinical and practical reasons. For example, once having accrued helping skills, they can directly ameliorate problems in their own homes rather than pursue the time-consuming path of going indirectly through a professional counselor. These new skills may also generalize so that trained parents may subsequently apply their new knowledge to other members of their families, as well as to the particular child about whom they might have initially been concerned. Moreover, although many parents are still reluctant to seek professional mental health services, they may find it easier to deal with trained and qualified peers. Rieff (1966, 1969) has suggested that "professionalism" does not necessarily reflect a particular degree or level of talent, but rather the tendency of some interest groups to hold on to specific reflects the fact that mental health professionals are beginning to share a variety of direct and indirect helping skills with parents.

In this chapter, there has been a description of a variety of avenues by which professionals have attempted to reach parents. With respect to the range and effectiveness of such activities, this concluding section will deal with general observations and then summarize some specific conclusions that can be drawn from the thirty studies evaluated in this chapter. The target populations of these programs, have involved individual parents or groups of parents. While approximately one-third of these programs were aimed more specifically at direct service or remedial needs, the remaining programs were more concerned with either ameliorating minor problems or preventing their occurrence. Of note is that, relative to other types of nonprofessional helper programs, those for parents seem to have best utilized consultation, education, and training approaches. With respect to training, the parent programs have ranged from informal to didactic-experiential with the majority being in the latter category. The general implication emerging from most of these studies was that a combination of teaching and practice was the most effective means for developing parent helper roles for both direct and indirect services.

However, very little of the research evaluated the actual effectiveness of these approaches in terms of comparative controlled studies. In view of the numerous empirical problems in researching such programs, the overall results remain somewhat inconclusive. Although nearly two-thirds of these projects were close to a suggestive research level, only one (Johnson et al. 1974) approximated quality research and this too, as noted, had some shortcomings. Only four studies dealt with the issue of actual helpee outcome, and the problems in these programs have already been cited (Gluckstern 1973; Johnson et al. 1974; Larson 1972; Stover and Guerney 1967).

Many promising avenues for further program development are indicated by a more specific appraisal of the field of parent training. If we divide the area into educational approaches, parents as helpers with their own children, and general peer helping programs, the following conclusions may be made.

(1) Educational programs in the form of discussion groups, courses, or workshops have increasingly emerged as an important preventive means for providing parents with knowledge and strategies for coping with actual or potential problems. In fact, Hawkins (1971) made a plea for universal parent-hood training to ideally ensure the adequacy of parents' basic childrearing skills. Despite the wide variety of such endeavors, little evaluative data are available with the exception of findings concerning the highly visible PET program (Gordon 1970). As noted, the research relating to this program, while promising, is in general not empirically adequate (e.g., Larson 1972).

(2) While educational approaches may serve important preventive and ameliorative functions, situations frequently arise where parents must be more specifically trained to deal with their children's current problems. For example, low-income mothers can acquire various techniques which will hopefully facilitate the cognitive and emotional growth of their children. While the research in this area has often been negligible, one recent study by Johnson et al. (1974) was relatively systematic and empirically sound. It also clearly suggested the benefits of the didactic-experiential training approach in preparing mothers to more effectively deal with their children. But the crucial question regarding the long-term effects on both the parents' and the children's level of functioning is unanswered in the evaluation of this and other related programs.

(3) Parents have also been trained using the client-centered, filial therapy model as direct service therapists with their own children. To date, there have been few studies evaluating this program (e.g., Stover and Guerney 1967), and while generally positive results were reported, it was suggested that more and better controlled studies are needed.

(4) There is also extensive work concerning the teaching of behavior modification techniques to parents. These programs vary considerably in terms of goals, training format, technology, and evaluation. Although there is some support for the didactic-experiential approach as being superior, little comparative research is available. Numerous empirical problems inherent in these studies were cited, and it was suggested that greater utilization of factorial designs and control groups is necessary to best evaluate parent behavior management programs. There does appear, however, to be enough relatively systematic data to at least tentatively conclude that parent behavior management programs can contribute to positive gains for both parents and children.

(5) As was the case with programs to train teachers in various mental health roles (Chapter 4), the most extensive work with parents has also been in filial therapy (client-centered play therapy) and behavior modification approaches. Here, too, despite apparent conceptual and methodological differences, there are similarities in both approaches. In particular, there is the frequent use of the didactic-experiential format by which both client-centered and behavior modification approaches are presented and practiced. The didactic-experiential model receives some support as perhaps the most ideal training mode even in the context of different program goals. Tavormina (1974) has suggested specific assessment of the comparative utility and cost efficiency of the client-centered and behavioral models.

(6) Another thrust described in this chapter was that of training parents as peer helpers in counseling, supportive, and consulting roles. The outstanding example of such efforts is seen in Gluckstern's (1973) extensive work. She selected and systematically trained parents to serve as drug counselors and community organizers. Evaluation suggested that a wide range of direct service and community skills were successfully accrued by the trainees and benefited their clients. However, various methodological shortcomings noted in the research make any conclusions rather tentative. As with the other types of programs reviewed in this chapter, further research is certainly needed to assess the effectiveness of parent peer helping programs.

One final point is relevant in ending this chapter: while "parents" were the particular nonprofessional group on focus, it was essentially mothers who were involved in most of these programs. This is unfortunate, for recent studies have begun to emphasize the important role played by fathers on the cognitive, social and emotional development of their children (e.g., Biller 1974; Biller and Meredith 1974). There is a definite need for better balanced parent self-help programs with both fathers and mothers included.

10 Mental Health Volunteers

Previous chapters of this book have examined the work of a variety of nonprofessional mental health helpers. Both paid paraprofessionals and a range of lay and allied professionals involved in some aspect of mental health care on either an informal or a formal basis have been discussed. The present chapter deals with perhaps the largest group of the new mental health workforce—those individuals who often volunteer their time or skills in the delivery of services in a variety of school, psychiatric, or related settings. College and high school students and interested homemakers typically comprise the personnel for these volunteer programs. Reiff and Riessman (1965) refer to these individuals as "ubiquitous nonprofessionals" (in contrast to indigenous). They are usually similar to professionals with respect to their middle-class background, life experiences, attitudes, and values.

Student Programs

Students have been at the forefront of the nonprofessional movement. They seem to possess a combination of characteristics which allows them to very quickly become involved in helping relationships. For example, students often appear more eager, flexible, committed, and idealistic in their involvement than other nonprofessionals. Similarly, their very naiveté concerning pathology and treatment along with their lack of experience and relative youth seems to enable them to establish trust and meaningful relationships with even the most disturbed individuals.

Gruver (1971) has critically examined much of the available literature on students as mental health helpers. This section will provide a more focused look at college helpers, highlighting the basic issues, tasks, and problems inherent in student volunteer mental health work. The interested reader is urged to read the Gruver (1971) article for a much more detailed account of this area.

Psychiatric Patient Companions

Probably the most extensive use made of college volunteers has been in companion programs for inpatient psychiatric adults (e.g., Beck, Kantor, and Gelineau 1963; Chinsky and Rappaport 1970a; Fischer 1970; Golann, Baker, and Frydman 1973; Greenblatt and Kantor 1962; Poser 1966; Rappaport and Chinsky 1970; Rappaport, Chinsky, and Cowen 1971).

Despite there being over 500 such programs, adequate objective research in this area has been scarce (Zax and Cowen 1972). Screening of student helpers has tended to be minimal; students receive no actual preparation in some programs (e.g., Poser 1966), while in others there is on-the-job training and ongoing supervision (e.g., Holzberg, Knapp, and Turner 1967). Similarly, there has been a wide variety in the type of companion services being provided. For example, while students generally offer supportive services (recreation, talking, liaison work, and mild one-to-one counseling), other programs have failed to work out meaningful roles for students which have relevance for the larger hospital (Brown and Ishiyama 1968).

Methodological shortcomings abound in most of the evaluations of student programs. Deficiencies include a lack of basic research design, control groups, premeasures and postmeasures, specific attention to outcome, and appropriate follow-up (e.g., Greenblatt and Kantor 1962). Even when nontreatment control groups are included, there is an absence of alternative treatment or attention-placebo groups. Such controls seem imperative given the diversity of treatment-like experiences on the psychiatric ward and the strong possibility that the youthful, energetic demeanors of the students might contribute to any reported patient changes. In addition, all the problems in defining and measuring inpatient and ex-patient progress or deterioration (e.g., discharge and readmission rates), which were discussed in Chapter 7, are equally relevant in evaluating these programs.

Notable contrasts to the generally poorly researched student companion programs are the Connecticut Valley Companion project (Holzberg 1963; Holzberg, Gewirtz, and Ebner 1964; Holzberg and Knapp 1965; Holzberg, Knapp, and Turner 1966, 1967; Knapp and Holzberg 1964) and the Connecticut Service program (Hersch, Kulik, and Scheibe 1969; Scheibe et al. 1969). The organizers of these programs have demonstrated great concern for appropriate training, supervision, and process and outcome research. Their reported positive findings regarding both patient and student volunteer progress are thus particularly meaningful.

Perhaps the biggest problem in many of the companion programs has been the failure to carefully evaluate outcome for patients; there has been a greater concentration on program effects on the student helpers themselves (Bergman and Doland 1974). Gains for student helpers seem particularly evident when they can be appropriately matched with responsive patients (Fisher 1970; Tomlinson, Barthol, and Groot 1969). There have been reports of positive changes in students' attitudes toward patients (Beckman 1972; Chinsky and Rappaport 1970a; Kish and Hood 1974), self-acceptance and self-confidence (Golann, Baker, and Frydman 1973), moral judgment (Holzberg, Gewirtz, and Ebner 1964; King, Walder, and Pavey 1970), self-understanding (Reinherz

1962), and ability in choosing further academic and occupational training (Kish and Stage 1973).

Most of the reports examining student outcome have tended to be more objective and better controlled than those more specifically interested in patient outcome. One could conclude that hospital-based student companion programs have a signficant impact on the student helper's psychological functioning, but systematic data regarding the effects of these programs on patients have been minimal (e.g., Bergman and Doland 1974; Holzberg, Knapp, and Turner 1967; Poser 1966; Rappaport, Chinsky, and Cowen 1971). If the ultimate goal of utilizing student nonprofessional workers is primarily for patient care and secondarily for the helper's personal growth, then it behooves future investigators to direct more sophisticated empirical attention toward patient outcome. In any case, outcome research should be but one component of a comprehensive model for student involvement. There should also be ample consideration given to selection, training, supervision, inservice education, clarity of role and job description, and nonprofessional student-professional relationships (Brown and Ishiyama 1968).

Programs with Children

The youth and activity levels of students have made them well suited for mental health-related programs for children as well as for adults (Brennen 1967). Students have been reported to have effectively worked as companions with emotionally disturbed children in the hospital (Megenity, Russell, and Kerkoski 1972; Reinherz 1963) and out of the hospital (Goodman 1967, 1972a; Kraft 1966; Mitchell 1966), as friends to children from unstable or broken homes (Patterson and Patterson 1967), and as "therapeutic" tutors for Headstart and disadvantaged children (Jason, Clarfield, and Cowen 1973; Spector and Cowen 1971).

In general, these programs seem somewhat more concerned with selection and training issues than did the hospital-based student companion projects, perhaps because the children in these studies tend to be outpatients and more amenable to treatment. Gruver (1971) suggested that college volunteers prefer to work with children because improvement in youngsters is apparent much more quickly and hence is more rewarding. Training in the child-oriented programs, while not extensive, is usually in the form of some ongoing individual and group supervision with the emphasis on "learning by doing."

Research on the student-child programs has been minimal, with positive claims essentially supported only by anecdotal data. Goodman's (1967, 1972a) work is an exception. He developed an extensive project aimed at studying behavioral and attitudinal changes in preadolescent boys who had participated in a companion-activity relationship with highly selected undergraduate men. The participating boys were viewed as emotionally troubled by parents and/or teachers. In the initial phase of the program, the boys and counselors were divided into "outgoing" and "quiet" categories; then like and unlike dyads were formed to compare the relative success of different combinations of helper-helpee personality types. The actual interventions consisted of a range of supportive activities with dyads usually meeting 2 or 3 times per week for a period of 1 to 5 hours throughout the academic year. As compared to a no-treatment control group, experimental boys and students were reported to have achieved significant changes, with perhaps the greatest gains occurring in pairs consisting of outgoing students and quiet boys.

A particularly important dimension of Goodman's (1972a) project was the systematic evaluation of the effects of varied student training levels. His results suggested that trained and supervised students were perceived by the youngsters as more disclosive and empathic than untrained and unsupervised undergraduates. Similarly, parent ratings of the children's behavior reflected the same differential effectiveness of trained and untrained students. Although the Goodman (1967, 1972a) program lacked a sufficient number of control groups and comparative criteria measures, it was still of value in pointing out that adequate research is indeed possible in the area of student-child mental health work.

Another comprehensive use of student helpers is seen in the innovative school prevention program developed at the University of Rochester (e.g., Cowen 1969a). This program was noted earlier in the discussion on retirees as paraprofessionals (Chapter 7). In the after-school activities program, primary-grade children experiencing school adjustment difficulties were seen by student volunteers once or twice a week for about 75 minutes either individually or in a group (Cowen, Zax, and Laird 1966; Zax and Cowen 1967). Results of this program were favorable and suggestive of the variety of contexts (e.g., play, conversation, trips) in which students may provide therapeutic experiences (Cowen, Carlisle, and Kaufman 1969). Research in this program can be rated only as suggestive since no control groups were utilized. Training followed a didactic-experiential format with students involved in a year-long seminar consisting of lectures, classwork, practicum experiences, and ongoing discussion groups.

Perhaps the most extensive programming in the area of student-child interventions is seen in the work of Stollak and his associates (Stollak 1968, 1973a, 1973b; Stollak et al. 1973). Students are trained as basically client-centered play therapists. This particular mode of nonprofessional training was previously discussed in Chapter 4 in the section concerning teachers as play therapists. The process involved trainees learning the fundamentals of Rogerian theory, examining the techniques of client-centered play therapy, observing demonstrations by trainers and peers, actually practicing the skills with selected children, and receiving feedback and supervision from the rest of the training group (Guerney 1964).

In Stollak's (1973a) program for undergraduates, screening and training were intensive, involving at least a 2-year commitment from the students, and were presented in a well-balanced didactic-experiential framework including a sequence of academic courses and fieldwork. Extensive use was made of role playing and videotapes. The goal of this program involved helping the student volunteers, as well as the children, make positive psychological gains (Guerney, Stollak, and Guerney 1970, 1971). Once again, it may be noted that the training process in this program is, with certain variations, rather consistent with the skill-building, social learning, and group training model of many of the more sophisticated nonprofessional programs cited earlier.

Research on this program has been ongoing since the late 1960s. The researchers have developed extensive process and outcome measures and utilized relatively sophisticated empirical designs. The bulk of the reported findings indicate significant changes for both students and youngsters. This program is quite promising because it demonstrates the feasibility of doing quality evaluative research on a sophisticated nonprofessional training program.

Peer Helpers

Undergraduates are also becoming increasingly involved as peer helpers, frequently participating in campus counseling and drop-in centers (Wolff 1969). This new development may be seen as a reflection of recent innovations by mental health personnel at colleges struggling to enhance the quantity and quality of their services (Berns 1972; Delworth, Sherwood, and Casaburri 1974; Kirk et al. 1971; McCarthy 1970; Morrill and Hurst 1971; Oetting 1967; Winer et al. 1974; Wolff 1974).

The expansion of campus mental health services has created a need for the involvement of selected undergraduates to supplement the already depleted professional staff. A survey by Steenland (1973) found a great range of services performed by student paraprofessionals. Students are often involved in crisis center or hot line work (e.g., Berman 1973; Berman, Davis, and Phillips 1973; Kalafat and Tyler 1973; McCarthy and Berman 1971; Tucker, Megenity, and Vigil 1970); companion or befriending programs for alienated, foreign, or maladjusted freshman students (e.g., Boylin 1971, 1973); academic adjustment counseling programs (e.g., Brown 1965; Brown et al. 1971; Brown and Zunker 1966; Zunker and Brown 1966); dormitory residence hall helping projects (e.g., Davis 1974; Holbrook 1972; McBride 1973; Schilling 1974; Thompson and Fiddleman 1973); and relatively extensive individual and group peer counseling services (Delworth et al. 1974; Edgar and Kotrick 1972; Ferree, Wasserman, and McCarthy 1973; *Guidepost* 1974; McCarthy and Michaud 1971; Persons et al. 1973; Wrenn and Mencke 1972).

These programs appear to be more concerned with effective selection and training measures than those programs utilizing undergraduates as interveners with chronic patients and troubled children. Many of the programs have devoted considerable time to didactic-experiential training which has often included coursework, practicums, sensitivity training, individual and group supervision, and continuing education. Probably the most extensive college programs are emerging in university counseling centers interested in developing student self-help networks. An example is the Colorado State University program where students, at various training levels, function as integral members in a range of direct and indirect mental health services (Delworth et al. 1974; Delworth, Sherwood, and Casaburri 1974).

There is an especially well-developed and comprehensive peer counseling program at American University (Ferree, Wasserman, and McCarthy 1973). This program utilizes a selection process which includes psychological testing, screening interviews, and stressful role-playing situations. Eligible students then receive a variety of intensive training experiences geared to specific services. The major goal is to develop a student-centered peer counseling program so that within 3 years 10 percent of the student body will have been directly trained in this program (*Guidepost* 1974). Services include academic aid, resident hall counseling, crisis intervention and hot line work, dropout prevention, and research and evaluation. Whether students are serving as models, counselors, tutors, liaison contacts, companions, or empathic listeners, they are usually carefully screened, trained, and supervised and generally they seem to have an important impact.

Although much attention is usually paid to quality training, there is typically little time spent on systematic research of the outcome effects of these programs. What data are available present gross figures regarding such information as the consumption of services. Basic control groups generally have not been employed, and often data have been gathered only by the use of simple self-report measures and questionnaires. Despite the fact that these programs entail some of the most creative examples of nonprofessional training and utilization, there is a dearth of appropriate evaluation appraising process as well as outcome.

One exception to the general lack of systematic evaluative research is the assessment of the peer academic adjustment programs developed by Brown and his associates (Brown 1965, 1974; Brown et al. 1971; Zunker and Brown 1966). Utilizing relatively sophisticated experimental designs (e.g., nontreatment or professional counselor control groups), Brown investigated the intervention effects of student paraprofessionals working with a range of peers experiencing academic problems. Overall results led to the conclusion that paraprofessional counseling was effective and practical in a variety of preventive and corrective contexts (Brown 1974).

High School and Junior High School Helping Programs

In addition to undergraduates, high school and junior high school students also have been utilized as paraprofessional workers (Pasework 1974; Staton, Tiller, and Weyler 1969). Particular service experiences have involved working with geriatric patients (Friedman and Spada 1970); troubled peers (Hamburg and Varenhorst 1972; Leibowitz and Rhoads 1974; Varenhorst 1974); and emotionally disturbed, handicapped, and underachieving grade school students (Clarfield and McMillan 1973; Durlak 1973b; McWilliams and Finkel 1973; Perlmutter and Durham 1965; Rath and David 1973; Rogeness and Bednar 1973a, 1973b; Rouse and Farb 1974; Winters and Arent 1969).

The same features characterizing the undergraduate helping programs are generally found in the projects involving high school and junior high school students. Rather favorable results are also reported with the major emphasis, however, being on the gains achieved by the helpers. There is often considerable concern for the selection of helpers, and training models typically contain both cognitive and directly experiential dimensions. Another similarity is that the projects focusing specifically on peer helping appear to be the most comprehensive in terms of training and diversity of services.

The peer counseling secondary school project developed by Hamburg and Varenhorst (1972) involved intensive small group training sessions to help other students with personal problems or situational stress. Peer helpers taught social skills, provided vocational information, and served as a bridge to the professional staff. High school and junior high school students are thus functioning in a range of helping services which are quite similar in thought, structure, and ultimate goals to the larger peer helping models currently in operation at campuses such as American University.

A regrettable parallel between the undergraduate and public school programs concerns the general lack of outcome data, particularly concerning helpees. Here, too, the research is scanty with gross measures regarding helper changes. Where outcome data are available, they are in the area of maladapting grade school children evidencing both emotional and academic adjustment problems (Clarfield and McMillan 1973; McWilliams and Finkel 1973; Rogeness and Bednar 1973b). Although evaluation of such programs tends to suffer from some methodological inadequacies, it does attain a suggestive research level and, importantly, have attempted to include control groups. Interestingly, the more methodologically sound peer counseling programs at the undergraduate level were also concerned with academic-emotional adjustment difficulties (e.g., Zunker and Brown 1966).

A final comment should be made regarding the functioning of secondary school helpers. As was the case with other nonprofessionals, the key element in most of these programs is probably their dual preventive approach. They attempt to create a therapeutic environment for troubled students by utilizing helping peers who themselves at times may be having adjustment problems and who will hopefully also grow in the process—again consistent with the helper therapy principle (Clarfield and McMillan 1973; McWilliams and Finkel 1973).

Summary

This relatively brief examination of the vast student helping literature has described the range of services, selection and training, and research issues involved in such programs. As a whole, the group of articles describing student intervention lacks sufficient empirical outcome data to warrant firm conclusions. Generally, the better studies were more concerned with helper process rather than helpee outcome results. However, there are more outcome studies in this chapter on student helping than in any of the other previous chapters concerning other types of nonprofessional programs. Perhaps this reflects the greater number of articles concerning student helping appearing in the literature, plus the fact that nowhere else are nonprofessional programs so closely tied to the professional research campus community.

Most of these studies involved helping services essentially supportive in nature. All report positive findings although only three begin to approach an empirically adequate level of research sophistication (Bergman and Doland 1974; Rappaport, Chinsky, and Cowen 1971; Zunker and Brown 1966). The remaining articles tend to have various methodological flaws such as an insufficient number of control groups. The least sophisticated evaluations concern student helpers in inpatient programs, and the most well developed are related to the various projects pairing student helpers with maladjusted school children.

Some of the conclusions reached by Gruver (1971) regarding the effectiveness of student helping are particularly pertinent. Noted below are some of Gruver's (1971) more salient observations which are consistent with the authors' perceptions.

(1) Most of the studies are methodologically inadequate (i.e., lack of control groups, of pretesting and posttesting, and of objective measures), and few of the programs appear similar enough in any respect to warrant general conclusions in a given area. The target populations are quite diverse as are the extent and type of training, degree of student motivation, and the actual amount of helper-helpee contact.

(2) There do appear to be some sound empirical data attesting to the positive attitudinal, personality, and behavioral changes that student helpers themselves accrue as a function of participating in these programs—at least for the short run.

(3) General issues that need to be more fully investigated concern the problems arising from professional-student helper interactions, the most effective types of training, and kinds of student helping interventions.

Gruver (1971) concluded that further consideration of these issues in the framework of systematic evaluation is necessary in order to justify the use of students working with a variety of distressed individuals. The authors agree with this overall conclusion, but are somewhat more optimistic regarding the efficacy of student helpers. Both indirect and direct evidence indicates some particularly promising work in the areas of peer (e.g., Delworth, Sherwood, and Casaburri 1974) and child counseling (e.g., Rogeness and Bednar 1973b; Stollak 1968). These programs at least suggest that students at times can be effective in specific helping services and can grow personally in these roles, and that future work utilizing student personnel as mental health nonprofessionals should certainly be explored further.

Homemakers

Another mental health workforce development relates to the large number of volunteer homemakers in numerous helping and service roles. These volunteers tend to be middle-class and have grown children. Many became bored with their life situation and considered securing employment, returning to school, or finding meaningful volunteer work. Their life experiences, maturity, and sense of commitment and responsibility make them ideal candidates for any number of volunteer/paraprofessional training programs (Sata 1972).

NIMH Training Programs for Mental Health Counselors

Much of the impetus for utilizing homemakers derived from the now classic National Institute of Mental Health training program for mental health counselors. This was one of the groundbreaking efforts at providing concentrated, high-level training for lay people in new mental health roles (Rioch 1962, 1967; Rioch et al. 1963).

This program attempted to demonstrate that carefully selected middle-aged women, with little previous mental health experience, could be trained over a 2 year period, on a part-time basis, to function as counselor-therapists for troubled adolescents and adults in hospital, outpatient, and school settings. Training included didactic and experiential features with the primary emphasis on observation, practicum experience, and thorough supervision.

There was evaluation of the program, both during the 2-year training period and at a 3-year follow-up. The data, based on such criteria as self-report, employer evaluations, peer ratings, and supervisor assessments, suggested that these women were effective in therapeutic roles (Golann, Breiter, and Magoon 1966; Magoon and Golann 1966; Magoon, Golann, and Freeman 1969). Also these trainees were subsequently able to obtain employment in mental health facilities (Golann 1970).

The Rioch et al. (1963) program seems promising, but further solid data are needed to carefully assess its merits and outcome effects. Despite its importance as a prototype for intensive nonprofessional training, the Rioch et al. program (1963) has not received adequate empirical support. Aside from a lack of control groups, there were no appropriate premeasures and postmeasures and unbiased self-report, peer, and employer ratings. Similarly, such criteria as subsequent job placement and longevity may reflect other factors than effective helpee intervention. It is possible that these helpers did make a very significant impact as helping agents. However, the question arises as to whether such program effects were really due to the high selectivity, intensive training, and ongoing supervision provided to these women or whether the effects were the result of middle-class professionals comfortably working with middle-class women volunteers who in turn were intervening with essentially middle-class patients.

A related, rather innovative, project which grew out of the Rioch program was the District of Columbia Children's Hospital Training Program for Child Development Counselors (Lourie, Rioch, and Schwartz 1967). The major aim of this program was preventive rather than therapeutic. Selected women were trained to provide lower-class mothers (or expectant mothers) with emotional support and information concerning various areas of child development. This service was conducted at well-baby clinics and in maternity wards. The selection and training of the participants were similar to the previously mentioned pioneering NIMH mental health counselor program, but not quite as stringent or structured. Evaluation and follow-up were poorly conceived and failed to reveal results which were as successful as these reported in the earlier program. For example, despite favorable supervisor ratings, trainees were more frustrated in their new, relatively unstructured role. They were less likely to be committed to continuing with this kind of work, especially since subsequent related job placement was difficult to obtain (Golann 1967, 1970). The seeming ineffectiveness of this program may in part be explained by the pronounced social class differences between mental health aides and expectant mothers which probably contributed to interpersonal frustrations and communication gaps.

Other Homemaker Helping Programs

The Rioch programs tended to utilize highly selected, bright, relatively well-educated women and gave extensive training experiences. Most other homemaker volunteer programs have been less selective and more limited in scope, but nonetheless have attempted to broaden the helping skills of their participants. Homemakers have been reported to have effectively served as companions and advocates to psychiatric inpatients (Davidoff, Lauga, and Walzer 1969; Gendlin et al. 1966; Reding and Goldsmith 1967; Verinis 1970b) and outpatients (Cohen 1966; Hodgman and Stein 1966; Smitsom 1970). They have also served as adjunct counselors at mental health centers (Cooper and Southard 1966), crisis interveners at suicide prevention centers (Heilig et al. 1968; Neleigh et al. 1971), and as supportive aides for children with mild to severe academic and emotional problems (Moser 1973; Nichtern et al. 1964; Sperber and Reiser 1971; Tolor and Lane 1968).

There has been no training in some of these programs (e.g., Smitson 1970) while in others training has been comprehensive (Heilig et al. 1968). However, systematic program evaluation has usually been minimal or nonexistent, with generally only a report of favorable impressions. An exception is the work of Verinis (1970b) who did make a concerted effort at developing and assessing an inpatient companion program. Chronic hospitalized patients (matched for diagnoses, sex, age, length of hospitalization, and education) were divided into a treatment and a control group. All the patients were involved in the usual custodial-oriented hospital routines, but in addition the experimental patients were each assigned a volunteer with whom they met for weekly counseling sessions for a period of 5 months.

The helpers received only a brief orientation to the program and their patients. At best, available supervision was minimal. A major goal of the project was to test the hypothesis that clinical performance is often a function of one's attitude and set. The volunteers (unknown to them) were subdivided into two groups, one of which was given an "optimistic" set regarding their interventions, the other a "pessimistic" orientation concerning their clinical tasks and probable outcome.

Premeasures and postmeasures included independent ratings by psychiatric aides of patients' ward behaviors. At termination of the 5-month project it was found that the experimental treatment group patients showed significantly more improvement than the control group on many of the behavior ratings. They were rated as having more successful interactions with the aides and as evidencing improved social behavior on the wards. In fact, by the end of the program, at least five different treatment group patients had left the hospital while none of the members of the control group had been discharged. Patients in the experimental group did not seem to be affected by the optimistic or pessimistic set initially given the volunteers. Such results again raise the possibility previously noted in discussing nursing and student helpers—that simply the attention and concern expressed by the nonprofessional may facilitate positive change. The prior attitude or type of training of the nonprofessional may at most be a relatively minor factor.

Although promising, the findings in this study must be considered quite tentative because of some inherent design problems: a few of the volunteers had prior psychiatric experience while others did not; retrospective ratings were made on some patients already discharged at the time of assessment; some patients changed wards while others did not; and the "independent" psychiatric aides in reality may have been biased in their ratings. Obviously, more systematic research is necessary to provide a firm empirical foundation for this program.

Primary Mental Health Project

A program cited earlier in discussions of retired and undergraduate nonprofessional workforce is the ongoing Primary Mental Health Project (PMHP) at the University of Rochester (Cowen 1969b; Cowen, Dorr, Izzo, Madonia, and Trost

1971). Homemakers have perhaps played the largest role in this extensive well-researched project. As previously described, the overall focus of the program is the early detection and prevention of school adjustment problems by using nonprofessional child aides. These aides receive focused, short-term didactic-experiential training under the supervision of psychologists and social workers, and they learn how to provide various helping services to problem children.

The early phase of the program, from 1958 to 1969, reflected the development of screening and assessment techniques. There was an emphasis on identifying children who were school adjustment difficulties, expanding the use of nonprofessional workers, and the beginning of direct services and initial secondary preventive programs in a single elementary school (Cowen 1971; Cowen et al. 1963; Zax and Cowen 1967, 1972; Zax et al. 1966). The aides' effectiveness was suggested by ratings of the children's educational and behavioral progress and the generally positive reactions of teachers and parents (Cowen 1969b; Cowen et al. 1972, 1973).

By 1969 the PMHP had expanded to eleven elementary schools, involving over 4000 students with increasing and diverse programs and greater use of nonprofessional aides (Cowen 1971; Cowen, Dorr, Sandler, and McWilliams 1971; Dorr, Cowen, and Kraus 1973). There have been extensive and detailed studies in the following areas: aides' personality and demographic characteristics (Cowen, Dorr, and Pokracki 1972; Dorr, Cowen, and Sandler 1973; Dorr et al. 1973; Sandler 1972); aides' actual intervention activities with the children such as individual counseling, group work, and consultation (Cowen, Trost, and Izzo 1973; McWilliams 1972; Terrell, McWilliams, and Cowen 1972); the changes in aides' attitudes and response styles as a result of this work experience (Dorr, Cowen, and Sandler 1973); and the aides' own evaluation of the children they were seeing (Dorr and Cowen 1973).

There has also been evaluation with respect to the homemakers' overall functioning (Dorr, Cowen, and Kraus 1973) and particularly their effectiveness in working with the children (e.g., Cowen 1971; Cowen and Schochet 1973; Dorr and Cowen 1973). The results have clearly suggested the positive value of using nonprofessional homemakers if their training experience involves well thought out selection, training, goals, and assessment.

Later reports also described the expansive nature of the PMHP, particularly its continued growth in effectively reaching maladaptive target children, the further use of nonprofessional homemaker aides, and the efficient utilization of professional input (Cowen et al. 1974; Lorion, Cowen, and Kraus 1974). Out of all the many nonprofessional programs so far reviewed in previous chapters, the PMHP program stands out as being the broadest in concept and application and the most durable over time. It is also the most well planned and thought out with respect to the use of a wide range of nonprofessional personnel and concern for the rather sensitive area of professional-nonprofessional relations.

A vital and consistent attribute of this program has been the strong commitment to evaluative research. The majority of the above studies have approximated at least a suggestive research level with attention given to adequate measures, pre-post designs, and control groups. However, most of the focus has tended to be directed at process data relating to such variables as the selection, training, personality characteristics, and behavior of the helpers (e.g., Dorr, Cowen, and Kraus 1973; Dorr, Cowen, and Sandler 1973; Sandler 1972). In contrast, the studies which have specifically dealt with the issue of child outcome effects have suffered methodologically from a lack of control groups and seemingly biased ratings of parents and nonprofessional aides (e.g., Cowen 1971; Cowen et al. 1972; Dorr and Cowen 1973). Cowen (1971) himself recognized these limitations when describing all the research problems inherent in an intervention program of the magnitude of the PMHP.

Fortunately, the developers of the PMHP, particularly in their commitment to continued programming and further evaluation, will most likely deal adequately with such complex empirical issues. The PMHP parallels the importance of the earlier projects developed by Stollak (1968) for college student helpers, in providing the most promising training and intervention programs for homemaker helpers.

Summary

Most of the counseling work of homemakers is generally supportive in nature and takes place in hospitals, community agencies, and school settings. Of the 30 homemaker programs reviewed here, nearly 50 percent were of at least a suggestive research level and over 63 percent included high-level training. However, even when these programs have included basic experimental design features, too often attention is on process data and helper variables rather than on actual program effectiveness. The outcome studies are too few and too limited to permit more than suggestive conclusions. The heralded Rioch (1967) NIMH program, despite its historical significance to nonprofessional training, has not received sufficient empirical support. The most potentially promising homemaker volunteer programming, in terms of selection, training, and evaluation, is the Primary Mental Health Project (PMHP) at the University of Rochester (Cowen 1971). This long-term program has struggled with most of the basic issues inherent in utilizing nonprofessional mental health personnel, and may hence serve as a viable prototype for such program development. Hopefully, more outcome data will emerge from PMHP studies, providing specific findings regarding the effectiveness of homemaker volunteers as child mental health aides.

Overview

This chapter has described and analyzed perhaps the largest area of nonprofessional mental health work. More and more programs are having to turn to unpaid volunteers to help provide services in the face of ever-increasing needs and decelerating funding. Given their relative enthusiasm, commitment, and available time, students and homemakers are particularly likely to be willing and well-received volunteers. Their typically middle-class background also fits with the needs of the professionals running these programs.

In comparison to most other programs for nonprofessionals, student and homemaker volunteer programs tend to be more concerned with selection, training, and evaluation issues. In the better developed programs training frequently was based on a didactic-experiential model. Other issues grappled with included the need for a supportive group atmosphere, the importance of some kind of continuing education, the necessity of clear role definitions and advancement possibilities, and attention to the problems inherent in professional-nonprofessional relationships.

While suggestive to adequate research characterized 35 percent of the reported programs, the focus was more on process than on outcome data, delimiting the positive conclusions which may be drawn regarding volunteer effectiveness.

Interestingly, the most viable programs for student (e.g., Stollak 1968) and homemaker volunteers (e.g., Cowen 1971) involve services for academically and emotionally troubled children. As data continue to emerge from such projects, we will probably be on a stronger footing to positively endorse the effectiveness of volunteer mental health aides in these child-oriented supportive roles. Other promising leads are also emerging from peer helping programs at the undergraduate (e.g., Zunker and Brown 1966) and secondary school levels (e.g., Clarfield and McMillan 1973). Similarly these programs have been directed at academic-emotional supportive counseling. Perhaps then the common target helpee problem underlying all the above programs—namely, school adjustment—may inspire research efforts which include specific goals, concrete and objective criteria, and more valid measures. In contrast, many of the other volunteer helping activities reviewed in this chapter (e.g., companions, advocates) were more nebulous and hence perhaps more difficult to research in terms of actual outcome effectiveness.

11

Final Summary, Training Models, and Implications for Mental Health Professionals

A major goal of this book was to adequately portray the vastness and range of the nonprofessional mental health movement, as well as the historical and contemporary factors underlying its emergence and continued growth. A second aim was to organize the material into a source book from which the interested reader might focus on specific types of helpers in particular areas of functioning. A central emphasis throughout the book was the evaluation of relevant research projects concerning program effectiveness.

Analysis of the Research

This section will not rereview all the previously cited research. The reader is referred to previous chapters for much more detailed accounts of specific nonprofessional mental health programs. A very clear implication from the research reviewed in this book is that it is fallacious to ask a question such as, Are nonprofessionals effective? Rather, relevant questions pertain to the particular kinds of helpers, target populations, and helping interventions in a given program. As is the case with the professional psychotherapy research, evaluation must consider specific as well as more general issues and data.

Given this caveat, the present section is an attempt to tease out the overall trends and implications apparent in the book. A total of 275 studies are systematically reviewed with respect to such factors as target populations, purposes of intervention, specific types of helping, levels of training, and levels of evaluation. Included are any outcome studies which were at at least a suggestive or adequate empirical level.

Methods, Targets, and Purpose of Nonprofessional Intervention

Great claims have been made regarding the utilization of nonprofessionals in a wide range of helping roles. Drum and Figler (1973) have examined numerous nonprofessional programs and have differentiated two general directions in training. First there are those subprofessional counseling tasks which comprise activities related to certain limited roles such as orientation to programs, tutoring, classroom and home observation, chauffering of clients, recreational and occupational activities, program organization, public relations and outreach, and supportive counseling for minor problems.

Training for such tasks is distinguished from the other major thrust, namely, the preparation of nonprofessionals to provide professional-level helping and counseling skills. It is at this level of training, as indicated previously, that professionals and nonprofessionals may be at odds with one another (in terms of territoriality, quality of care, etc.). Professionals are much more accepting of the subprofessional support roles. This chapter concentrates more on training for professional-level helping and counseling skills although the guidelines which will be presented may apply equally well to developing training programs for the more supportive, adjunctive tasks.

With respect to the actual programs reviewed in this book approximately 47 percent of the studies described nonprofessionals as involved in the more adjunctive supportive types of roles. However, 32 percent of the programs concerned the utilization of nonprofessionals in helping services quite consistent with typical professional level counseling activities. This finding clearly indicates that a large proportion of nonprofessionals are not serving just in an assistant capacity, but rather as primary helping agents.

Direct helping services constitute a broadly defined area, and nonprofessionals are increasingly involved in an expanding range of such activities. Crisis intervention, client-centered play therapy, and behavior modification, in particular, are becoming more frequent activities for nonprofessionals. Such services, though different in many respects, may actually overlap in the ways they may be concretized, taught, practiced, and refined. Approximately 10 percent of the programs used nonprofessionals in consultative and educational roles. Nonprofessionals are thus engaging in tasks which were previously professionally dominated.

However, despite such gains, the nonprofessional role is usually still quite limited in scope. For example, 63 percent of the studies involved nonprofessionals working with individuals (alone or in groups) and 33 percent in peer helping activities. Relatively little nonprofessional work was evident in the areas of family relationships or with the larger institutions within the community. This implies that intervention on both these levels is still very much in the province of professionals. This trend is similarly seen in terms of the rationale and goals given for providing helping services, with 90 percent of these programs undertaken for essentially remedial purposes—with developmental and preventive work generally remaining in professional hands. While nonprofessionals and professionals may be engaging in rather similar helping activities, differences are still evident with respect to who receives such services and why. Professionals still seem to have greater latitude in terms of target populations and generally have a wider range of mental health intervention roles.

Levels and Types of Nonprofessional Training

As has been noted in earlier chapters, training experiences for nonprofessional helpers have been very diverse. Approximately 30 percent of the programs involved minimal or no training. In contrast, there is a growing trend for programs to provide broader training experiences involving highly experiential (33 percent) or combined didactic-experiential (23 percent) features. Over 55 percent of the programs focused on a variety of practical training experiences as opposed to the traditional structured lecture approach (10 percent). The trend appears to be increasingly in the direction of didactic-experiential training. However, this development is still more promising than substantive since, as noted previously, little comparative data are available to examine differential training effectiveness. Nevertheless, nearly 50 percent of the outcome studies at suggestive or adequate empirical levels utilized some didactic-experiential skill-building features. Additional support for this type of model is presented in a later section of this chapter in which there is a discussion of the expansive professional and nonprofessional training programs developed by Carkhuff (1969b) and Ivey (1971).

Evaluation of Nonprofessional Programs

The general dearth of evaluative research is readily apparent: over 52 percent of the programs are of a purely descriptive or inadequate empirical level. However, 34 percent of the programs, in reporting essentially positive findings, did achieve at least a suggestive or somewhat better research level. It should be emphasized that only 2 out of 275 studies achieved a clearly adequate research level according to the criteria outlined in Chapter 2 (Kroeker, Forsyth, and Haase 1974; Paul, McInnis, and Mariotto 1973).

Among the numerous methodological problems contributing to this rather sparse and empirically limited research output are small sample sizes; insufficient use of control groups; failure to match or randomize subjects; poor use of preassessment and postassessment designs; inadequate objective measures; rater bias; questionable criteria for selection, training, and evaluation; greater focus on process than on outcome variables; and unsophisticated use of basic statistical procedures.

Helpee Outcome Results

As noted repeatedly, the ultimate test of program effectiveness rests on the actual impact the nonprofessioal helper has on the target population. Only 13 percent of the articles specifically included evaluations of the effects that programs had on helpee recipients. Obviously more outcome work must be undertaken if there is to be an assessment of program influence on the target population. Of the 37 reported outcome studies, 29 were at a suggestive empirical level with 8 almost reaching an adequate level of evaluation.

Since some measurable comparison between professional and nonprofessional helpers was attempted in only three of the studies, we are in no position to comment about differential effectiveness. The sparsity of such studies and their basic methodological flaws (such as the failure to keep treatment approaches constant across helper groups) preclude any definitive conclusions. This issue is important as much subjective and emotional fervor would suggest that nonprofessionals are as good as, if not better than, their professional colleagues. The research has not adequately tested this assumption. Certainly the available data indicate that nonprofessionals fare no worse than professionals. However, it is urged that there be some caution in interpreting these studies. It was rare for any of the articles to present negative findings, which suggests a pervasive halo effect and also a reluctance to report unfavorable program findings.

What we know of the impact and effectiveness of nonprofessionals on their helpee recipients is at best promising and suggestive. The dearth of adequate outcome studies makes it premature to talk definitively about nonprofessional helping in terms of outcome effectiveness. As indicated in the beginning of this chapter, it appears more productive to discuss particular types of helpers, target populations, methods and goals of services, and the quality of specific evaluative studies. Nevertheless, consistent with previous writers, the authors are tentatively willing to draw generally positive conclusions about the viability of training, utility, and impact of nonprofessional helpers (e.g., Brown 1974; Durlak 1971, 1973; Karlsruher 1974; Siegel 1973). As Brown (1974) notes, despite the dearth of well-controlled studies, the avalanche of programs over the last fifteen years, from so many sources, compellingly suggests that nonprofessionals contribute meaningfully to the mental health field.

More definitive statements regarding the training and utilization of nonprofessional workers will be possible only with additional quality evaluative studies. The typical methodological shortcomings, and the rationale given by many nonprofessional programmers in explanation for their limited research productivity, have been noted and challenged throughout this book. Valid empirical approaches are not only possible, but essential to demonstrate accountability to supportive and funding agencies, professional colleagues, and the lay public. They are also crucial for the further refinement and development of the nonprofessional programs themselves.

The Necessity of Evaluation

The utilization and assessment of the new mental health workforce must be viewed in the broader context of the many exciting changes occurring in the mental health field within the last ten to fifteen years. This vibrancy is seen in the numerous mental health-related programs and activities in hospitals, community mental health centers, neighborhoods, schools, and other settings. An almost constant furor arises, with new programs almost continually surfacing to meet various needs and interests, only to be quickly followed by still more "innovative" programs or techniques.

In such a climate programs come and go with little apparent time or interest devoted to properly investigating their actual merits. Instead there is too often a dedication to invention but not to accountability (Tourney 1967). Certainly the "nonprofessional revolution" fits quite well with this description, and too often programs have evolved as being "in" or "relevant" and as meeting urgent needs (e.g., workforce shortage, etc.).

Oetting and Hawkes (1974) suggested that three other factors inhibit appropriate evaluation: first, evaluation may be feared by staff because they feel it reflects on their competency and training ability; second, evaluative research is confused with laboratory or basic research which is viewed as devoid of practical value for real field situations; and third, few trainers or administrators have adequate experience with evaluative research and, particularly, a solid knowledge of research design, instrumentation, and necessary consultation skills. Bloom (1972) also noted that adequate evaluation may require additional financial expenditures that are just not available unless there is a postponement of certain seemingly necessary program services.

Over and above these particular issues, it is becoming imperative that some system of accountability and assessment be built into mental health programming. Edgerton (1971) strongly underscored this point when he urged that we can just no longer afford, ethically and financially, the luxury of simply developing any mental health program in the hope that it will be a contribution. We must have a means for making reasonable choices as to the most effective types of mental health services.

The following are strong but necessary statements which have many implications for nonprofessional mental health personnel.

1. Program developers should be able to really determine just what their training liabilities and assets are as well as the most effective selection, training, and placement of nonprofessionals.
2. Nonprofessionals should better understand themselves and the reality of what they can and cannot do in delivering effective helping services.
3. The target community and particularly the prospective recipients should have available to them facts and answers regarding the viability of the nonprofessional services being rendered.
4. Evaluation should provide hard data for any funding sources to enable them to make appropriate choices as to which programs are indeed effective.

Now that the obvious need for evaluation has been discussed, it is helpful to identify exactly what we mean by "evaluation" and "basic research" and how these two approaches relate to nonprofessional programs. We will then be in a better position to explore effective designs and research strategies which may overcome the flaws and obstacles indicated above.

Evaluative Research and Basic Research

The terms *evaluative research* and *basic research* are often used interchangeably in describing program assessment. However, some distinction is needed since these approaches often mean quite different things to the individuals responsible for the assessment of training programs.

Basic research is aimed primarily at discovering new knowledge for its own sake, often independent of the utility, practicality, and political effects of the results (Edgerton 1971). Unless the research evidences appropriate experimental design and control, the results are usually considered suspect. Such stringent guidelines are, however, generally ignored by developers of training programs because they see them as unrealistic and irrelevant (e.g., Levine 1974; Raush 1974).

Evaluative research, in contrast, has as its major thrust a quick and practical determination of the degree of success a program has in reaching predetermined goals. Its basic purpose is to collect information with which to improve methods, techniques, or whole programs. Such research can be generated while either modifying or discarding less successful approaches. Evaluative efforts are not concerned with advancing theory and science per se, but rather with the immediacy of dealing with particular needs (Burck and Peterson 1975; Oetting and Hawkes 1974).

It seems necessary to reach a better balance between evaluative and basic research approaches. Strict adherence to the "laboratory" research model may too easily inhibit and frustrate even minimal attempts at evaluation. It may also lead to discarding programs which are in actuality effective and of heuristic value but are poorly designed. On the other hand, a flippant disregard for assessment is also irresponsible. Programmers, trainers, and prospective helpers must be accountable for the services they provide. Ethical, professional, and financial demands necessitate some objective evaluative process beyond the usual conjectures and inferences that emerge from articles regarding a program's merits.

A greater research-evaluation orientation hopefully will facilitate more movement away from a gross level of subjective appraisal to a far more objective level of assessment. More careful assessment will make it easier to deduce meaningful conclusions, modify existing procedures, and generate more responsible training efforts. That this can be accomplished without losing sensitivity to practical considerations is illustrated by various programs cited in prior chapters. Such programs have generally attended to meaningful issues and needs while still attempting to utilize relatively adequate research methodology.

Given the need for an effective appraisal process of nonprofessional training, it is essential that evaluation be an ongoing, built-in feature of the program and not tacked on as an afterthought once the project has already started. Bloom's (1972) general evaluation strategy, for example, conceptualizes quantifiable objectives which can be carefully monitored to demonstrate whether preconceived program goals have been achieved. His model encompasses a continuing process of objective setting, activity selection, evaluation, revision of objectives and activities, and reevaluation.

Delworth et al. (1974) also agree with clearly specifying and measuring program objectives. They distinguished two different levels where such behavioral goal setting should take place in adequately assessing nonprofessional programs. First, there is the general level which may involve evaluating the real needs for a program, determining selection and screening of professional and lay personnel, and formulating overall program objectives. Ways of obtaining such data include checklists, opinion polls and surveys, interviews, and more objective research methods. A second level consists of the specific program evaluation which examines the actual nonprofessional program itself. Here we may be interested specifically in evaluating the nonprofessionals themselves, the helpees served, program outcome effectiveness, and trainer and supervisor performances. Evaluation here may consist of self-assessments, helper-helpee ratings, and objective measures of attitudinal and behavioral changes.

What emerges from both the Bloom (1972) and Delworth et al. (1974) articles is a fairly comprehensive evaluative approach which stresses concrete behavioral goals; the setting and monitoring of objectives before, during, and after a nonprofessional program; a multiplicity of outcome criteria for goal attainment at both the general and the specific levels; and a variety of assessment tools ranging in focus and degree of objectivity. D'Augelli (1973c) has also developed a very systematic approach to evaluating nonprofessional training programs which embodies these same features.

Implications from Psychotherapy Research

The very issues and general research concerns that nonprofessional programs must tackle similarly have been struggled with by evaluators of professional psychotherapy. We shall only briefly examine these extensive developments to cull out suggestions and implications which have relevance to nonprofessional program research.

A comparison between professional and nonprofessional helpers seems justified for at least two general reasons. First, psychotherapy research findings seem directly applicable to those lay programs which utilize nonprofessional helpers in specific direct service counseling roles. Even when the service is not psychotherapy per se, but rather a more supportive type of role (e.g., companion-helper), comparisons may still be useful. Most nonprofessional services can be considered to be helping interventions and, as such, seem related to the goals of psychotherapy research. Second, programs for nonprofessionals which are more concerned with the process of training or with comparing the effectiveness of one or more training formats (rather than with helpee outcome) may also be explored within a psychotherapy research framework. Different training approaches may be considered to be "treatments" or interventions as experienced by the particular group of trainees in a given program.

Within the last few years there have been numerous reviews of the professional psychotherapy research, all aimed at determining whether therapy is indeed effective (e.g., Bergin and Garfield 1971; Meltzoff and Kornreich 1970). From the writings of such investigators as Bergin (1971), Fiske et al. (1970), Kiesler (1966, 1971), Luborsky et al. (1971), Malan (1973), and Strupp (1971, 1972), it is possible to draw a number of major conclusions.

(1) Much of the psychotherapy research during the last twenty years has been methodologically inadequate. Problems have involved lack of agreement about what psychotherapy is and what constitutes a therapeutic relationship. Deficiencies in research have included poorly defined terms and goals, inadequate description of the intervention(s), lack of controls and randomization, unreliable and invalid measures, restricted or vague predictive outcome criteria, and insufficient follow-up. In general the research often has had little relevance and application to actual clinical practices.

(2) We can no longer ask, Is psychotherapy effective? Therapy is no longer considered to be a unitary process simply applied to singular problems. It is a highly complex type of interaction meaning different things to different people, both to the providers of the service as well as to the recipients. Questions must be raised regarding the specific types of interventions, changes, therapists, clients, and the particular conditions.

(3) It is necessary to have a more focused examination of the major components comprising the psychotherapeutic interaction both singularly and in combination:

Therapist variables: training experiences, orientation, attitudes and interests, background, personality, and demographic data

Client factors: demographic data, personality, intelligence, skills, particular problem areas, prior help, persuadability

Nature of the therapy: description of orientation and focus, particular philosophical and practical features, number of sessions

Situational-environmental factors: home, social, and work influences, medication, outside helping interventions

Obviously systematic consideration of these factors is similarly relevant for improving the quality of research concerning nonprofessional mental health programs.

(4) Given the complexity and interdependence of these variables, there is an increasing emphasis in the psychotherapy research on breaking down these

factors into more concrete, measurable parts, with the recognition that behavioral types of strategies might be particularly amenable to this type of specificity (Bergin 1971).

(5) What emerges is a suggested multilevel approach to psychotherapy research involving ingredients such as the following:

a. Incorporating as best as possible basic essential research tenets (e.g., control groups, randomization, homogeneous samples, standardization, valid and reliable measures, etc.).

b. Greater description regarding the nature of treatment, the individuals providing and receiving the therapy, the environmental context, and particularly the interactions between these variables. This would be greatly facilitated by breaking down these variables into more concrete, measurable units.

c. The need for multiple outcome criteria since diverse measures are necessary in order to effectively tap the numerous overt and subtle changes occurring in the psychotherapy process.

d. A combination of process and outcome measures as both types of evaluation are really quite similar and perhaps merely different points on the continuum of therapist-client change.

e. Case studies, correlation research, and simple experimental manipulative designs are all part of the psychotherapy research approach. However, Kiesler (1971) and others urge the greater use of factorial level strategies to fully explore the multiplicity of variable interactions which are undoubtedly affecting the psychotherapy process.

f. It seems possible to develop effective psychotherapy research paradigms if the investigator takes a two-pronged perspective. On the one hand, he or she must be more concrete, examining closely the specific elements in therapy. Yet, the researcher must also broaden his focus and recognize the multi-dimensional changes and numerous interactions occurring in the process. This dual perspective of breadth and specificity necessitates a methodological orientation balancing precision and flexibility. As Fiske et al. (1971) suggested, psychotherapy research may require, either singularly or in combination, experimental or quasi-experimental designs, the inventiveness of effective designs only being limited by our limited knowledge of the variables affecting the psychotherapy process.

g. It should be noted, however, that the most relevant and well-designed research efforts will be ineffective unless investigators have the cooperation of the therapists and clients in the study. For example, evaluators may have to inform these individuals of the reasons for and possible benefits of the research. Without adequate public relations, research efforts may be undermined.

These are but a sample of the findings and ideas emerging from the psychotherapy research literature. They do touch on some of the more salient points and reasonably parallel many of the concerns confronting nonprofessional program evaluation. In fact, the similarity between professional, nonprofessional, and general mental health program evaluation concerns is striking in that all three areas seem to converge in their ideas regarding research issues, attitudes, and suggested strategies. Perhaps then, in the case of both professional and nonprofessional helping, it is inappropriate to ask, Are these effective mental health helpers? Rather the ideal question might be, Is this particular mental health helper, selected according to these particular criteria and exposed to this particular orientation or training program, effective in those particular skills, with these particular helpees?

Variables Contributing to the Success of Nonprofessionals

An analysis of psychotherapy research clearly points to the complex nature of any mental health helping relationship, and the need to consider the various elements inherent in this type of transaction such as helper/helpee variables, the actual nature of the interaction, and the internal and external context in which the helping occurs. These observations are consistent with the findings noted in the previous chapters on nonprofessionals. Specifically, a variety of factors have been previously mentioned as explanations for the apparent positive impact of nonprofessional mental health helpers. For example, their generally high interest, enthusiasm, and dedication combined with a naiveté about psychopathology typically lead to positive expectations concerning helpees. Also of key importance appears to be their nonthreatening "lay" status and sociocultural similarity to clients.

Interestingly while the Chapter 8 summary of indigenous and exotic helping revealed a paucity of systematic research, it nevertheless offered some of the most promising leads in attempting to understand the seeming impact of nonprofessional mental health helpers. Various observers have suggested basic "universals" in effective helping regardless of whether the counselor is a voodoo healer or Western psychiatrist (Frank 1971; Kiev 1972; Torrey 1969). The essential ingredients underlying all helping interchanges include clearly defined helper and helpee participant roles; a culturally or subculturally sanctioned problematic situation; intervention attempts utilizing a variety of emotional, cognitive, and behavioral strategies to help the troubled person(s); and the operation of faith, trust, and hope. Other factors which were mentioned as influential in the helping transaction were the social background and personality characteristics of the helper (e.g., status, reputation). Also, the role of the helpee's expectations coupled with the placebo aspects of the helper's role was seen as particularly important. Scientific support for the above ideas is derived from social psychological research concerning the factors influencing persuadability and attitude change in individual and group contexts (e.g., Karlins and Abelson 1970).

Robert Carkhuff's (e.g., 1969a, 1969b) work has dealt largely with the issue that the essential elements in effective helping might be more important than the particular training, educational background, or specific techniques of the helper. His major findings concerning universal helping ingredients are summarized here. Carkhuff and his associates have investigated those Rogerian-derived, facilitative, and therapeutic conditions which have been reported to be significantly related to helpee change and improvement (Berenson and Carkhuff 1967; Carkhuff 1969b, 1969c, 1969d; Carkhuff and Berenson 1967; Truax 1967; Truax and Carkhuff 1967).

A major finding in this research is that effective change agents compared to less effective helpers, regardless of professional or nonprofessional status, demonstrate higher levels of such client-centered conditions as warmth, empathy, and genuineness. Carkhuff (1969b) further indicated that these presumably essential helping qualities are often personality attributes already inherent in many people, and that lay training programs can be developed to further enhance these skills and attitudes (Carkhuff and Truax 1965b). He strongly emphasized that most traditional graduate/professional programs fail to attend to these therapeutic ingredients, too often relying on didactic and skill training methods which may be quite unrelated to helpee change (Carkhuff, Kratochvil, and Friel 1968). It is also important to point out that the admission criteria such as grade point averages and academic test scores that are used by professional mental health programs have been found to have little correlation with helper effectiveness (e.g., Arbuckle 1968; Marston 1971; Wittmer and Lister 1971).

There are therefore a variety of leads, derived from both the professional and nonprofessional literature, as to why the relatively less trained, inexperienced nonprofessional apparently is able to function quite effectively in particular helping situations. As noted earlier, despite the general lack of systematic research in this area, the overall trend still strongly points to the positive impact various types of helpers may have. The specific personality and helping "ingredients" noted in this section suggest why these individuals may be, in fact, influential irrespective of the quality of research and degree of training.

General Issues in Program Development and Training

There are various issues that must concern program developers no matter how well they design their projects or how cognizant they are of successful helping intervention characteristics. Aside from the primary issue of evaluation, particular attention needs to be directed toward the planning of the program, the actual development and execution of the program, and the importance of postprogram considerations (Eisdorfer and Golann 1969; Gordon 1965; Lynch and Gardner 1970; Riessman 1967b).

Planning the Program

When designing nonprofessional training programs particular concern should be given to the needs of the community. Prospective trainers should be cautious as to whether the utilization of nontraditional mental health manpower is in fact appropriate for their particular community. Before too hastily training nonprofessionals, because it is innovative and popular to do so, there should be careful consideration of the actual need for such a program. If there is a need for a nonprofessional program the feasibility (in terms of staff, time, and financial allocation) of providing such a program must also be realistically examined.

An accurate assessment of the target community's attitude and feelings regarding nonprofessionals is essential in the planning phase. Trainers must first determine if there will be some ground level support for nontraditional personnel (e.g., McWilliams and Morris 1974). The best designed programs will be subsequently undermined if community members are unwilling to be served by paraprofessionals. As most trainees are likely to be indigenous to the catchment area, the community's responsiveness to recruitment efforts will be a further indication of acceptance of the program.

Maierle (1973) also urged that the various categories of professional caregivers be systematically consulted to determine their reactions and commitment to the intended training program. This step is important since as the community's leaders and professionals wield much clout in legitimizing a program, they can influence attitudes toward the program, usage of its services, and often stimulate much needed legislation and financial backing.

Even after defining a definite training need and securing community support, trainers must then consider the attitudes of their peers, particularly if they are professional mental health personnel. Nonprofessional training may involve quite intensive and complex programs. There is often the necessity of considerable staff cooperation in the actual training, in providing direct or indirect practicum experiences for trainees, and in subsequently absorbing program graduates into various activities and job placements. The trainer should do a good deal of exploratory ground work to assess the attitudinal and behavioral commitment of his staff before embarking on any program.

Professionals may be very negative or ambivalent concerning nonprofessionals and their potential roles. They may react with great resistance to the "infringement" of these new personnel into previously professional territory. It seems essential to explore the implicit as well as explicit concerns of one's peers before beginning specific program development. For example, there is a need to carefully work through professionals' concerns regarding the nonprofessionals' assumed lack of clinical sophistication and potential danger to clients. Also involved may be a more subtle resistance by professionals because of their feeling threatened by the competition of traditional mental health roles and services (e.g., Visotsky 1970; Whittaker 1970; Wigfall and Mace 1972).

It is not difficult to see the problems facing professionals if they are to truly accept, on a comfortable and equal footing, nonprofessional peers. Nonprofessionals may be relatively untrained and uneducated in mental health matters, yet they are often zealously described in the literature as being an inexpensive and quite capable resource for providing many basic helping services as well as, if not better than, their professional counterparts. These delicate issues have been considered by various writers ranging in opinion from strong concern about utilizing nonprofessionals (e.g., Gust 1968; Odgers 1964; Marler 1971; Steisel 1972; Rosenbaum 1966) to more cautious acceptance given legal and organized controls (Blau 1969; Nelson 1968; Patterson 1965) to enthusiastic support for mutual professional/nonprofessional collaboration (Rioch 1966, 1972; Reiff 1972; Shapiro 1970). In any event, prospective developers of nonprofessional programs must carefully consider attitudes and stereotypes held by both professionals and nonprofessionals, or else their program may be doomed to failure (Durlak 1973; O'Donnell 1970; Toban 1970).

In addition to the cost in terms of professional manhours in running a training program, there may need to be consideration of other financial expenditures. Programs examined in this volume have run the gamut from requiring little or no financial outlay, to some agency expenditure and private endowments, to extensive funding at the city, state, or federal level. Eisdorfer and Golann (1969) suggest that in developing *funded* programs, trainers should simultaneously consider alternative resources. This is necessary because of potential financial cutbacks and the real possibility that a program might have to be terminated midway if its initial source of revenue is withdrawn.

Financing may be a particularly important issue in programs using indigenous nonprofessionals. Trainers should consider possible stipends or scholarships for indigenous nonprofessionals as they will probably be unable to commit much time to a program unless supplemented financially for their involvement.

Another crucial step in the development of nonprofessional programs is the clear definition of roles and activities expected of trainees. They should know what is or is not expected of them, their actual duties, lines of responsibility, and the criteria used in judging their performance and acquisition of skills. As Riessman (1967b) pointed out, too often the term "nonprofessional" describes what he is not, but does not clearly indicate what he is.

Similarly, Gordon (1965) stressed that a challenge faced by the helping professions is that of attempting to break down the professional roles into subprofessional classifications or subroles, each of which may be filled by people with less than complete professional training and whose training is specific to their roles. On the other hand, it would be just as important for nonprofessionals to have a clear idea as to the particular roles and functions actually performed by professionals.

Selection and Preparation of Trainers

This step in program planning appears to be extremely crucial. Not enough attention has been given to the qualifications of trainers. It seems essential that the trainer be an interpersonally effective individual, one to whom trainees can easily relate, without having to overcome professional distancing and jargon. Such a comfort level would be highly important given the natural inhibitions and uncertainty nonprofessionals may initially bring to the training sessions. This would be particularly true in programs dealing with trainees indigenous to poor neighborhoods. In such programs much time may have to be devoted to carefully working through differences between trainers and trainees.

It is also essential that the professional possess the necessary training ability to appropriately convey whatever information and skills the program is intending to impart to participants. A given professional may have acquired considerable clinical expertise which in fact may be quite unrelated to the consultative and educational skills needed to conduct a successful training program. The prospective trainer may first have to be trained in effective teaching strategies as well as thoroughly familiar with the proposed program content. The trainer should have a thorough working knowledge of the particular skills and roles to be assumed by trainees. The professional may be quite attuned to more traditional services, and may even be adept in clinical teaching, but not be cognizant of, or experienced in, the specific duties trainees are to take on. To remedy this situation Eisdorfer and Golann (1969) suggested that the trainer be put into the situation to be occupied by the trainee so that he can understand the setting in which the new professionals will have to function, as well as the demands of the role.

The primary reason a trainer's personality, teaching ability, and familiarity with both traditional and new roles are so important is that much of a program's success is dependent on the image he presents. For example, new trainees are likely to imitate, at least in part, the values and attitudes of their program leaders. Thus, a serious problem may arise if a given trainer has little actual experience or interest in the activities and jobs to be assumed by trainees, yet at the same time attempts to effectively teach these skills to them.

The trainer's modeling role is considered by Carkhuff (1969b) to be one of the most critical variables in successful nonprofessional training. He cited much data suggesting that unless trainers are themselves functioning at reasonably high levels in terms of the attitudes and skills they are trying to teach, there is unlikely to be much constructive growth in trainees. Delworth, Sherwood, and Casaburri (1974) and Moore (1974) have built upon Carkhuff's ideas and have developed specific training models by which to teach professionals the target helping skills, educate them in the important elements of effective nonprofessional supervision, and the means by which to develop positive professional-nonprofessional collaborative relationships.

Recruitment and Selection of Trainees

Programs have rarely dealt in an adequate way with recruitment and selection of trainees. Programs usually develop out of specific interests or pressing needs with trainees often recruited in a rather haphazard manner. Trainees tend to enter programs by "word of mouth," referral or recommendation by others, or by direct outreach to lay and professional organizations. In some programs, potential trainees may be interviewed or administered questionnaires or personality tests. There may be an attempt to uncover blatant personal problems, intellectual capabilities, motivation for joining the program, and expectations about present and future jobs and roles. Usually such procedures involve gross selection measures which are often of dubious validity and reliability.

In contrast to the above approach, there have been more systematic attempts at selecting nonprofessionals. In some programs, specific attention has been given to an initial determination of the degree to which trainees possess those very skills and attitudes for which they would be trained (Carkhuff 1969b; Chinsky and Rappaport 1970; D'Augelli 1973a; Delworth and Moore 1974; Rappaport 1973a). If, for example, future interpersonal helping effectiveness is the goal of a training program then it is suggested that a real life or simulated sample of that actual helping behavior be used as a selection criterion (D'Augelli 1973a).

Behaviorally oriented procedures can greatly add to the precision of the initial assessment and the predictability of the trainees' performance both during and following the training program. This type of selection approach may also be seen as consistent with much of the social learning research. Such research has demonstrated that the most accurate predictor of specific future behavior is a sample of that same behavior as presently assessed in the same or highly similar situations (Bandura 1969; Mischel 1968; Wolff and Merrens 1974).

The behavioral operationalizing of training goals and desired behavior is itself a difficult task particularly when so many different schools of thought exist as to how to define helping and therapeutic effectiveness. It appears, however, that the client-centered orientation can be readily translated into a well defined working model for nonprofessional helper selection (Goodman 1972b). This is another example of the possible interface between the client-centered and behavioral modification approaches. As noted earlier, despite their apparent differences, the approaches really have a good deal of overlap and can be effectively utilized in an integrated fashion.

There will now be a presentation of two behaviorally oriented screening techniques derived largely from Rogerian theory. These appear to be particularly effective selection and assessment measures.

Carkhuff's Standard Indexes of Communication
and Discrimination

Carkhuff and his associates have discussed the development of their communication and discrimination scales as necessary steps in providing good selection and training effectiveness measures (e.g. Carkhuff 1969a, 1969b, 1969c; Carkhuff, Kratochvil, and Friel 1968). These scales are aimed at assessing levels of interpersonal helping effectiveness at different stages of training. The basis for both measures is a series of sixteen standard client or "helpee" statements, presented in written or taped form, which are designed to represent a variety of emotional and problem areas. The emotional expressions involve depression-distress, anger-hostility, and elation-excitement. Conflict areas include child rearing, sexual-marriage, social-interpersonal, and educational-vocational issues.

The Communication Index calls for trainees to assume a helping role and respond in a manner that they perceive to be most helpful and appropriate in particular situations. Expert raters assess these responses in terms of their level of interpersonal and therapeutic effectiveness (i.e., empathy, genuineness, etc.). The Index of Discrimination is based upon the trainees' own ratings of the effectiveness of a series of four helper responses (ranging from low to high facilitativeness) which have been made to each of the same sixteen helper statements. Trainees rate each of the helper responses along a continuum ranging from 1 to 5 with 5 being a general description of the ideal effective helper response. Thus the standard indexes are assessing trainees' skills in the following two helping areas: the ability to communicate effectively and the ability to evaluate the quality of helper responses.

Carkhuff (1969b) presented extensive research which has utilized both measures for selection and pre- and post-training assessment purposes. In general, the findings he reported in these studies are positive, supporting the reliability and validity of the indexes and particularly their predictive value in training programs involving such diverse groups as teachers (Carkhuff 1969d), undergraduates (Carkhuff, Collingwood, and Renz 1969), parents (Carkhuff and Bierman 1970), and minority groups (Carkhuff and Banks 1970; Carkhuff and Griffin 1971).

The findings also suggest that on the five point rating scale, scores above three, between two and three, and below two correspond to high, moderate, and low levels of interpersonal functioning respectively. In addition, while individuals may be adept at discriminating quality of responses, this does not mean they automatically can communicate effectively, thus suggesting that a trainee's initial level of communication is the best overall selection criterion. Although most trainees are likely to increase their level of interpersonal functioning .8 to 1.2 points, very low level trainees (1.0 or below) seem much less likely to make as much progress as initially higher level prospective trainees.

Goodman's Group Assessment for Interpersonal Traits (GAIT)

Goodman (1967, 1972a, 1972b) developed a structured group procedure for the selection of college students to work as companions to troubled children. The procedure involves a two-phased process in which groups of six to eight participants, plus staff observers, meet for one and a half hour sessions. During these sessions participants are expected to perform several specific tasks relating to both self-disclosure of interpersonal concerns and the understanding of the concerns of others.

During the evaluation phase each group participant is rated by both peers and trained staff observers on a six-point rating scale along dimensions for the following seven interpersonal traits: understanding, depressed, open, quiet, accepting-warm, rigid, and relaxed. The understanding, open, and accepting-warm qualities comprise a therapeutic talent (TT) score which is directly derived from the Rogerian (1957) conditions of therapeutic effectiveness and is considered a predictor of helping ability. Investigators have generally utilized the TT score as a major selection variable with, for example, the cut-off criterion for acceptance of trainees set at the median split of all TT scores. Also, although both peer and observer ratings have been found to be significantly correlated (e.g., Chinsky and Rappaport 1970a; Goodman 1972a, 1972b) the observer ratings are considered more objective and accurate appraisals of the GAIT TT interactions (Dooley 1973; D'Augelli 1973a; Rappaport, Chinsky, and Cowen 1971).

Research with the GAIT has revealed that it has significant split-half and test-retest reliability (Dooley 1973; Goodman 1972a; Rappaport, Chinsky and Cowen 1971). The GAIT has also proved to be a reasonable predictor since the effectiveness of high therapeutic talent trainees has been positively related to various outcome measures of subsequent improvement in troubled boys (Goodman 1972b) and psychiatric in-patients (Rappaport, Chinsky, and Cowen 1971).

Other investigators have reported that high TT trainees were likely to be more open and disclosive, and less anxious than low TT's in sensitivity-type group experiences (D'Augelli 1973b; D'Augelli and Chinsky 1974; D'Augelli, Chinsky, and Getter 1974). D'Augelli and Chinsky (1974) found that high TT trainees were more responsive to interpersonal communication training on a subsequent follow-up than were low TT trainees. The GAIT appears to measure current level of interpersonal skill as well as trainability for later social and helping interactions.

Research on the GAIT suggests it is an effective procedure of adequate reliability and promising predictive validity. It seems best used for selection and prediction purposes and not for pre- and post-training evaluations (D'Augelli 1973d; Rappaport 1973b). The precision of the GAIT has been enhanced by various pre-GAIT training exercises, greater elaboration of instructions, more detailed scoring procedures and, perhaps most important, considerable practice for expert raters in scoring prior to the actual exercise (D'Augelli 1973d; D'Augelli and Chinsky 1974; Rappaport 1973b; Rappaport, Gross, and Lepper 1973).

Both the GAIT and the Carkhuff Indexes certainly have their share of methodological problems (e.g., Carkhuff 1969b; Goodman 1972b). There is particular difficulty in attempting to translate such vague, client-centered concepts as "empathy" and "genuineness" into objective and measured processes. However, the recent spurt of research using these procedures has led to continuing refinement and clarification of the measures, their methodological properties, and selection and assessment utility.

Common Trends in Training Programs

From the better researched training programs, one may abstract a number of common elements. For example, these programs tend to be fairly eclectic in theory and often have client-centered, behavioral modification, and sensitivity training components. Similarly, such programs tend to combine job-specific didactic and experiential (learning-by-doing) approaches. A wide variety of techniques may be used, including lecturettes, role playing, modeling, specific directions and instructions, simulation exercises, information feedback, audiovisual instruction, and constant practicing.

Although programs differ in the extent to which they incorporate these various modalities into their training package, research strongly suggests that some flexible combination of these features is important in both professional and nonprofessional training effectiveness (e.g., Goldstein and Goedhart 1973; Paul, McInnis, and Mariotto 1973; Rappaport, Gross, and Lepper 1973; Truax 1967; Vander Kolk 1973).

Brammer (1973) has conceptualized a particular didactic-experiential training model often seen in some of the more sophisticated programs. He describes this as the microskills training approach which is essentially a strategy that divides a large category of skills into simple, teachable behavioral components. The elements in this model include: 1) breaking down a helping skill, such as empathic listening into small sequential steps; 2) explaining and modeling the skill to trainees; 3) providing trainees opportunities to practice the skills; 4) giving feedback regarding initial performance; and 5) repeating steps three through four until acceptable levels of performance are achieved (Delworth, Sherwood, and Casaburri 1974).

Many helping skills may be broken down and taught in this manner. These skills can be categorized under the following three major intervention areas: understanding (usual verbal-listening type of counseling), comfort and crises (including such crisis intervention tasks as hot line, suicide prevention, drug counseling), and positive action (e.g., problem solving, goal setting, and skill building). It should again be emphasized that although this approach to nonprofessional mental health training has focused on professionallike counseling skills, the model is just as applicable to the development of activities which are more supportive and subprofessional in nature (Brammer 1973).

Programs have varied in how much they adhere to such an eclectic microtraining type of model. Specifically, the particular emphasis, and the amount and breadth of training, will reflect the actual needs of the program, the required and desired skills, time and workforce available, and type of population to be served. For example, training of indigenous minority nonprofessionals has usually emphasized a more practical, concrete paradigm rather than a didactic orientation. Riessman (1967b) specifically suggested a "phased training" approach. He advised trainers to first utilize a short preservice period involving simple knowledge and skills so as to lessen the usual insecurity and anxiety experienced by the novice indigenous worker. There should be a gradual phasing in of training for more difficult skills, with aides being placed on the job as quickly as possible. They should then continue to be exposed to inservice training and ongoing supervision. Despite the particular training emphasis in Riessman's approach, the common threads of breaking job skills down into manageable units, repeated practice and feedback, and didactic and experiential meetings are still prominent.

Programs with a Microtraining Skill-Building Approach

Training programs have been developed for both nonprofessional and professional mental health workers which clearly embody eclectic skill-building principles. The training approaches of Danish and Hauer (1973), Ivey (1971), and Carkhuff (1969b, 1969c) are perhaps the best conceptualized and researched programs. These programs were only briefly cited in earlier chapters of this book as their goals are much broader in scope, encompassing both professional and nonprofessional training development (Danish and Brock 1974). These more expansive projects will now be briefly examined with a focus on the applicability of their training models to nonprofessional mental health work.

(1) *Danish and Hauer* (1973) have developed a university-based Counseling Adjunct Program, described as an attempt to utilize trained undergraduate counselors to work cooperatively with professional helpers. Their six-stage program involves training in the following areas: understanding of one's need to

be a helper, nonverbal behavior, effective verbal interventions, self-involving behavior, helpers' interactions and verbalizations, and establishing effective relationships. Hauer (1973) described the program as having a step-by-step microskills training format. It requires between 18 and 30 hours to complete and is followed by ongoing weekly training sessions aimed at providing additional skills in such areas as desensitization, leading encounter groups, and assertiveness training. While Hauer's presentation was more descriptive than empirical, the indication was that more substantive evaluative studies are underway.

(2) *Ivey and his associates* (Ivey 1971, 1973a, 1973c, 1974a; Ivey et al. 1968) have been at the forefront in developing focused, eclectic training programs for both professional and lay mental health personnel. Ivey's micro-counseling approach is quite consistent with the Delworth et al. (1971) model but relies more heavily on videotape feedback. Each step is repeated until the desired level of competence is achieved for a particular helping skill. The usual training session lasts between 45 minutes and 1 hour with repeated trials for trainees having difficulties acquiring the skills. Depending upon level of ability a trainee may focus on only one particular skill or may simultaneously work on a few skills in combination.

Twelve specific helping skills have been taught under the following four clusters: skills of the beginning counselor (i.e., attending behavior, open-ended questions, minimal encouragement); listening skills (i.e., reflection of feelings, paraphrasing, summarizing); sharing skills (i.e., expression of feelings, direct mutual communication); and interpretation skills (i.e., analysis, cognitive re-structuring).

The microcounseling model has been reported to have been effectively employed to teach helping and communication skills to paraprofessionals (Haase and Dimattia 1973), dormitory counselors (Ivey et al. 1968), beginning graduate student counselors (Ivey et al. 1968), homemaker drug counselors (Gluckstern 1973), medical students (Moreland, Ivey, and Phillips 1973), elementary school children and junior high students (Aldridge 1972), and psychiatric patients (Higgins, Ivey, and Uhlemann 1970; Ivey 1973a).

As a group, these studies are of a relatively more adequate empirical quality than much of the nonprofessional research that has been reviewed in this book. Generally there has been greater concern for predesign and postdesign issues, conceptual and methodological precision, use of control groups, objective instrumentation, and outcome results. However, the writers themselves suggest that further studies are needed to determine the generalizability and main-tenance of microcounseling skills from the more laboratory analogue situation to actual *in vivo* helper functioning. While it appears that these skills may be readily learned and applied in the typically highly structured microcounseling paradigm, research efforts are needed to investigate outcome effects on actual helpee recipients. Such data would lend more solid support to this highly promising training approach.

(3) *Systematic human relations training:* Perhaps the training approach best illustrating the didactic-experiential microskills model is embodied in the research of Carkhuff and his associates (e.g., Carkhuff 1969b). Currently, this program appears to be the most thoroughly researched training approach for either professionals or nonprofessionals. Originally derived from Rogerian theory, the initial Truax and Carkhuff (1967) training program aimed at developing a systematic procedure from which graduate student trainees could acquire certain helping skills that previous research had shown to be correlated with therapeutic changes. They attempted to reformulate the classic Rogerian "necessary and sufficient conditions" for client movement (i.e., empathy, unconditional positive regard, congruence) and translate these into their own, presumably more heuristic, essential therapeutic ingredients—warmth, empathy, and genuineness.

The work of Carkhuff (1969b, 1969c) and others has attempted to further elaborate the training program and refine its conceptual model and scales. The emerging Systematic Human Relations Training (SHRT) approach as developed for both professional and lay mental health personnel has been operationalized into a series of didactic-experiential training modules. A typical sequence is the following.

Phase 1. There is an introduction to the model; intensive *in vivo*, taped, and simulated training; continual explanation, practice, and shaping in such core conditions as empathy, respect, and warmth. For example, growth in empathy skills might be determined by Carkhuff's five-point scale which delineates the following: Level 1: the helper's response either does not attend to or significantly detracts from the expression of the helpee. Level 3: the helper's responses are interchangeable with the helpee's in that they express essentially the same feelings and meanings. Level 5: the helper's responses add significantly to the helpee's feelings and meanings and lead to clearer communication.

Similar training and assessment scales have been developed for the other core conditions, and a given trainee may continue practice in one area, moving to other helping dimensions only when a level score of 3 or above is achieved and consistently maintained.

Phase 2. There is further training in such initiative and facilitative helping skills as being concrete, genuine, and self-disclosive. Again, scales may be used to train, monitor, and refine a helper's level of achievement in a particular core condition.

Phase 3. With mastery of the basic helping skills comes additional training in more active helper interventions such as appropriate confrontation and ways to fully explore the helper-helpee relationship.

Phase 4. At this stage helpers can be taught a variety of action responses and strategies which go beyond the initial trust building, listening, and relationship skills training. These are the types of interventions which a helper can use to further promote helpee changes once a meaningful relationship has been established.

What emerges in the SHRT model is a highly eclectic, systematic training format that closely parallels the Delworth and Ivey programs. In these approaches there is supposed to be the basic development of attending and listening skills, followed by more involved helping interventions and finally the evolution of a high-level repertoire of counseling procedures. A good example of a Carkhuff-derived SHRT model combining client-centered and behavioral theory is seen in the work of Sydnor, Akridge, and Parkhill (1973). These trainers have developed action training skill development (phase 4) in such areas as problem solving, modeling and staging, homework and assignments, logo therapy, relaxation, desensitization, physical activities, assertiveness training, and goal reorientation and life planning.

Depending on the needs of the program and the trainees' previous experiences, SHRT programs have ranged anywhere from a few to over 100 hours of training. Three essential elements of the programs are intensive training in program-related rating and discrimination scales, a trainer-supervisor who expertly models the core helping dimensions, and a cohesive group atmosphere for trainees to explore feelings, practice skills, and receive continual feedback. There have been many extensive reviews of programs involving the SHRT model (e.g., Carkhuff 1966, 1969b, 1969c; Matarazzo 1971; Truax 1967, 1970; Truax and Carkhuff 1967; Truax, Carkhuff, and Douds 1964; Truax and Mitchell 1968, 1971).

SHRT studies of particular relevance to the review of nonprofessional mental health workers are listed below:

1. Undergraduate Volunteers: Berenson, Carkhuff, and Myrus 1966
2. Resident Hall Assistants: Mitchell et al. 1971
3. Psychiatric Attendants: Brockhaus, Marshall, and Dustin 1973; Carkhuff and Truax 1965a, 1965b; Vander Kolk 1973
4. Nurses: Goldstein and Goedhart 1973; Kratochvil 1969
5. Indigenous Workers: Carkhuff 1970, 1971a, 1971b; Carkhuff and Berenson 1972; Carkhuff and Griffin 1971
6. Teachers: Bierman, Carkhuff, and Santilli 1972; Carkhuff 1969d; Carkhuff and Banks 1970; Gazda et al. 1973
7. Parents: Carkhuff and Bierman 1970
8. Psychiatric Patients: Pierce and Drasgow 1969; Vitalo 1971

Many of the above studies have been fairly well designed and conceptualized and clearly suggest the effectiveness of SHRT-based programs. The SHRT research literature has, however, promoted some controversy on both theoretical and methodological grounds, particularly with respect to Carkhuff's earlier work. For example, the basic core condition of "empathic understanding" has been challenged by some writers as being a rather vague, unreliable concept (e.g., Chinsky and Rappaport 1970b; McNally and Drummond 1974; Means 1973; Rappaport and Chinsky 1972; Zelhart and Davis 1973), yet it is defended by other investigators as being an empirically and conceptually viable construct (e.g., Bozarth and Krauft 1972; Truax 1972; Truax and Mitchell 1971).

A definite problem with the term *accurate empathy* has been the too frequent lack of agreement as to just what behaviors are being referred to, as well as how best to measure them. This may be as much a problem for raters within the same SHRT program as for raters and trainers offering training in empathy with approaches other than the SHRT model. The variety of training and measurement approaches to empathy is reflected in the work of Chapman (1971); Delaney and Heimann (1966); Dalton, Sunblad, and Hylbert (1973); Saltmarsh (1973); and Wogan (1969). Kurtz and Grumman (1972) compared six different measures of helper level of empathy as utilized in previous research (including Carkhuff's) and correlated these scales with one another and with various outcome and process measures such as a client's depth of self-exploration. Results indicated that these different measures of empathy were relatively unrelated, suggesting that the scales may actually be measuring very different variables which are misleadingly subsumed under the general label of empathy.

Most probably there will be a continuation of the controversy surrounding the efficacy of the theory, training format, conceptual schema, and methodology of SHRT programs. Gormally and Hill (1974) have critically examined the massive Carkhuff-related SHRT literature and have presented a highly heuristic model consisting of specific guidelines for evaluating both present and future studies. These writers have pinpointed various areas that need further empirical attention in order to clear up the inconsistencies and methodological and theoretical problems surrounding the SHRT model. These include clearer delineation of treatment and control groups and inclusion of attention-placebo groups; more precision in measuring outcome with particular specification of what behaviors are to be measured; greater attention to the potential pitfalls presented by utilizing particular rating scales; further examination of individual as well as group assessment; and the inclusion of more follow-up measures to determine the durability of skills.

Although the Danish and Hauer, Ivey, and Carkhuff programs may differ somewhat in structure and technology, they appear to have much in common. These programs clearly adopt and operationalize particular characteristics considered facilitative of effective helping, provide comprehensive didactic-experiential training procedures, and have a strong concern for systematically evaluating process and outcome changes. There are also other similar training programs which have been developed and presented in either manual or research form (Brammer 1973; Gilmore 1973; Hackney and Nye 1973; Johnson 1972; Kagan 1971). These programs incorporate many of the principles outlined above and are equally applicable to both professional and nonprofessional mental health personnel.

As Danish and Brock (1974) suggest, the data really do not point to a specific program as being significantly superior to the others, particularly in view of the apparent absence of comparative studies. Until such information is available, Danish and Brock (1974) offer some highly realistic consumer guidelines for programmers wishing to employ didactic-experiential training programs. For example, they recommend that prospective trainers consider whether such factors as the program objectives, length, cost, and the number of people to be trained are compatible with the resources and needs of the consumer.

The goals of this section were threefold: to pull together common ingredients which have comprised some of the previously reviewed programs; to closely examine the didactic-experiential microskills training model; and to review training programs which most clearly embody this type of model. The eclectic skill-building approach appears to hold much promise in the training of specific or complex skills for either counseling or supportive roles. As was evident from earlier chapters of this book, programs may differ greatly in terms of theory, goals, format, and type of trainee. Nevertheless, the particular training approach described here would seem to be quite adaptable in fulfilling most training needs and objectives. This model has a promising research potential for meeting evaluation and accountability requirements.

In some ways this model appears most applicable to the lay/volunteer type of nonprofessional, such as homemakers or students, who may be clearly seeking involvement in some short term, formalized, skill-building training experience. However, the model, or parts of it, may also be adopted for training experiences aimed at the numerous other types of nonprofessional mental health helpers such as lawyers, clergy, police, physicians, and nurses. Similarly, the principles described here may even be applied in developing particular skills for natural community helpers such as exotic healers and bartenders, or at least provide some framework for understanding their potential effectiveness. In addition, salaried paraprofessional level workers are increasingly being exposed to more extensive mental health didactic and experiential training.

Unfortunately, a review of typical nonprofessional and professional programs (in hospitals, schools, social agencies, clinics, and counseling centers) reveals a generally rigid reliance by professionals on traditional training formats. According to Berlin (1969) and Ivey (1973b, 1974b), professionals may stick with outmoded training models because of an unwillingness to acquire new knowledge and skills and to consider recent research data. Understandably, many professionals want to hold on to comfortable habits and resist the threat any new approaches may pose to the status quo. It is hoped that professionals involved in graduate training and nonprofessional training will increasingly consider more systematic approaches. The Danish and Hauer (1973), Ivey

(1971), and Carkhuff (1969b, 1969c) programs, in particular are more conceptually and methodologically sound than traditional training procedures and most importantly, seem to be associated with more desirable changes in both helpers and helpees.

Posttraining Program Considerations

Various additional factors appear to be important to the success and the continuance of nonprofessional mental health programs. Some of these factors may be considered overlapping with the actual training phase of the program but they will be shown to be essential once the formal training period is over.

Group Format

The group approach to training nonprofessionals is frequently discussed in previous chapters. At times these groups are relatively unstructured with little focus on the group process per se, with more emphasis on the material being presented. In other programs group process is a strong focal point and frequently quite structured. In such cases, the emphasis may be a T-group, sensitivity group, or more traditional group therapy. Regardless of its emphasis, a group approach may provide a tremendous growth and learning component and should not be viewed simply as an expedient way of meeting a need to deal with large numbers of trainees (see Bradford, Gibb, and Benne 1964; Lifton 1967; Rosenbaum and Berger 1963 for reviews of theory, process, and techniques of group work).

As outlined earlier, much of a training program is typically experiential in nature. Usually participants continually practice the particular skills they are working on, provide constant feedback for one another, and use each other for simulated helper/helpee roles. The group therefore provides a forum for shared learning and modeling. On another level, the group provides a supportive base from which a sense of cohesiveness and trust can develop. This enables group members to share the initial frustrations, anxieties, and role ambiguities which nonprofessional training programs are certain to engender.

On still another level a group may provide a growth/therapeutic climate for its participants. Nonprofessional helpers may enhance their own abilities through exploration of their attitudes, feelings, and strengths and weaknesses in a group context. As Lynch and Gardner (1970) suggested, the group experience can help challenge the trainee to look beyond his preconceived self-concept, to think critically and to grapple with his deficiencies as well as his assets.

Much of Carkhuff's (e.g., 1969b) work on the helper's emotional level indicates that the trainee's receptivity, trainability, and subsequent performance are a function of his level of interpersonal effectiveness. There is some research examining the functioning of paraprofessionals which similarly suggests a strong relationship between self-concept and later job performance (e.g., Bushweiler and Gershon 1973). Homemakers who had a consistently high self-image evidenced a greater degree of helping effectiveness than those manifesting a poor self-concept. In fact, it seemed that trainees who felt good about themselves consistently achieved higher levels of performance regardless of the nature of the task. As Carkhuff (1969b, 1969c) has indicated, training individuals with poor self-concepts may prove more time consuming and be much less productive.

Another important feature of a training group, assuming it evolves into a cohesive unit, is the power it gives nonprofessionals in negotiating with the professional training facility. Certain nonprofessionals may, in union fashion, serve as advocates to the professional staff to air any needs and concerns, provide feedback about current programs, and participate in future developments and planning (Riessman 1967b). For example, Bushweiler and Gershon (1973) included trained nonprofessional representatives at all relevant mental-health-agency policy and planning meetings. This helped to insure greater cooperation and reduced role confusion between lay and professional staff. Sloane (1973) found that such contented and involved nonprofessional volunteers could serve a highly visible and positive public relations function for their participating mental health center.

Continuing Education and Training

Skill development should not end with the completion of the basic training program. Continued growth can be better ensured through different types of ongoing training experiences. First, there can be continued on-the-job training whereby trainees receive practice and feedback in their acquired skills with, hopefully, these additional experiences further refining their levels of competency. Perhaps just as important for a successful program are new learning opportunities for trainees as they begin to broaden their talents and interests. For example, some nonprofessionals are interested in doing community outreach work, but they lack necessary interviewing and canvassing skills. In Gluckstern's (1973) drug counselor program, additional training in community organization strategies was provided to the trainees (parents) so that they could more effectively provide counseling and advisory skills.

Continuing inservice training may be provided by seminars, workshops, courses, and additional practice either at the training site or at other agencies. Regardless of the particular format, continuing education seems essential for maintaining the trainees' enthusiasm and level of competency, as well as meeting new training needs. Haase, DiMattia, and Guttman (1972), in a one-year, follow-up study, found that trainees began reverting back to pretraining skill levels, strongly indicating the need for further educative experiences to maintain previously achieved gains.

Ongoing Supervision

Earlier in this chapter the importance of careful trainer selection was discussed. Supervisors as well as trainers need to possess effective personalities and interpersonal skills, teaching ability, and familiarity with professional and nonprofessional roles. The posttraining period may be a particularly stressful time as the trainees' new skills are actually put to the test and competency is carefully evaluated. Capable supervision is very important. This point is highlighted by the growing motivation to develop training programs specifically designed for professionals interested in supervising nonprofessional personnel (e.g. Delworth and Moore 1974; Delworth, Sherwood and Casaburri 1974; MacLennan, et al. 1966; Nash and Mittlefehedt 1974).

Moore (1974) provided guidelines for preparing professional supervisors. He described a training approach which closely parallels the model for nonprofessional skill-building outlined earlier. Specifically, the general skill of supervision is broken down into smaller behavioral subskills which are to be mastered by the professional. These skills are then discussed, modeled, and practiced until a particular level of performance is achieved.

Whether the supervision is provided in groups and/or individually, additional guidelines seem important in maximizing the possibility of a successful supervisor-supervisee relationship. For example, it must be kept in mind that recently trained nonprofessionals may experience a good deal of anxiety regarding their new roles and ambiguous status. It is important for supervisors to be readily available to provide support for any needs or issues that may arise. Support, however, must be balanced with flexibility on the supervisor's part and a determined willingness not to be paternalistic and overprotective (Nash 1974).

A prime reason for utilizing nonprofessional mental health manpower is the unique attributes these individuals may bring to their roles, qualities which may be lacking in the professional staff. For example, low-income indigenous workers may have ethnic backgrounds which can greatly enhance their entry into particular target communities. Similarly, physicians or ministers by their very roles often have quicker access to people in trouble than do professional mental health helpers. It is important for professionals, both during training and supervision, to respect the particular assets of their trainees and not make the too frequent mistake of trying to convert them into mini-psychologists, psychiatrists, or social workers (Gordon 1965).

The above guidelines may be seen to be basically an extension of the interpersonal, supportive, and leadership skills needed by the effective trainer. What is further needed during supervision is a capacity to really let trainees grow and test out their abilities. They should have the possibility of discovering paths for themselves, perhaps not even considered at the beginning of the program. Supervision must thus be reasonably sensitive to a trainee's sense of autonomy as well as his needs for dependence and structure. A potential conflict may be the degree to which professionals are willing to sacrifice control while still being consistent with program structure and objectives.

Job Placement and Career Ladders

Although group training, continuing education, and on-going supervision are important factors in the longevity and success of a program, these experiences may be wasted unless trainees are ultimately placed in relevant positions. Many nonprofessional programs flounder because of the failure to effectively utilize participants in those very duties for which they have been prepared. By the end of the training period, participants usually feel both anxious and enthusiastic about finally being able to implement their new skills. Their dedication may even surpass the level of commitment of the professional staff. Even if subsequent job placement is thought out in advance there is a strong likelihood that the high interest level of the nonprofessional trainees will diminish once the harsh realities, frustrations, and limitations of helping are experienced. This let-down effect is even more likely when little provision has been made for proper utilization of their talents. Posttraining placement should be an essential component of program planning.

While the issue of proper posttraining placement is important for any of the volunteer types of programs it becomes a particularly crucial factor for programs dealing with salaried paraprofessional or indigenous nonprofessional workers. They have concerns not only about meaningful placement, but also about salary levels, job security and benefits, promotions, credentials, role relationships and competition, upward mobility, and career ladders. The reader is urged to review earlier chapters on paraprofessional and indigenous mental health workers and to particularly note the discussion on the "new careers movement" which has been concerned with all these issues (e.g., Gartner 1971). The real test and "guts" of the nonprofessional movement is often seen at the stage of job placement. This phase of the program will or will not demonstrate several things: the effectiveness and importance of nonprofessionals, the real commitment of the professional staff to the program, and the acceptance of other agencies and clientele within the community to the services being offered.

Implications for Professional Mental Health Training

True acceptance and utilization of nonprofessional workers by professional personnel has additional implications beyond simply working out collaborative interpersonal relationships or expanding mental health ideology and activity. There is a need for professionals to develop appropriate training and supervisory skills for the preparation of nonprofessional support personnel—abilities which are essentially not taught in most professional schools (Woods 1971). If a major goal in the expansion of nonprofessional mental health services is to free professionals to devote more time to supervision, program evaluation, consultation and education, and other indirect service tasks, then professionals also need to develop more proficiency in these areas. However, graduate school training and subsequent professional practice have traditionally been deficient in preparing mental health professionals for such roles (Bouhoustos 1970).

Fortunately, there has been some recent practical expansion in the training of professional mental health personnel. More and more training opportunities are being made available to professionals in the areas of organizational development (e.g., Burke 1970; Walsh et al. 1974), consultation and education (e.g., Broskowski, Khajavi, and Mehryar 1973; Norman and Forti 1972; Signell and Scott 1971, 1972; Walsh 1973), and models for mental health research and program evaluation (e.g., Brogan and Greenberg 1973; Broskowski and Schulberg 1974; Oetting and Hawkes 1974).

Turning to the specific professional mental health disciplines themselves, we see more clearly the above changes. For example, Peplau (1972) has described numerous advances occurring in the training of psychiatric nurses. There has been a vast improvement in undergraduate, graduate, and postgraduate programs which are increasingly devoted to new theories and techniques for effectively dealing with a wide range of troubled people in different settings. Relevant training has replaced the traditional lecture format with a greater emphasis on a didactic-experiential approach, including courses, casework and case studies, participant experiences, observations and conferences, cotherapy in groups, follow-up visits with individuals and families, and participation in interdisciplinary helping teams.

Clinical social work has similarly evidenced considerable change in recent years. It has increasingly moved away from traditional casework approaches to models of thinking and action much more consistent with new and innovative mental health practices. Various writers have attributed this change to an attempt to cope with the professional workforce shortage and the necessary utilization of nonprofessional support personnel (Blum 1969; Wittman 1974), to concerns with greater community accountability and social action (Epstein 1968; Meyer 1969; Mueller and James 1972), and to the development of training and educational approaches much more responsive to relevant needs and practices (Parad and Rapoport 1972; Rothman 1969).

Clinical psychiatry has also manifested recent ideological and technical upheavals. Much of the furor concerns differences regarding trends away from traditional medical practices toward greater community involvement and responsibility for broader delivery of services [see Sarason (1974) for a historical synopsis of this development]. Psychiatry is beginning to show growth in its usual consulting and treatment practices (e.g., Gray 1974; Poser 1970) and in the evolution of the community psychiatry specialty area. There is an increasing concern with such issues as prevention, accountability and consumerism, nonprofessional involvement, the politics of mental health, racism and sexism, and the need for specialized psychiatric training in these new helping areas (e.g., Berlin 1965b; Caplan 1964; Cohen and Hirschowitz 1972; Cottrell 1964; Daniels

1966; Freed 1967; Halleck 1968; Margolis and Bonstedt 1970; Mendel 1966; Zuithoff 1970). Not only are continuing education and specialized training becoming available, but much reexamination is also going on regarding the most effective teaching of psychiatry at the predoctoral, medical school level (e.g., Ables and Brandsma 1973; Hansell 1973; Small 1975).

Perhaps the greatest changes in thinking, education, and practice are evident in the fields of applied psychology. Psychology, like other mental health professions, has been faced with accelerating problems regarding workforce needs as well as all the issues raised by the "third revolution" in mental health (Chapter 1). Most psychology departments in graduate and professional schools are doing much soul searching regarding the professional's role within the complex and changing mental health arena. Specific struggles are concerned with such issues as the size of undergraduate and graduate psychology programs; the job market and subsequent employment, selection, and screening criteria for admissions; explicit and implicit goals underlying the preparation of students; continuing education; and, particularly, the theory and technology used to achieve training and applied objectives (e.g., Arnhoff and Boneau 1972; Cuca 1974; Katahn 1970; Marston 1971; Nyman 1973; Proshansky 1972; Ross 1974).

There has been a vigorous emergence of a community psychology specialty similar to the community psychiatry movement (e.g., Adelson and Kalis 1970; Newbrough 1970; Reiff 1970). Various reports have carefully analyzed the need for specialized training in community psychology at the undergraduate, graduate, and postgraduate levels (e.g., Cowen, Chinsky, and Rappaport 1970; Golann, Wurm, and Magoon 1964; Jacob 1971). More and more programs are offering to individuals at various levels of training a variety of experiences and workshops relevant to community psychology (Iscoe 1971; Iscoe and Spielberger 1970; Kalis 1973; Rosenblum 1973; Spielberger and Iscoe 1972).

Alternative levels of training and academic degrees have emerged so as to meet both the conceptual and the practical demands implicit in the community psychology approach (e.g., Arnhoff and Jenkins 1969; Knott 1969). Related developments have included the establishment of a new doctor of psychology degree (Peterson 1968) and a refocusing and recognition of the viability of masters-level psychologists (e.g., Pinkus and Korn 1973). It is at the bachelors level of training that psychology has most moved into the nonprofessional area. Some psychology departments are turning out a new breed of bachelor-level psychology technicians. These individuals are essentially paraprofessional personnel who provide a range of services including assisting in research, psychological testing, direct and indirect supportive counseling, and community organization (e.g., Cohen 1969, 1974; Gentry 1974a, 1974b; Musante 1974; Sloop and Quarrick 1974).

All these changes "came to a head" most dramatically at the National Conference on Levels and Patterns of Professional Training in Psychology, better known as the Vail Conference (e.g., Korman 1974). Not only did this conference have far-reaching implications for the field of psychology, but it was also significant for all mental health disciplines. Recommendations of this important conference foreshadow the probable struggles that professional mental workers and their nonprofessional colleagues will contend with in the future.

Recommendations dealt head-on with the issues of values and responsiveness to community needs, appropriate or inappropriate handling of nontraditional intervention groups, alternative levels of helping personnel, the necessity for continuing education and evaluation of professionals, and the place for both the professional psychologist and scientist-professional training models. While these issues certainly have been examined in previous professional conferences, Ivey and Leppaluoto (1975) emphasized that the Vail Conference had a much greater sense of urgency and mission. Members of most major professional and nonprofessional groups, and various consumers of services, attended the conference. Much emphasis was given to possible practical resolutions and building up follow-up networks of local and national groups to perpetuate the momentum of the conference. The goal of the conference planners was to provide psychology and related mental health disciplines with a "launching pad" for entering a new era of thinking and commitment to quality mental health training and delivery.

Closing Note

Although this book was essentially directed at exploring all the issues inherent in the "nonprofessional revolution," it is really not all that surprising that we end up talking about issues concerning professional personnel. Professional and nonprofessional mental health resources are becoming more and more intertwined. For example, professionals are often the key people initiating nonprofessional program development and working out collaborative relationships. Professionals often take the responsibility for the selection and training of nonprofessionals and frequently provide funding for them.

All the issues on which nonprofessionals have been examined and critiqued in this book are equally relevant for evaluating the work of mental health professionals. An examination of the psychotherapy literature suggested that our knowledge of professional helping is just as vague, poorly researched, and inconclusive as is our understanding of nonprofessional intervention. Before professionals continue to "critique" nonprofessional programming, they would be wise to first "clean up their own house," do more systematic evaluation of what they themselves actually do or do not do, and recognize their own frailties. In particular, they must confront their anxieties in the face of the growing nonprofessional revolution. This movement challenges many of the professionals' assumptions regarding theory, selection and training approaches, and actual helping effectiveness.

Both nonprofessionals and professionals are here to stay. Rather than the usual antipathy often expressed by both sides, further team building both within and across the professional/nonprofessional fields is essential. This chapter has specifically noted various developments consistent with this positive trend. In a sense this book has come full circle, focusing first on nonprofessional rather than professional mental health personnel, only to return to the key role professional helpers may have in relation to their nonprofessional colleagues as well as in their own continuing development.

Bibliography

Ables, B.S., and Brandsma, J. The effectiveness of different learning experiences for teaching psychiatry. *Comprehensive Psychiatry* 1973, 14: 29-33.

Abrahams, R.B. Mutual help for the widowed. *Social Work* 1972, 17: 54-61.

Addelson, F. Induced abortion: Sources of guilt or growth? *American Journal of Orthopsychiatry* 1973, 43: 815-23.

Adelson, D., and Kalis, B.L. *Community psychology and mental health: Perspectives and challenges.* Scranton, Pa.: Chandler, 1970.

Adler, H.M., and Hammett, V.B. Crisis, conversion, and cult formation: An examination of a common psychosocial sequence. *American Journal of Psychiatry* 1973, 130: 861-64.

Adler, L.M., and Enelow, A.J. An instrument to measure skill in diagnostic interviewing: A teaching and evaluation tool. *Journal of Medical Education* 1966, 3: 281-88.

_____ ; Ware, J.E.; and Enelow, A.J. Changes in medical interviewing style after instruction with two closed-circuit television techniques. *Journal of Medical Education* 1970, 45: 21-28.

Adler, P.T. The community as a mental health system. *Mental Hygiene* 1972, 56: 28-32.

Ahmed, M.B., and Young, E.L. The process of establishing a collaborative program between a mental health center and a public health nursing division: A case study. *American Journal of Public Health* 1974, 64: 880-85.

Albee, G.W. *Mental health manpower trends.* New York: Basic Books, 1959.

_____ . The relation of conceptual models to manpower needs. In E.L. Cowen, E.A. Gardner, and M. Zax (eds.), *Emergent approaches to mental health problems.* New York: Appleton-Century-Crofts, 1967.

_____ . Conceptual models and manpower requirements in psychology. *American Psychologist* 1968a, 23: 317-20.

_____ . Models, myths, and manpower. *Mental Hygiene* 1968b, 52: 168-79.

Alcohol and Health Notes. Al-Anon, Alateen aid friends, relatives of alcoholic people. December 1973.

Aldridge, E.E. The microtraining paradigm in the instruction of junior high school students in attending behavior. *Dissertation Abstracts International* 1972, 32: 7300.

Allen, R.R.; Pilnick, S.; and Silverzweib, S. Conflict resolution—team building for police and ghetto residents. *Journal of Criminal Law, Criminology and Police Science* 1969, 60: 251-55.

Alschuler, A.S.; Tabor, D.; and McIntyre, J. *Teaching achievement motivation: Theory and practice in psychological education.* Middletown, Conn.: Education Ventures, 1971.

Altman, K.I., and Linton, L.E. Operant conditioning in the classroom setting: A review of the research. *Journal of Educational Research* 1971, 64: 278-86.

Alvord, J. *Home token economy: An incentive program for children and their parents.* Champaign, Ill.: Research Press, 1973.

Anderson, D.A., and Jones, B. The paraprofessional management and delivery of professional human services. *American Journal of Orthopsychiatry* 1972, 42: 267-68.

Andrews, J.K. The results of a pilot program to train teachers in the classroom application of behavior modification techniques. *Journal of School Psychology* 1970, 8: 37-42.

Andronico, M.P.; Fidler, J.; Guerney, B.; and Guerney, L.F. The combination of didactic and dynamic elements in filial therapy. *International Journal of Group Therapy* 1967, 17: 10-17.

_____ , and Guerney, B.G. The potential application of filial therapy to the school situation. *Journal of School Psychology* 1967, 6: 2-7.

Anker, J.M., and Walsh, R.P. Group psychotherapy: A Special activity program and group structure in the treatment of chronic schizophrenics. *Journal of Consulting Psychology* 1961, 25: 476-81.

Appleby, L. Evaluation of treatment methods for chronic schizophrenia. *Archives of General Psychiatry* 1963, 8: 8-21.

Arbuckle, D.S. Current issues in counselor education. *Counselor Education and Supervision* 1968, 7: 244-51.

Armstrong, J.C. Perceived intimate friendship as a quasi-therapeutic agent. *Journal of Counseling Psychology*, 1969, 16: 137-41.

Arnhoff, F.N. Realities and mental health manpower. *Mental Hygiene* 1968a, 52: 181-89.

_____ . Reassessment of the triology: Need, supply, and demand. *American Psychologist* 1968b, 23: 312-16.

_____ , and Boneau, C.A. Manpower needs and resources for community psychology and mental health. In S.E. Golann and C. Eisdorfer (eds.), *Handbook of community mental health.* New York: Appleton-Century-Crofts, 1972.

_____ , and Jenkins, J.W. Subdoctoral education in psychology: A study of issues and attitudes. *American Psychologist* 1969, 24: 430-43.

_____ ; Rubenstein, E.A.; Shriver, B.; and Jones, D.R. The mental health fields: An overview of manpower growth and development. In F.N. Arnhoff, E.A. Rubenstein, and J.C. Speisman (eds.), *Manpower for mental health.* Chicago: Aldine, 1969.

_____ ; Rubenstein, E.A.; and Speisman, J.C. (eds.), *Mental health manpower.* Chicago: Aldine, 1969.

Ashbaugh, W.H. The therapeutic curriculum. *Psychology in the Schools* 1965, 2: 126-29.

Atkeson, P. Alternative career opportunities for the neighborhood worker. *Social Work* 1967, 12: 81-88.

Atkinson, R.M. Current and emerging models of residential psychiatric treatment, with special reference to the California situation. *American Journal of Psychiatry* 1975, 132: 391-96.

Autor, S.B., and Zide, E.D. Master's-level professional training in clinical psychology and community mental health. *Professional Psychology* 1974, 5: 115-21.

Bailey, M.B. Al-Anon family groups as an aid to wives of alcoholics. *Social Work* 1965, 10: 68-74.

Baker, E.J. The mental health associate: A new approach in mental health. *Community Mental Health Journal* 1972, 8: 281-91.

_____. The mental health associate: One year later. *Community Mental Health Journal* 1973, 9: 203-14.

Baker, F. From community mental health to human service ideology. *American Journal of Public Health* 1974, 64: 576-81.

_____, and Schulberg, H.C. The development of a community mental health ideology scale. *Community Mental Health Journal* 1967, 3: 216-25.

Balinsky, B. Outside consultants to industry: Strengths, problems, and pitfalls. Symposium II. Some experiences and problems in appraising executive personnel. *Personnel Psychology* 1964, 17: 107-14.

Bandura, A. *Principles of behavior modification.* New York: Holt, 1969.

Bard, M. Family intervention police teams as a community mental health resource. *Journal of Criminal Law, Criminology and Police Science* 1969, 60: 247-50.

_____. *Training police as specialists in family crisis intervention.* Washington: U.S. Government Printing Office, 1970.

_____. The role of law enforcement in the helping system. *Community Mental Health Journal* 1971a, 7: 151-60.

_____. Iatrogenic violence. *The Police Chief* 1971b, 38: 16-17.

_____. Immediacy and authority in crisis management. Presented at an NIMH Crisis Intervention Seminar, Washington, D.C., 1973.

_____, and Berkowitz, B. Training police as specialists in family crisis intervention: A community psychology action program. *Community Mental Health Journal* 1967, 3: 315-17.

_____, and _____. A community psychology consultation program in police family crisis intervention: Preliminary impressions. *International Journal of Social Psychiatry* 1969, 15: 209-15.

Barnes, K.E.; Wootton, M.; and Wood, S. The public health nurse as an effective therapist-behavior modifier of preschool play behavior. *Community Mental Health Journal* 1972, 8: 3-7.

Barnett, C.D., and Bensberg, G.J. Evaluation: A basic tool in training attendant personnel. *Mental Retardation* 1964, 2: 224-30.

Barocas, H.A. Police crisis intervention and the prevention of violence. *American Journal of Psychoanalysis* 1972, 32: 211-15.

_____. Urban policemen: Crisis mediators or crisis creators? *American Journal of Orthopsychiatry* 1973, 43: 632-39.

Barocas, H.A. Iatrogenic and preventive intervention in police-family crisis situations. *International Journal of Social Psychiatry* 1974, 20: 113-21.

Barrett, C.J.; Berg, P.I.; Eaton, E.M.; and Pomeroy, E.L. Implications of women's liberation and the future of psychotherapy. *Psychotherapy: Theory, Research and Practice* 1974, 11: 11-15.

Baudry, F., and Wiener, A. Initiation of a psychiatric teaching program for surgeons. *American Journal of Psychiatry* 1969, 126: 1192-97.

Beach, D.R.; Levine, M.; and Goldberg, S. Teacher discussion groups: A community mental health approach. *International Journal of Social Psychiatry* 1973, 19: 102-9.

Beale, A.V. Working with parents: A guidance drama. *Elementary School Guidance and Counseling* 1974, 8: 182-88.

Beard, J.H., Schmitt, J.R., Smith, M.R., and Dinson, J. Three aspects of psychiatric rehabilitation at Fountain House. *Mental Hygiene* 1964, 48: 11-21.

Beck, J.C.; Kantor, D.; and Gelineau, V.A. Follow-up study of chronic psychotic patients "treated" by college case-aid volunteers. *American Journal of Psychiatry* 1963, 120: 269-71.

Becker, R.E.; Wintrob, R.M.; Cancro, R.; and Stabenau, J.R. Psychiatry in the functionally organized undergraduate curriculum. *American Journal of Psychiatry* 1973, 130: 571-73.

Becker, W.C. *Parents are teachers: A child management program.* Champaign, Ill.: Research Press, 1971.

_____; Madsen, C.H., Jr.; Arnold, C.R.; and Thomas, D.R. The contingent use of teacher attention and praise in reducing classroom behavior problems. *Journal of Special Education* 1967, 1: 287-307.

Beckman, L. Locus of control and attitudes toward mental illness among mental health volunteers. *Journal of Consulting and Clinical Psychology* 1972, 38: 84-89.

Beigel, A. Law enforcement, the judiciary, and mental health: A growing partnership. *Hospital and Community Psychiatry* 1973, 24: 605-9.

Beit-Hallahmi, B. Salvation and its vicissitudes: Clinical psychology and political values. *American Psychologist* 1974, 29: 124-29.

Belkin, M.; Suchman, E.A.; Rosenblatt, D.; and Jacobziner, H. Effect of physician training in mental health principles on mothers' appraisal of child health conferences. *Mental Hygiene* 1965, 49: 104-12.

Bell, R.L.; Cleveland, S.E.; Hanson, P.G.; and O'Connell, W.E. Small group dialogue and discussion: An approach to police-community relationships. *Journal of Criminal Law, Criminology and Police Science* 1969, 60: 242-46.

Bellak, L. A psychiatric training program for general practitioners and nonpsychiatric specialists. In L. Bellak (ed.), *Handbook of community psychiatry and community mental health.* New York: Grune & Stratton, 1964.

Bennett, V.D.; Taylor, P.; and Ford, S. An experimental course in sex education for teachers. *Mental Hygiene* 1969, 53: 625-31.

Bensberg, G.J.; Barnett, C.P.; and Hurder, W.P. Training of attendant personnel in residential facilities for the mentally retarded. *Mental Retardation* 1964, 2: 144-51.

Bentz, W.K. Consensus between role expectations and role behavior among ministers. *Community Mental Health Journal* 1968, 4: 301-6.

Berenson, B.G., and Carkhuff, R.R. *The sources of gain in counseling and psychotherapy.* New York: Holt, 1967.

_____; Carkhuff, R.R.; and Myrus, P. The interpersonal functioning and training of college students. *Journal of Counseling Psychology* 1966, 13: 441-46.

Bergin, A.E. The evaluation of therapeutic outcomes. In A.E. Bergin and S.L. Garfield (eds.), *Handbook of psychotherapy and behavior change.* New York: Wiley, 1971.

_____, and Garfield, S.L. (eds.), *Handbook of psychotherapy and behavior change.* New York: Wiley, 1971.

Bergman, J.S., and Doland, D.J. The effectiveness of college students as therapeutic agents with chronic hospitalized patients. *American Journal of Orthopsychiatry* 1974, 44: 92-101.

Bergman, R.L. A school for medicine men. *American Journal of Psychiatry* 1973, 130: 663-66.

Berkowitz, B.P., and Graziano, A.M. Training parents as behavior therapists: A review. *Behavior Research and Therapy* 1972, 10: 297-317.

Berlin, I.N. Mental health consultation in the schools: Who can do it and why? *Community Mental Health Journal* 1965a, 1: 19-23.

_____. Training in community psychiatry: Its relation to clinical psychiatry. *Community Mental Health Journal* 1965b, 1: 357-60.

_____. Resistance to change in mental health professionals. *American Journal of Orthopsychiatry* 1969, 39: 109-15.

Berman, A.L. Experiential training for crisis intervention. In G.A. Specter and W.L. Claiborn (eds.), *Crisis Intervention.* New York: Behavioral Publications, 1973.

Berman, P.J.; Davis, A.W.; and Phillips, E.L. George Washington University volunteer hotline, a descriptive study. *Psychological Reports* 1973, 33: 364-66.

Berman, S.P. A report on a CWLA pilot project to train new child care workers. *Child Welfare* 1970, 49: 156-60.

Berns, R.S. College students as peer counselors. *American Journal of Orthopsychiatry* 1972, 42: 269.

Bernstein, B.E. Lawyer and counselor as an interdisciplinary team: One lawyer's suggestions. *Family Coordinator* 1974, 23: 41-44.

Bernstein, S., and Herzberg, J. Small group experience with psychiatric aides. *Mental Hygiene* 1970, 54: 113-17.

Bettis, M.C. Mental health, growth, and your national association. *Mental Hygiene* 1968, 52: 190-96.

Bettis, M.C., and Roberts, R.E. The mental health manpower dilemma. *Mental Hygiene* 1969, 53: 163-75.

Bierman, R.; Carkhuff, R.R.; and Santilli, M. Efficacy of empathic communication training groups for inner city preschool teachers and family workers. *Journal of Applied Behavioral Science* 1972, 8: 188-202.

Biller, H.B. Paternal deprivation, cognitive functioning and the faminized classroom. In A. Davids (ed.), *Child personality and psychopathology: Current topics*, vol. 1. New York: Wiley, 1974.

_____, and Meredith, D.L. *Father Power*, New York: McKay, 1974.

Birnbaum, M.L., and Jones, C.H. Activities of the social work aides. *Social Casework* 1967, 48: 626-32.

Bittner, E. Police discretion in emergency apprehension of mentally ill persons. *Social Problems* 1967, 14: 278-92.

Blau, T.H. The professional in the community views the nonprofessional helper: Psychology. *Professional Psychology* 1969, 1: 25-31.

Bloom, B.L. Mental health program evaluation. In S.E. Golann and C. Eisdorfer (eds.), *Handbook of community mental health*. New York: Appleton-Century-Crofts, 1972.

_____. *Community mental health: A historical and critical analysis*. Morristown, N.J.: General Learning Press, 1973.

Blum, A. Differential use of manpower in public welfare. In B.G. Guerney (ed.), *Psychotherapeutic agents: New roles for nonprofessionals, parents, and teachers*. New York: Holt, 1969.

Blum, E.M., and Blum, R.H. *Alcoholism, modern psychological approaches to treatment*. San Francisco: Jossey-Bass, 1967.

Blumberg, D. The ex-patient as change agent. *Mental Hygiene* 1970, 54: 159-60.

Bockhoven, J.S. *Moral treatment in American psychiatry*. New York: Springer, 1963.

Boer, B.L., and McIver, B.C. Human relations training: Laboratories and team policing. *Journal of Police Science and Administration* 1973, 1: 162-67.

Bornstein, P.H. Training parents as behavior modifiers: A bibliography 1959-1973. *JSAS Catalog of Selected Documents in Psychology* 1974, 4: 130.

Borton, T. Teaching for personal growth: An introduction to new materials. *Mental Hygiene* 1969, 53: 594-99.

Borus, J.F. Community mental health center and the private practitioner: First step. *Psychiatry* 1971, 34: 274-88.

Bouhoustos, J.C. The nontraditionally trained mental health worker: Fad or future? *Professional Psychology* 1970, 2: 455-59.

Bourne, P.G. Human resources: A new approach to the dilemmas of community psychiatry. *American Journal of Psychiatry* 1974, 131: 666-69.

Bouska, D.; Briggs, H.; Deming, B.; Goodenough, B.; Oakes, R.; and Werner, S. *Education for modern parents: New ways in family living*. Mission, Kans.: Johnson County Mental Health Center, 1974.

Bowden, C.L., and Barton, D. Goals of medical student psychiatric education. *Journal of Medical Education* 1975, 50: 257-63.

Boyer, L.B. Folk psychiatry of the Apaches of the Mescalero Indian reservation. In A. Kiev (ed.), *Faith, magic and healing: Studies in primitive psychiatry today.* Glencoe, Ill.: Free Press, 1964.

Boyette, R.; Blount, W.; Petaway, K.; Jones, E.; and Hill, S. The plight of the new careerist: A bright horizon overshadowed by a dark cloud. *American Journal of Orthopsychiatry* 1972, 42: 596-602.

Boylin, E.R. The use of peers in psychotherapy. *Psychotherapy: Theory, Research and Practice* 1971, 8: 285-86.

_____. The companion program: Students as helpers. *Psychotherapy: Theory, Research and Practice* 1973, 10: 242-44.

Bozarth, J.D., and Krauft, C.C. Accurate empathy ratings: Some methodological considerations. *Journal of Clinical Psychology* 1972, 28: 408-10.

Bradford, L.P.; Gibb, J.; and Benne, K.D. (eds.). *T-group theory and laboratory method.* New York: Wiley, 1964.

Brager, G. The indigenous worker: A new approach to the social work technician. *Social Work* 1965, 10: 33-40.

Braginsky, B.M.; Braginsky, D.D.; and Ring, K. *Methods of madness: The mental hospital as a last resort.* New York: Holt, 1969.

Brammer, L.M. *The helping relationship: Process and skills.* Englewood Cliffs, N.J.: Prentice-Hall, 1973.

Branch, C.H. Psychiatric training and the general practitioner. *American Journal of Psychiatry* 1965a, 122: 485-89.

_____. Should the medical student be trained to refer or handle his own psychiatric patients? *American Journal of Psychiatry* 1965b, 121: 847-51.

Brennen, E.C. College students and mental health programs for children. *American Journal of Public Health* 1967, 57: 1767-71.

Brockhaus, J.P.; Marshall, J.C.; and Dustin, E.R. The effect of a training program on the empathic ability of psychiatric aides. *Journal of Community Psychology* 1973, 1: 431-35.

Brodsky, A. The consciousness-raising group as a model for therapy with women. *Psychotherapy: Theory, Research and Practice* 1973, 10: 24-29.

Brodsky, C.J. The systematic incompatibility of medical practice and psychotherapy. *Diseases of the Nervous System* 1970, 31: 597-604.

Brodsky, C.M. Clergymen as psychotherapists: Problems in interrole communication. *Community Mental Health Journal* 1968, 4: 482-91.

Brody, M.; Golden, M.M.; and Lichtman, H.S. Experience with small group seminars for practicing physicians. *American Journal of Psychiatry* 1965, 122: 497-500.

Brogan, D.R., and Greenberg, B.G. An educational program in mental health statistics. *Community Mental Health Journal* 1973, 9: 68-78.

Brook, B.D. Crisis hostel: An Alternative to psychiatric hospitalization for emergency patients. *Hospital and Community Psychiatry* 1973, 24: 621-24.

Brooks, C.M. New mental health perspectives in the black community. *Social Casework* 1974, 55: 489-96.

Broskowski, A., and Baker, F. Professional, organizational, and social barriers to primary prevention. *American Journal of Orthopsychiatry* 1974, 44: 707-19.

_____ ; Khajavi, F.; and Mehryar, A. An evaluation of an in-service training seminar on community consultation and education. *Journal of Community Psychology* 1973, 1: 174-76.

_____ , and Schulberg, H.C. A model training program for clinical research and development. *Professional Psychology* 1974, 5: 133-39.

Brotman, H.B. The fastest growing minority: The aging. *American Journal of Public Health* 1974, 64: 249-52.

Broverman, I.K.; Broverman, D.M.; Clarkson, F.E.; Rosenkrantz, P.; and Vogel, S.R. Sex-role stereotypes and clinical judgments of mental health. *Journal of Consulting Psychology* 1970, 34: 1-7.

Brown, B.S., and Ishiyama, T. Some reflections on the role of the student in the mental hospital. *Community Mental Health Journal* 1968, 4: 509-18.

Brown, D.G. *Behavior modification in child, school, and family mental health: An annotated bibliography.* Champaign, Ill.: Research Press, 1972.

Brown, W.F. Student-to-student counseling for academic adjustment. *Personnel and Guidance Journal* 1965, 43: 811-17.

_____ . Effectiveness of paraprofessionals: The evidence. *Personnel and Guidance Journal* 1974, 53: 257-63.

_____ ; Wehe, N.O.; Zunker, V.G.; and Haslam, W.L. Effectiveness of student-to-student counseling on the academic adjustment of potential college dropouts. *Journal of Educational Psychology* 1971, 64: 285-89.

_____ , and Zunker, V.G. Student counselor utilization at four-year institutions of higher learning. *Journal of College Student Personnel* 1966, 7: 41-46.

Brownstone, J.E., and Dye, C.J. *Communication workshop for parents of adolescents.* Champaign, Ill.: Research Press, 1973.

Bruder, E.E. The clergyman's contribution to community mental health. *Hospital and Community Psychiatry* 1971, 22: 207-10.

Bruhn, J.G., and Parsons, O.A. Attitudes toward medical specialties: Two follow-up studies. *Journal of Medical Education* 1965, 40: 273-80.

Budner, S.; Chazin, R.M.; and Young, H. The indigenous nonprofessional in a multiservice center. *Social Casework* 1973, 54: 354-59.

Buie, L.C.; Goldfelder, J.; and Saba, T.H. A psychiatrist participates in a county health program. *Children* 1962, 9: 227-31.

Burck, H.D., and Peterson, G.W. Needed: More evaluation, not research. *Personnel and Guidance Journal* 1975, 53: 563-69.

Burgess, M.M. Alcohol: America's most widely misused drug. *Journal of Drug Education* 1971, 1: 25-31.

Burke, W.W. Training organization development specialists. *Professional Psychology* 1970, 1: 354-58.

Bushweiler, G.L., and Gershon, M. The use of an interactional model for the training of volunteers. Paper presented at the Annual Meeting of the Rocky Mountain Psychological Association, May 1973.

Butterfield, W.H. Modeling and shaping by parents to develop chewing behavior in their retarded child. *Journal of Behavior Therapy and Experimental Psychiatry* 1973, 4: 285-87.

Cain, A.C. The perils of prevention. *American Journal of Orthopsychiatry* 1967, 37: 640-42.

Callan, J.P. Meeting mental health needs of Puerto Rican families. *Hospital and Community Psychiatry* 1973, 24: 330-33.

Campbell, D.T., and Stanley, J.C. *Experimental and quasiexperimental designs for research.* Chicago: Rand McNally, 1966.

Campbell, E.H. Consultation and supervision of student teachers in a program of therapeutic tutoring. *Journal of School Psychology* 1967, 6: 7-13.

Cantor, E.M. The challenge of volunteer services. *Child Welfare* 1968, 47: 538-41.

Caplan, G. *An approach to community mental health.* New York: Grune and Stratton, 1961.

_____. *Principles of preventive psychiatry.* New York: Basic Books, 1964.

_____. *The theory and practice of mental health consultation.* New York: Basic Books, 1970.

_____. *Support systems and community mental health: Lectures on concept development.* New York: Behavioral Publications, 1974a.

_____. *The nurse's role in changing health services.* In G. Caplan, *Support systems and community mental health: Lectures on concept development.* New York: Behavioral Publications, 1974b.

Caplan, R.B. *Psychiatry and the community in nineteenth-century America.* New York: Basic Books, 1969.

_____. *Helping the helpers to help.* New York: Seabury Press, 1972.

Carkhuff, R.R. Training in the counseling and therapeutic practices: Requiem or reveille? *Journal of Counseling Psychology* 1966, 13: 360-67.

_____. *Helper communication as a function of helpee affect and content.* *Journal of Counseling Psychology* 1969a, 16: 126-31.

_____. *Helping and human relations.* Vol. 1: *Selection and training.* New York: Holt, 1969b.

_____. *Helping and human relations.* Vol. 2: *Practice and research.* New York: Holt, 1969c.

_____. The prediction of the effects of teacher-counselor education: The development of communication and discrimination selection indexes. *Counselor Education and Supervision* 1969d, 8: 265-72.

_____. The development of effective courses of action for ghetto school children. *Psychology in the Schools* 1970, 7: 272-74.

Carkhuff, R.R. Principles of social action in training new careers in human services. *Journal of Counseling Psychology* 1971a, 18: 147-51.

_____. *The development of human resources: Education, psychology, and social change.* New York: Holt, 1971b.

_____, and Banks, G. Training as a preferred mode of facilitating relations between races and generations. *Journal of Counseling Psychology* 1970, 17: 413-18.

_____, and Berenson, B.G. *Beyond counseling and therapy.* New York: Holt, 1967.

_____, and _____. The utilization of black functional professionals to reconstitute troubled families. *Journal of Clinical Psychology* 1972, 28: 92-93.

_____, and Bierman, R. Training as a preferred mode of treatment of parents of emotionally disturbed children. *Journal of Counseling Psychology* 1970, 17: 157-61.

_____; Collingwood, T.; and Renz, L. The prediction of the effects of didactic training in discrimination. *Journal of Clinical Psychology* 1969, 25: 460-61.

_____, and Griffin, A.H. Selection and training of functional professionals for a concentrated employment program. *Journal of Clinical Psychology* 1971, 27: 163-65.

_____; Kratochvil, D.; and Friel, T. Effects of professional training: Communication and discrimination of facilitative conditions. *Journal of Counseling* 1968, 15: 68-74.

_____, and Truax, C.B. Training in counseling and psychotherapy: An evaluation of an integrated and experiential approach. *Journal of Consulting Psychology* 1965a, 29: 333-36.

_____, and _____. Lay mental health counseling: The effects of lay group counseling. *Journal of Consulting Psychology* 1965b, 29: 426-31.

Carlson, J. Consulting: Facilitating school change. *Elementary School Guidance and Counseling* 1972, 7: 83-88.

_____, and Pietrofesa, J.J. A tri-level guidance structure: An answer to our apparent ineffectiveness. *Elementary School Guidance and Counseling* 1971, 5: 190-95.

Carlson, R. Understanding women: Implications for personality theory and research. *Journal of Social Issues* 1972, 28: 17-32.

Carter, J.H. Psychiatry's insensitivity to racism and aging. *Psychiatric Opinion* 1973, 10: 21-25.

Carter, R.D. *Help! These kids are driving me crazy.* Champaign, Ill.: Research Press, 1972.

Casper, E.G., and Philippus, M.J. Fifteen cases of embrujada: Combining medication and suggestion in treatment. *Hospital and Community Psychiatry* 1975, 26: 271-74.

Castelnuova-Tedesco, P. How much psychiatry are medical students really learning? *Archives of General Psychiatry* 1967, 16: 668-75.

_____. The "20-minute" hour revisited: A follow-up. *Comprehensive Psychiatry* 1970, 11: 108-22.

Cates, J., and Dawson, W. Master's in psychology. *American Psychologist* 1971, 26: 928-30.

Chafetz, M.E. Addictions. III: Alcoholism. In A.M. Freedman and H.I. Kaplan (eds.), *Comprehensive textbook of psychiatry*. Baltimore, Md.: Williams and Wilkins, 1967.

Chapman, J.L. Development and validation of a scale to measure empathy. *Journal of Counseling Psychology* 1971, 18: 281-82.

Cherkas, M.S. Synanon Foundation—a radical approach to the problem of addiction. *American Journal of Psychiatry* 1965, 121: 1065-68.

Chesler, P. *Women and madness*. New York: Doubleday, 1972.

Chien, C.P., and Cole, J.O. Landlord-supervised cooperative apartments: A new modality for community-based treatment. *American Journal of Psychiatry* 1973, 130: 156-59.

Chinsky, J.M., and Rappaport, J. Attitude change in college students and chronic patients: A dual perspective. *Journal of Consulting and Clinical Psychology* 1970a, 35: 388-94.

_____, and _____. Brief critique of the meaning and reliability of "accurate empathy" ratings. *Psychological Bulletin* 1970b, 73: 379-82.

Christ, J. Volunteer training as an education. *Mental Hygiene* 1967, 51: 433-39.

Christensen, K.C., and Magoon, T.M. Perceived hierarchy of help-giving sources for two categories of student problems. *Journal of Counseling Psychology* 1974, 21: 311-14.

Christmas, J.J. Group methods in training and practice: Nonprofessional mental health personnel in a deprived community. *American Journal of Orthopsychiatry* 1966, 36: 410-19.

_____. Sociopsychiatric rehabilitation in a black urban ghetto. I. Conflicts, issues, and directions. *American Journal of Orthopsychiatry* 1969, 39: 651-61.

_____; Wallace, H.; and Edwards, J. New careers and new mental health services: Fantasy or future? *American Journal of Orthopsychiatry* 1970, 127: 1480-86.

Clancy, J.; Brodland, G.; and Fahr, S. A psychiatric clerkship for law students. *American Journal of Psychiatry* 1972, 129: 322-26.

Clarfield, S., and McMillan, R. Tuned-out secondary school students as mental health aides in the elementary school. *American Journal of Community Psychology* 1973, 1: 212-18.

Clayton, T. The changing mental hospital: Emerging alternatives. *Hospital and Community Psychiatry* 1974, 25: 386-92.

Cleland, C.C. Selection and training of attendants: a review of research. *American Journal of Mental Deficiency* 1962, 67: 205-10.

Cline, D.W., and Garrard, J.N. A medical interviewing course: Objectives, techniques, and assessment. *American Journal of Psychiatry* 1973, 130: 574-78.

Cline, T.R. Effectiveness of you-messages and I-messages on the helping relationship. Unpublished master's thesis, 1971.

Cobb, C.W. Community mental health services and the lower socioeconomic classes: A summary of research literature on outpatient treatment (1963-1969). *American Journal of Orthopsychiatry* 1972, 42: 404-14.

Cochran, I.L., and Steiner, K.E. Evaluation of an inservice training program using the SREB Information test. *American Journal of Mental Deficiency* 1966, 70: 913-17.

Cohen, J., and Struening, E.L. Opinions about mental illness in the personnel of two large mental hospitals. *Journal of Abnormal and Social Psychology* 1962, 64: 349-60.

_____, and _____. Opinions about mental illness: Mental hospital occupational profiles and profile clusters. *Psychological Reports* 1963, 12: 111-24.

Cohen, L.D. Training psychologists. In C. Grosser, W.E. Henry, and J.G. Kelly (eds.), *Nonprofessionals in the human service*. San Francisco: Jossey-Bass, 1969.

_____. Overview: Past, present, future. *Professional Psychology* 1974, 5: 222-26.

Cohen, M. Hospitality House: Volunteer companionship therapy through a community center. *Mental Hygiene* 1966, 50: 34-35.

Cohen, R.E. Principles of preventive mental health programs for ethnic minority populations: The acculturation of Puerto Ricans to the United States. *American Journal of Psychiatry* 1972, 128: 1529-33.

_____. The collaborative coprofessional: Developing a new mental health role. *Hospital and Community Psychiatry* 1973, 24: 242-46.

_____, and Hirschowitz, R.G. Training in community psychiatry. In S. Golann and C. Eisdorfer (eds.) *Handbook of community mental health*. New York: Appleton-Century-Crofts, 1972.

Cole, J.P., and Cole, W.E. Volunteers helping families of the mentally ill. *Mental Hygiene* 1969, 53: 188-95.

Collins, A.H. Natural delivery systems: Accessible sources of power for mental health. *American Journal of Orthopsychiatry* 1972, 42: 247-48.

Collins, J.A. The paraprofessional: 1. Manpower issues in the mental health field. *Hospital and Community Psychiatry* 1971, 22: 362-67.

Comer, J.P. The need is now. *Mental Hygiene* 1973, 57: 3-6.

Cone, J.D., and Sloop, E.W. Parents as agents of change. In A. Jacobs and W.W. Spradlin (eds.), *Group as agent of change*. Chicago: Aldine-Atherton, 1971.

Cook, D.W.; Kunce, J.T.; and Sleater, S.M. Vicarious behavior induction and training psychiatric aides. *Journal of Community Psychology* 1974, 2: 293-97.

Cooper, M., and Southard, C.G. The Mental Health Exchange: An important function of a community mental health center. *Community Mental Health Journal* 1966, 2: 343-46.

Cote, R.W. Behavior modification: Some questions. *Elementary School Journal* 1973, 74: 44-47.

Cottrell, L.S. Social planning, the competent community, and mental health. In *Urban America and the planning of mental health services.* Group for the Advancement of Psychiatry, Vol. V, Symposium No. 10, November 1964.

Cowen, E.L. Combined graduate-undergraduate training in community mental health. *Professional Psychology* 1969a, 1: 72-73.

_____. Mothers in the classroom. *Psychology Today* 1969b, 3: 36-39.

_____. Emergent directions in school mental health. *American Scientist* 1971, 59: 723-33.

_____. Social and community interventions. In P. Mussen and M. Rosenzweig (eds.), *Annual Review of Psychology* 1973, 24: 423-72.

_____; Carlisle, R.L.; and Kaufman, G. Evaluation of a college student volunteer program with primary graders experiencing school adjustment problems. *Psychology in the Schools* 1969, 6: 371-75.

_____; Chinsky, J.; and Rappaport, J. An undergraduate practicum in community mental health. *Community Mental Health Journal* 1970, 6: 91-100.

_____; Dorr, D.; Izzo, L.D.; Madonia, A.; and Trost, M.A. The Primary Mental Health Project: A new way to conceptualize and deliver school mental health services. *Psychology in the Schools* 1971, 8: 216-25.

_____; Dorr, D.A.; and Pokracki, F. Selection of nonprofessional child aides for a school mental health project. *Community Mental Health Journal* 1972, 8: 220-26.

_____; Dorr, D.A.; Sandler, I.N.; and McWilliams, S. Utilization of a nonprofessional child-aide school mental health program. *Journal of School Psychology* 1971, 9: 131-36.

_____; Dorr, D.; Trost, M.A.; and Izzo, L.D. Follow-up study of maladapting school children seen by nonprofessionals. *Journal of Consulting and Clinical Psychology* 1972, 39: 235-38.

_____; Gardner, E.A.; and Zax, M. (eds.), *Emergent approaches to mental health problems.* New York: Appleton-Century-Crofts, 1967.

_____; Izzo, L.D.; Miles, H.; Telschow, E.F.; Trost, M.A.; and Zax, M.A. A mental health program in the school setting: Description and evaluation. *Journal of Psychology* 1963, 56: 307-56.

_____; Leibowitz, E.; and Leibowitz, G. Utilization of retired people as mental health aides with children. *American Journal of Orthopsychiatry* 1968, 38: 900-909.

_____; Lorion, R.P.; Kraus, R.M.; and Dorr, D. Geometric expansion of helping services. *Journal of School Psychology* 1974, 12: 288-95.

Cowen, E.L.; Pederson, A.; Babigian, H.; Izzo, L.D.; and Trost, M.A. Long-term follow-up of early detected vulnerable children. *Journal of Consulting and Clinical Psychology* 1973, 41: 438-46.

_____, and Schochet, B.V. Referral and outcome differences between terminating and nonterminating children seen by nonprofessionals in a school mental health project. *American Journal of Community Psychology* 1973, 1: 103-12.

_____; Trost, M.A.; and Izzo, L.D. Nonprofessional human-service personnel in consulting roles. *Community Mental Health Journal* 1973, 9: 335-41.

_____; Zax, M.; and Laird, J.D. A college student volunteer program in the elementary school setting. *Community Mental Health Journal* 1966, 2: 319-28.

Cowne, L.J. Approaches to the mental health manpower problem: A review of the literature. *Mental Hygiene* 1969, 53: 176-87.

_____. Case studies of volunteer programs in mental health. *Mental Hygiene* 1970, 54: 337-45.

Cozzarelli, L.A., and Silin, M.W. The application of psychodynamic concepts to education: A proposed model for inservice training. *American Journal of Orthopsychiatry* 1974, 44: 227-28.

Crabbs, M.A. Listening workshops for teachers. *School Counselor* 1972, 20: 61-63.

Craighead, W.E., and Mercatoris, M. Mentally retarded residents as paraprofessionals: A review. *American Journal of Mental Deficiency* 1973, 78: 339-47.

Cuca, J. Graduate enrollments leveling off. *APA Monitor* 1974, 5: 16, 19.

Cullen, J.S. The effectiveness of parent discussion groups: A follow-up study. *Mental Hygiene* 1968, 52: 590-99.

Cumming, E. Phase movement in the support and control of the psychiatric patient. *Journal of Health and Human Behavior* 1962, 3: 235-41.

_____; Cumming, I.; and Edel, L. Policeman as philosopher, guide and friend. *Social Problems* 1965, 17: 276-86.

Cumming, J., and Cumming, E. *Ego and milieu: Theory and practice of environmental therapy.* New York: Atherton, 1969.

Dalton, R.F.; Sunblad, L.M.; and Hylbert, K.W. An application of principles of social learning to training in communication of empathy. *Journal of Counseling Psychology* 1973, 20: 378-83.

Daniels, A.M. Training school nurses to work with groups of adolescents. *Children* 1966, 13: 210-16.

Daniels, D.N. Task groups in the therapy of mental patients. *Current Psychiatric Therapies* 1969, 10: 186-94.

_____; Zelman, H.B.; and Campbell, J.H. Community based task groups in recovery of mental patients. *Archives of General Psychiatry* 1967, 16: 215-28.

Daniels, R.S. Community psychiatry—a new profession, a developing subspecialty, or effective clinical psychiatry? *Community Mental Health Journal* 1966, 2: 47-54.

Danish, S.J., and Brock, G.W. The current status of paraprofessional training. *Personnel and Guidance Journal* 1974, 53: 299-303.

_____, and Brodsky, S.L. Training of policemen in emotional control and awareness. *American Psychologist* 1970, 25: 368-69.

_____, and Hauer, A.L. *Helping skills: A basic training program.* New York: Behavioral Publications, 1973.

Danzig, M.E. Education of the community mental health assistant: Dovetailing theory with practice. *Mental Hygiene* 1970, 54: 357-63.

Darley, P.J. Who shall hold the conch? Some thoughts on community control of mental health programs. *Community Mental Health Journal* 1974, 10: 185-91.

D'Augelli, A.R. The assessment of interpersonal skills: A comparison of observer, peer, and self ratings. *Journal of Community Psychology* 1973a, 1: 177-79.

_____. Group composition using interpersonal skills: An analogue study on the effects of members' interpersonal skills on peer ratings and group cohesiveness. *Journal of Counseling Psychology* 1973b, 20: 531-34.

_____. Strategies for the comprehensive evaluation of training programs for nonprofessional human service workers. Paper presented at the Annual Meeting of the American Psychological Association, Montreal, Canada, 1973c.

_____. Personal communication, October 1973d.

_____, and Chinsky, J.M. Interpersonal skills and pretraining: Implications for the use of group procedures for interpersonal learning and for the selection of nonprofessional mental health workers. *Journal of Consulting and Clinical Psychology* 1974, 42: 65-72.

_____; _____; and Getter, H. The effect of group composition and duration on sensitivity training. *Small Group Behavior* 1974, 5: 56-64.

Davanzo, H. A method of teaching reparative psychotherapy to medical students. *Journal of Medical Education* 1965, 40: 785-91.

Davidoff, I.F.; Lauga, A.C.; and Walzer, R.S. The mental health rehabilitation worker: A new member of the psychiatric team. *Community Mental Health Journal* 1969, 5: 46-54.

Davis, K.L. Mental health consultative services in residence halls. *Journal of the American College Health Association* 1974, 23: 98-101.

Davis, M., and Mann, P.H. The psychologist as a consulttrainer. *Psychology in the Schools* 1973, 10: 407-10.

Dean, S.R. Self-help group psychotherapy: Mental patients rediscover will power. *International Journal of Social Psychiatry* 1970, 17: 72-78.

_____. The role of self-conducted group therapy in psychorehabilitation: A look at Recovery, Inc. *American Journal of Psychiatry* 1971, 127: 934-37.

Delaney, D.J., and Heimann, R.A. Effectiveness of sensitivity training on the perception on non-verbal communications. *Journal of Counseling Psychology* 1966, 13: 436-40.

DeLeon, G.; Holland, S.; and Rosenthal, M.S. Phoenix House: Criminal activity of dropouts. *Journal of the American Medical Association* 1972, 222: 686-89.

_____; Rosenthal, M.S.; and Brodney, K. Therapeutic community for drug addicts: Long-term measurement of emotional changes. *Psychological Reports* 1971, 29: 595-600.

_____; Skodol, A.; and Rosenthal, M.S. Phoenix House: Changes in psychopathological signs of resident drug addicts. *Archives of General Psychiatry* 1973, 28: 131-35.

Delk, J.L.; Urbancik, G.; Williams, C.; Berg, G., and Kahn, M.W. Drop-outs from an American Indian reservation school: A possible prevention program. *Journal of Community Psychology* 1974, 2: 15-16.

Delworth, U., and Moore, M. Helper plus trainer: A two-phase program for the counselor. *Personnel and Guidance Journal* 1974, 52: 428-33.

_____; Moore, M.; Millick, J.; and Leone, P. Training student volunteers. *Personnel and Guidance Journal* 1974, 53: 57-61.

_____; Sherwood, G.; and Casaburri, N. *Student paraprofessionals: A working model for higher education* (Student Personnel Series No. 17). Washington: American College Personnel Association, 1974.

Dibner, S.S. Newspaper advice columns as a mental health resource. *Community Mental Health Journal* 1974, 10: 147-55.

Dinges, N.G.; Yazzie, M.L.; and Tollefson, G.D. Developmental intervention for Navajo family mental health. *Personnel and Guidance Journal* 1974, 52: 390-95.

Dinkmeyer, D.C. *Developing understanding of self and others (DUSO).* Circle Pines, Minn.: American Guidance Service, 1970.

_____. The parent "C" group. *Personnel and Guidance Journal* 1973, 52: 252-56.

Dixon, M.C., and Burns, J.L. Crisis theory, active learning and the training of telephone crisis volunteers. *Journal of Community Psychology* 1974, 2: 120-25.

Donnelly, F.A.; Ware, J.E.; Wolkon, G.H.; and Naftulin, D.H. Evaluation of weekend seminars for physicians. *Journal of Medical Education* 1972, 47: 184-87.

Dooley, C.D. Effects of response interaction training on the group assessment of interpersonal traits. Unpublished doctoral dissertation, University of California, Los Angeles, 1973.

Dorr, D., and Cowen, E.L. Nonprofessional mental health workers' judgments of change in children. *Journal of Community Psychology* 1973, 1: 23-26.

_____; _____; and Kraus, R. Mental health professionals view nonprofessional mental health workers. *American Journal of Community Psychology* 1973, 1: 258-65.

_____ ; _____ ; and Sandler, I.N. Changes in nonprofessional mental health workers' response preference and attitudes as a function of training and supervised field experience. *Journal of School Psychology* 1973, 11: 118-22.

_____ ; _____ ; _____ ; and Pratt, D.M. Dimensionality of a test battery for nonprofessional mental health workers. *Journal of Consulting and Clinical Psychology* 1973, 41: 181-85.

Dorsey, J.R.; Matasunga, G.; and Bauman, G. Training public health nurses in mental health. *Archives of General Psychiatry* 1964, 11: 214-22.

Douglas, F.M. Prescientific psychiatry in the urban setting. *American Journal of Psychiatry* 1974, 131: 279-82.

Drabman, R., and Spitalnik, R. Training a retarded child as a behavioral teaching assistant. *Journal of Behavior Therapy and Experimental Psychiatry* 1973, 4: 269-72.

Driscoll, J.M.; Meyer, R.G.; and Schanie, C.F. Training police in family crisis intervention. *Journal of Applied Behavioral Science* 1973, 9: 62-82.

Drum, D.J., and Figler, H.E. *Outreach in counseling: Applying the growth and prevention models in schools and colleges.* New York: Intext Press, 1973.

_____ , and _____ . Achieving total outreach potential: A seven dimensional model. *Impact* 1974, 3: 5-17.

Dumont, M.P. Tavern culture: The sustenance of homeless men. *American Journal of Orthopsychiatry* 1967, 37: 938-45.

_____ . Self-help treatment programs. *American Journal of Psychiatry* 1974, 131: 631-35.

Dupont, H. Community mental health centers and services for the mentally retarded. *Community Mental Health Journal* 1967, 3: 33-66.

Durlak, J.A. The use of nonprofessionals as therapeutic agents: Research, issues, and implications. Unpublished doctoral dissertation, Vanderbilt University, 1971.

_____ . Myths concerning the nonprofessional therapist. *Professional Psychology* 1973a, 4: 300-4.

_____ . Ninth graders as student aides: Making use of the helper therapy principle. *Psychology in the Schools* 1973b, 10: 334-39.

_____ . Personal communication, October 1973c.

Duvall, H.J.; Locke, B.Z.; and Brill, L. Follow-up study of narcotic drug addicts five years after hospitalization. *Public Health Reports* 1963, 78: 185-93.

Dworkin, E.P. Implementation and evaluation of a clergy inservice training program in personal counseling. *Journal of Community Psychology* 1974, 2: 232-37.

Eberdt, M.G. Adopting secular post-graduate education in counseling to meet the needs of ministers. *Counselor Education and Supervision* 1970, 9: 122-25.

Ebersole, G.O.; Leiderman, P.H.; and Yalom, I.D. Training the nonprofessional group therapist. *Journal of Nervous and Mental Disease* 1969, 149: 294-302.

Eddy, W.B.; Paap, S.M.; and Glad, D.D. Solving problems in living: The citizen's viewpoint. *Mental Hygiene* 1970, 54: 64-72.

Edelstein, J.P. Mental health: Can the pediatrician help? *Mental Hygiene* 1965, 49: 453-60.

Edgar, K.F., and Kotrick, C. The development of a peer counseling center. *Psychotherapy: Theory, Research and Practice* 1972, 9: 256-58.

Edgerton, J.W. Evaluation in community mental health. In G. Rosenblum (ed.), *Issues in community psychology and preventive mental health.* New York: Behavioral Publications, 1971.

Edgerton, R.B., and Karno, M. Mexican-American bilingualism and the perception of mental illness. *Archives of General Psychiatry* 1971, 24: 286-90.

Edgerton, R.B.; Karno, M.; and Fernandez, I. Curanderismo in the metropolis: The diminished role of folk psychiatry among Los Angeles Mexican-Americans. *American Journal of Psychotherapy* 1970, 24: 124-34.

Edmondson, W.R. Long-term rehabilitation of the drug dependent person: The Odyssey House method. *Journal of the National Medical Association* 1972, 29: 595-600.

Egbert, L.D. Psychological support for surgical patients. *International Psychiatry Clinics* 1967, 4: 37-51.

Eisdorfer, C. Mental health in later life. In S.E. Golann and C. Eisdorfer (eds.), *Handbook of Community Mental Health.* New York: Appleton-Century-Crofts, 1972.

_____, and Golann, S.E. Principles for the training of "new professionals" in mental health. *Community Mental Health Journal* 1969, 5: 349-57.

Eldridge, M.S.; Barcikowski, R.S.; and Witmer, J.M. Effects of DUSO on the self-concepts of second grade students. *Elementary School Guidance and Counseling* 1972, 7: 256-60.

Elkins, A.M., and Papanek, G.O. Consultation with the police: An example of community psychiatry practice. *American Journal of Psychiatry* 1966, 123: 531-35.

Ellsworth, R.B. A behavioral study of staff attitudes toward mental illness. *Journal of Abnormal Psychology* 1965, 70: 194-200.

_____. *Nonprofessionals in psychiatric rehabilitation.* New York: Appleton-Century Crofts, 1968.

_____, and Ellsworth, J.J. The psychiatric aide: Therapeutic agent or lost potential. *Journal of Psychiatric Nursing* 1970, 8: 7-13.

Enelow, A.J., and Adler, L.M. Psychiatric skills and knowledge for the general practitioner. *Journal of the American Medical Association* 1964, 189: 91-96.

_____, and _____. Organization of postgraduate courses in psychiatry. *Archives of General Psychiatry* 1965, 12: 433-37.

_____ ; _____ ; and Manning, P.R. A supervised psychotherapy course for practicing physicians. *Journal of Medical Education* 1964, 39: 140-46.

_____ ; _____ ; and Wexler, M. Programmed instruction in interviewing: An experiment in medical education. *Journal of the American Medical Association* 1970, 212: 1843-46.

_____ , and Myers, V.H. Postgraduate psychiatric education: The ethnography of a failure. *American Journal of Psychiatry* 1968, 125: 627-31.

_____ , and Wexler, M. *Psychiatry in the practice of medicine.* New York: Oxford University Press, 1966.

Ennis, B.J. *Prisoners of psychiatry: Mental patients, psychiatrists, and the law.* New York: Avon, 1972.

_____ , and Siegel, L. *The rights of mental patients: The basic ACLU guide to a mental patient's rights.* New York: Avon, 1973.

Ephross, P.H., and French, P. Social service and the police. *Hospital and Community Psychiatry* 1972, 23: 61-63.

Epstein, I. Social workers and social action: Attitudes toward social action strategies. *Social Work* 1968, 13: 101-108.

Erickson, R.C. Outcome studies in mental hospitals: A search for criteria. *Journal of Consulting and Clinical Psychology* 1972, 39: 75-77.

Euster, G.L. Mental health workers: New mental hospital personnel for the seventies. *Mental Hygiene* 1971, 55: 283-90.

Evans, A.S., and Goldberg, M.F. Catholic seminarians in a secular institution. *Mental Hygiene* 1970, 54: 559-67.

Ewalt, P.L. *Mental health volunteers.* Springfield, Ill.: Charles C Thomas, 1967.

Fabian, A.E., and Tannor, H. The role of the psychiatric consultant to day care centers in ghetto communities. *American Journal of Orthopsychiatry* 1971, 41: 280.

Fairweather, G.W. *Social psychology in treating mental illness: An experimental approach.* New York: Wiley, 1964.

_____ ; Sanders, D.H.; Cressler, D.L.; and Maynard, H. *Community life for the mentally ill: An alternative to institutional care.* Chicago: Aldine, 1969.

Featherman, R.E., and Welling, M. Using volunteers in a community mental health center. *Hospital and Community Psychiatry* 1971, 22: 113-14.

Feldstein, D. The paraprofessional and the community college. *Social Work* 196, 14: 117.

Felton, G.S. Teaching internalization to middle-level mental health workers in training. *Psychological Reports* 1973, 32: 1279-82.

_____ ; Wallach, H.F.; and Gallo, C.L. Training mental health workers to better meet patient needs. *Hospital and Community Psychiatry* 1974a, 25: 299-302.

_____ ; _____ ; and _____ . New roles for new-professional mental health workers: Training the patient advocate, the integrator, and the therapist. *Community Mental Health Journal* 1974b, 10: 52-65.

Ferree, E.H.; Wasserman, C.V.; and McCarthy, B.W. The American University companion program: A model of paraprofessional counseling. *JSAS Catalog of Selected Documents in Psychology* 1973, 3: 92.

Fidler, J.W.; Guerney, B.G., Jr.; Andronico, M.P.; and Guerney, L. Filial therapy as a logical extension of current trends as psychotherapy. In B.G. Guerney (ed.), *Psychotherapeutic agents: New roles for nonprofessionals, parents, and teachers.* New York: Holt, 1969.

Finestone, S., and Sobey, F. *Nonprofessional personnel in mental health programs.* Chevy Chase, Md.: National Clearinghouse for Mental Health Information, 1969.

Fink, P.J., and Zerof, H. Mental health technology: An approach to the manpower problem. *American Journal of Psychiatry* 1971, 127: 1082-85.

Fink, R.; Goldensohn, S.S.; Shapiro, S.; and Dailey, E.F. Treatment of patients designated by family doctors as having emotional problems. *American Journal of Public Health* 1967, 57: 1550-64.

Fisch, S. Botanicas and spiritualism in a metropolis. *Transcultural Psychiatric Research* 1969, 6: 188-90.

Fischer, E.H. College students as companions to long-term mental health patients: Some considerations. *Journal of Consulting and Clinical Psychology.* 1970, 35: 308-10.

Fiske, D.W.; Luborsky, L.; Parloff, M.B.; Hunt, H.F.; Orne, M.T.; Reiser, M.F.; and Tuma, A.H. Planning of research on effectiveness of psychotherapy. *Archives of General Psychiatry* 1970, 22: 22-32.

Fitts, W.H. *Tennessee Self-Concept Scale.* Nashville, Tenn.: Counselor Recordings and Tests, 1965.

Fodor, I.E. The parent as a therapist. *Mental Hygiene* 1973, 57: 16-19.

Foley, A.R., and Gorham, P. Toward a new philosophy of care: Perspectives on prevention. *Community Mental Health Journal* 1973, 9: 99-107.

Fraleigh, P.W. A description and assessment of a procedure to train paraprofessional counselors to communicate understanding, acceptance, and sincerity. *Dissertation Abstracts International* 1971, 32: 173-74.

Frank, J.D. American psychotherapy in perspective. In A.R. Mahrer and L. Pearson (eds.), *Creative developments in psychotherapy.* Cleveland: Case Western Reserve University Press, 1971.

_____. *Persuasion and healing: A comparative study of psychotherapy.* New York: Schocken Books, 1974a.

_____. Psychotherapy: The restoration of morale. *American Journal of Psychiatry* 1974b, 131: 271-74.

Franks, C.M. (ed.). *Behavior therapy: Appraisal and status.* New York: McGraw-Hill, 1969.

Freed, H.M. The community psychiatrist and political action. *Archives of General Psychiatry* 1967, 17: 129-34.

Freeman, S.J., and George, R. Family life education: A case study of non-productive community intervention. *Canadian Psychiatric Association Journal* 1972, 17: 63-69.

Freitag, G.; Blechman, E.; and Berck, P. College students as companion aides to newly released psychiatric patients. In G.A. Specter and W.L. Claiborn (eds.), *Crisis intervention.* New York: Behavioral Publications, 1973.

Friedman, J.H., and Spada, A.R. A psychiatric training program for high school students assigned to a geriatric service. *Mental Hygiene* 1970, 54: 427-29.

Friedman, M.H. Community mental health education with police. *Mental Hygiene* 1965, 49: 182-86.

Fritz, K.M. Mental health personnel. *American Journal of Public Health* 1965, 55: 251-55.

Gabriel, H.P., and Danilowicz, D.A. Psychiatric concepts in pediatric residencies: A review of NIMH-supported training programs. *Journal of Medical Education* 1969, 44: 939-44.

Garcia, J. Preventive programs in parent education: A study of P.E.T. Unpublished research, 1971.

Gardner, E.A. Emotional disorders in medical practice. *Annals of Internal Medicine* 1970, 73: 651-53.

Gardner, J. Sexist counseling must stop. *Personnel and Guidance Journal* 1971, 49: 705-14.

Garfield, S.L. New developments in the preparation of counselors. *Community Mental Health Journal* 1969, 5: 240-46.

_____ . Research on client variables in psychotherapy. In A.E. Bergin and S.L. Garfield (eds.), *Handbook of psychotherapy and behavior change.* New York: Wiley, 1971.

Gartner, A. *Paraprofessionals and their performance: A survey of education, health, and social service programs.* New York: Praeger, 1971.

Gartner, A.; Kohler, M.C.; and Riessman, F. *Children teach children.* New York: Harper & Row, 1971.

Gazda, G.M.; Asbury, F.R.; Balzer, F.J.; Childers, W.C.; Desselle, R.E.; and Walters, R.P. *Human relations development: A manual for educators.* Boston: Allyn & Bacon, 1973.

Gendlin, E.; Kelly, J.J.; Raulinaitis, V.B.; and Spaner, F.E. Volunteers as a major asset in the treatment program. *Mental Hygiene* 1966, 50: 421-27.

Gentry, W.D. Three models of training and utilization. *Professional Psychology* 1974a, 5: 207-13.

_____ . Technicians' views of training and function. *Professional Psychology* 1974b, 5: 219-21.

Gerard, D.L.; Saenger, G.; and Wile, R. The abstinent alcoholic. *Archives of General Psychiatry* 1962, 6: 83-95.

Gerjouy, H.; Rosenberg, G.G.; Bond, J.G.; McDevitt, R.; and Balough, J.K. Mental hospital ward attendants' work attitudes and their work experience in "front" or "back" wards. *Journal of General Psychology* 1963, 68: 173-80.

Gerler, E. The Magic Circle program: How to involve teachers. *Elementary School Guidance and Counseling* 1973, 8: 86-91.

Gerson, B. Consciousness-raising groups with elementary school girls: A case study. *Psychotherapy: Theory, Research and Practice* 1974, 11: 30-35.

Gilbert, G.C. Counseling black adolescent parents. *Social Work* 1974, 19: 88-95.

Gilmore, S.K. *The counselor-in-training.* New York: Appleton-Century-Crofts, 1973.

Ginsberg, L.H. The mental patient liberation movement. *Social Work* 1974, 19: 3-4, 103.

Glass, T. Student companions for chronically ill patients. *Hospital and Community Psychiatry* 1966, 17: 224-25.

Glasscote, R.M.; Sussex, J.M.; Cumming, E.; and Smith, L. *The community mental health center: An interim appraisal.* Washington: Joint Information Service of the American Psychiatric Association, 1969.

Gluckstern, N.B. Training parents as drug counselors in the community. *Personnel and Guidance Journal* 1973, 51: 676-80.

Gobeil, O. El susto: A descriptive analysis. *International Journal of Social Psychiatry* 1973, 19: 38-43.

Goffman, E. *Asylums.* Garden City, N.Y.: Doubleday, 1961.

Golann, S.E. Initial findings of the follow-up study of child development counselors. *American Journal of Public Health* 1967, 57: 1759-66.

_____. Community psychology and mental health: An analysis of strategies and a survey of training. In I. Iscoe and C.D. Spielberger (eds.), *Community psychology: Perspectives in training and research.* New York: Appleton-Century-Crofts, 1970.

_____; Baker, J.; and Frydman, A. Demands and coping in the undergraduate therapeutic-companion experience. *American Journal of Community Psychology* 1973, 1: 228-37.

_____; Breiter, D.E.; and Magoon, T.M. A filmed interview applied to the evaluation of mental health counselors. *Psychotherapy: Theory, Research and Practice* 1966, 3: 21-24.

_____; Wurm, C.A.; and Magoon, T.M. Community mental health content of graduate programs in departments of psychology. *Journal of Clinical Psychology* 1964, 20: 518-22.

Goldman, A.E., and Lawton, M.P. The role of the psychiatric aide: A report on the Norristown Seminar. *Mental Hygiene* 1962, 46: 288-98.

Goldstein, A.P. Commonalities, differences, and directions in contemporary psychotherapy. In A.R. Mahrer and L. Pearson (eds.), *Creative developments in psychotherapy.* Cleveland: Case Western Reserve University Press, 1971.

_____. *Structured learning therapy: Toward a psychotherapy for the poor.* New York: Academic Press, 1973.

_____, and Goedhart, A. The use of structured learning for empathy enhancement in paraprofessional psychotherapist training. *Journal of Community Psychology* 1973, 1: 168-73.

————, and Simonson, N.R. Social psychological approaches to psychotherapy research. In A.E. Bergin and S.L. Garfield (eds.), *Handbook of psychotherapy and behavior change*. New York: Wiley, 1971.

Golland, J.H. Training army psychology technicians for intake and evaluation. *Hospital and Community Psychiatry* 1971, 22: 373-74.

Goodman, G. An experiment with companionship therapy: College students and troubled boys—assumptions, selection, and design. *American Journal of Public Health* 1967, 57: 1772-77.

————. *Companionship therapy: Studies in structured intimacy*. San Francisco: Jossey-Bass, 1972a.

————. Systematic selection of psychotherapeutic talent: Group assessment of interpersonal traits. In S.E. Golann and C. Eisdorfer (eds.), *Handbook of community mental health*. New York: Appleton-Century-Crofts, 1972b.

Gordon, I.J. Stimulation via parent education. *Children* 1969, 16: 57-58.

Gordon, J.E. Project Cause, the federal anti-poverty program, and some implications of subprofessional training. *American Psychologist* 1965, 20: 334-43.

Gordon, J.W. The psychologist as a consultant in an inservice program of child and youth study. *Journal of School Psychology* 1967, 6: 18-21.

Gordon, T. *Parent effectiveness training: The tested new way to raise responsible children*. New York: Wyden, 1970.

Gormally, J., and Hill, C.E. Guidelines for research on Carkhuff's training model. *Journal of Counseling Psychology* 1974, 21: 539-47.

Gottesfeld, H.; Rhee, C.; and Parker, G. A study of the role of paraprofessionals in community mental health. *Community Mental Health Journal* 1970, 6: 285-91.

Graff, H.; Kenig, L.; and Radoff, G. Prejudice of upper class therapists against lower class patients. *Psychiatric Quarterly* 1971, 45: 475-89.

Gray, J.J. Methods of training psychiatric residents in individual behavior therapy. *Journal of Behavior Therapy and Experimental Psychiatry* 1974, 5: 19-25.

Gray, R.M., and Kasteler, J.M. The effects of social reinforcement and training on institutionalized mentally retarded children. *American Journal of Mental Deficiency* 1969, 74: 50-56.

Greenbank, R.K., and Cameron, J.M. Mental health education for parents. *Mental Hygiene* 1968, 52: 587-89.

————, and Gilbert, A. Mental health education for parents. *Current Psychiatric Therapies* 1969, 9: 166-67.

Greenblatt, M., and Kantor, D. Student volunteer movement and the manpower shortage. *American Journal of Psychiatry* 1962, 118: 809-14.

Greene, R.J., and Hoats, D.L. Aversive tickling: A simple conditioning technique. *Behavior Therapy* 1971, 2: 389-93.

Grob, S. Psychiatric social clubs come of age. *Mental Hygiene* 1970, 54: 129-36.

Grosser, C. The role of the nonprofessional in the manpower development programs. In W. Amos (ed.), *Counseling the disadvantaged youth.* Englewood Cliffs, N.J.: Prentice-Hall, 1968.

_____ ; Henry, W.E.; and Kelly, J.G. (eds.). *Nonprofessionals in the human services.* San Francisco: Jossey-Bass, 1969.

Grossman, L., and Clark, D.H. Sensitivity training for teachers: A small group approach. *Psychology in the Schools* 1967, 4: 267-71.

Grundle, T.; Emiley, S.; and Webb, D. Entry credentialization and role change in consultation to a consultation program in a school system. *Journal of Community Psychology* 1973, 1: 383-86.

Gruver, G.G. College students as therapeutic agents. *Psychological Bulletin* 1971, 76: 111-27.

Guerney, B.G. Filial therapy: Description and rationale. *Journal of Consulting Psychology* 1964, 28: 304-10.

_____ . *Psychotherapeutic agents: New roles for nonprofessionals, parents, and teachers.* New York: Holt, 1969.

_____ , and Flumen, A.B. Teachers as psychotherapeutic agents for withdrawn children. *Journal of School Psychology* 1970, 8: 107-113.

_____ ; Guerney, L.F.; and Andronico, M.P. Filial therapy: A case illustration. *Yale Scientific Magazine* 1966, 40: 461-65.

_____ ; Stollak, G.E.; and Guerney, L. A format for a new mode of psychological practice. *Counseling Psychologist* 1970, 2: 97-104.

_____ ; _____ ; and _____ . The practicing psychologist as educator—an alternative to the medical practitioner model. *Professional Psychology* 1971, 2: 276-82.

Guess, D.; Smith, J.O.; and Ensminger, E.E. The role of nonprofessional persons in teaching language skills to mentally retarded children. *Exceptional Children* 1971, 37: 447-53.

Guidepost. American university tries peer counseling. 1974, 16: 5.

Gurin, G.; Veroff, J.; and Feld, S. *Americans view their mental health.* New York: Basic Books, 1960.

Gust, T. Support personnel vs. the counselor. *Counselor Education and Supervision* 1968, 7: 152-54.

Haak, M.A. The counselors workshop: Helping children learn about self. *Elementary School Guidance, and Counseling* 1972, 7: 226-30.

Haase, R.F., and DiMattia, D.J. The application of the microcounseling paradigm to the training of support personnel in counseling. In D.G. Zimpfer (ed.), *Paraprofessionals in counseling, guidance, and personnel services.* (APGA Reprint Series No. 5). Washington: American Personnel and Guidance Association, 1973.

_____ ; _____ ; and Guttman, M.A. Training of support personnel in three human relations skills: A systematic one-year follow-up. *Counselor Education and Supervision* 1972, 11: 194-99.

Hackney, H., and Nye, S. *Counseling strategies and objectives.* Englewood Cliffs, N.J.: Prentice-Hall, 1973.

Hadley, J.M.; True, J.E., and Kepes, S.Y. An experiment in the education of the pre-professional mental health worker: The Purdue program. *Community Mental Health Journal* 1970, 6: 40-50.

Halfacre, J., and Welch, F. Teacher consultation model: An operant approach. *Psychology in the Schools* 1973, 10: 494-97.

Hall, A.L., and Bourne, P.G. Indigenous therapists in a Southern black urban Community. *American Journal of Psychiatry* 1973, 28: 137-42.

Hall, R.V. Training teachers in classroom use of contingency management. *Educational Technology* 1971a, 11: 33-38.

_____. *Managing behavior. Part I: Behavior modification: The measurement of behavior.* Lawrence, Kans.: H & H Enterprises, 1971b.

_____. *Managing behavior. Part II: Behavior modification: Basic principles.* Lawrence, Kans.: H & H Enterprises, 1971c.

_____. *Managing behavior. Part III: Behavior modification: Applications in school and home.* Lawrence, Kans.: H & H Enterprises, 1971d.

Hall, S.M. Self-control and therapist control in the behavioral treatment of overweight women. *Behavior Research and Therapy* 1972, 10: 59-68.

Halleck, S.L. Psychiatry and the status quo: A political analysis of psychiatric practice. *Archives of General Psychiatry* 1968, 19: 257-65.

Hallowitz, E. The role of a neighborhood service center in community mental health. *American Journal of Orthopsychiatry* 1968, 38: 705-14.

_____, and Riessman, F. The role of the indigenous nonprofessional in a community mental health neighborhood service center program. *American Journal of Orthopsychiatry* 1967, 37: 766-78.

Halpern, W.I. The community mental health aide. *Mental Hygiene* 1969, 53: 78-83.

Hamburg, B.A., and Varenhorst, B.B. Peer counseling in the secondary schools: A community mental health project for youth. *American Journal of Orthopsychiatry* 1972, 42: 566-81.

Hammer, H.M. A ministerial training program in community mental health. *Mental Hygiene* 1965, 49: 520-24.

Hammerman, J. Health services: Their success and failure in reaching older adults. *American Journal of Public Health* 1974, 64: 253-56.

Hansell, N. The service context of psychiatric education. *Comprehensive Psychiatry* 1973, 14: 339-51.

_____; Wodarczyk, M.; and Visotsky, V. The mental health expediter. *Archives of General Psychiatry* 1968, 18: 392-99.

Hanson, P.G.; Rothaus, P.; O'Connell, W.E.; and Wiggens, G. Training patients for effective participation in back-home groups. *American Journal of Psychiatry* 1969, 126: 857-62.

_____. Some basic concepts in human relations training for patients. *Hospital and Community Psychiatry* 1970, 21: 137-43.

Harris, E.T. Parents Without Partners, Inc.: A resource for clients. *Social Work* 1966, 11: 92-98.

Hart, W.T., and Bassett, L. Delivery of services to lower socioeconomic groups by a suburban community mental health center. *American Journal of Psychiatry* 1972, 129: 191-96.

Harlage, L.C. Subprofessional therapists' use of reinforcement versus traditional psychotherapeutic techniques with schizophrenics. *Journal of Consulting and Clinical Psychology* 1970, 34: 181-83.

Hartog, J. A classification of mental health non-professionals. *Mental Hygiene* 1967, 51: 517-23.

Hauer, A.L. Adjunct counselors in college. *Personnel and Guidance Journal* 1973, 52: 43-46.

Hawkins, R.P. Universal parenthood training: A laboratory approach to teaching child-rearing skills to every parent. *Educational Technology* 1971, 11: 28-31.

_____; Peterson, R.F.; Schweid, E.; and Bijou, S.W. Behavior therapy in the home: Amelioration of problem parent-child relations with the parent in a therapeutic role. *Journal of Experimental Child Psychology* 1966, 4: 99-107.

Hawxhurst, D., and Walzer, H. Patients helping patients. *Mental Hygiene* 1970, 54: 370-73.

Haynes, S. Altering parental attitudes toward child-rearing practices using parent education groups. Unpublished research, 1972.

Heilig, S.M.; Farberow, N.L.; Litman, R.E.; and Shneidman, E.S. The role of nonprofessional volunteers in a suicide prevention center. *Community Mental Health Journal* 1968, 4: 287-95.

Henderson, J. Training groups for public health nurses. *Canada's Mental Health* 1973, 21: 12-14.

Hersch, C. The discontent explosion in mental health. *American Psychologist* 1968, 23: 497-506.

_____. Social history, mental health, and community control. *American Psychologist* 1972, 27: 749-54.

Hersch, P.D.; Kulik, J.A.; and Scheibe, K.E. Personal characteristics of college volunteers in mental hospitals. *Journal of Consulting and Clinical Psychology* 1969, 33: 30-34.

Hicks, J.M., and Spaner, F.E. Attitude change as a function of mental hospital experience. *Journal of Abnormal and Social Psychology* 1962, 65: 112-20.

Higgins, W.H.; Ivey, A.E.; and Uhlemann, M.R. Media therapy: A programmed approach to teaching behavioral skills. *Journal of Counseling Psychology* 1970, 17: 20-26.

Hiltner, S. Theological consultants in hospitals and mental health centers. *American Journal of Psychiatry* 1972, 128: 965-69.

Hirschowitz, R.G. Psychiatric education for nonpsychiatric physicians. *Archives of General Psychiatry* 1972, 27: 833-38.

_____. Foster grandparents program: Preventive intervention with the elderly poor. *Hospital and Community Psychiatry* 1973, 24: 558-59.

Hitchcock, J.E. Community mental health nursing: An innovative use of the nurses evolving role. *Community Mental Health Journal* 1971, 7: 3-12.

Hobbs, N. Mental health's third revolution. *American Journal of Orthopsychiatry* 1964, 34: 822-33.

Hodgman, E., and Stein, E. The cooperative apartment. *Community Mental Health Journal* 1966, 2: 347-52.

Holbrook, R.L. Student volunteers as helpers in residence halls. *Journal of College Student Personnel* 1972, 13: 559-61.

Hollander, M.A., and Plutchik, R. A reinforcement program for psychiatric attendants. *Journal of Behavior Therapy and Experimental Psychiatry* 1972, 3: 297-300.

Hollister, W.G. Five years' experience with lay discussion leaders in mental health education. *Mental Hygiene* 1958, 42: 106-17.

Holzberg, J.D. The companion program: Implementing the manpower recommendations of the joint commission on mental illness and health. *American Psychologist* 1963, 18: 224-26.

_____, and Gewirtz. H. A method of altering attitudes toward mental illness. *Psychiatric Quarterly Supplement* 1963, 37: 56-61.

_____; _____; and Ebner, E. Changes in moral judgment and self-acceptance as a function of companionship with hospitalized mental patients. *Journal of Consulting Psychology* 1964, 28: 299-303.

_____, and Knapp, R.H. The social interaction of college students and chronically ill mental patients. *American Journal of Orthopsychiatry* 1965, 35: 487-92.

_____; _____; and Turner, J.L. Companionship with the mentally ill: Effects on the personalities of college student volunteers. *Psychiatry* 1966, 29: 395-405.

_____; _____; and _____. College students as companions to the mentally ill. In E.L. Cowen, E.A. Gardner, and M. Zax (eds.), *Emergent approaches to mental health problems.* New York: Appleton-Century-Crofts, 1967.

Homme, L.; Cxanyi, A.P.; Gonzales, M.A.; and Rechs, J.R. *How to use contingency contracting in the classroom.* Champaign, Ill.: Research Press, 1970.

Huessy, H.H.; Marshall, C.D.; Lincoln, E.K.; and Finan, J.L. The indigenous nurse as crisis counselor and intervener. *American Journal of Public Health* 1969, 59: 2022-28.

Hunt, G.H., and Odoroff, M.E. Follow-up study of narcotic drug addicts after hospitalization. *Public Health Reports* 1962, 77: 41-54.

Hunt, W.J. *Training program for bartenders as mental health referral agents: Preliminary report.* Milwaukee, Wis.: Milwaukee County Mental Health Association, 1972.

Huntington, A.S. *The prevention and early recognition of mental illness: A guide for nurses.* Providence: Rhode Island Department of Social Welfare, 1968.

Hurvitz, N. Peer self-help psychotherapy groups and their implications for psychotherapy. *Psychotherapy: Theory, Research and Practice* 1970, 1: 41-49.

Huseman, R.C. Interpersonal communication training for police: An evaluation. *Journal of Police Science and Administration* 1973, 1: 355-61.

Iscoe, I. Professional and subprofessional training in community mental health as an aspect of community psychology. In G. Rosenblum (ed.), *Issues in community psychology and preventive mental health.* New York: Behavioral Publications, 1971.

_____. Community psychology and the competent community. *American Psychologist* 1974, 29: 607-13.

_____, and Spielberger, C.D. *Community psychology: Perspectives in training and research.* New York: Appleton-Century-Crofts, 1970.

Ishiyama, T.; McCulley, W.; and Rodriguez, O. Does the psychiatric aide have a treatment role? *Mental Hygiene* 1967, 51: 115-18.

Ivey, A.E. *Microcounseling: Innovations in interview training.* Springfield, Ill.: Charles C Thomas, 1971.

_____. Media therapy: Educational change planning for psychiatric patients. *Journal of Counseling Psychology* 1973a, 20: 338-43.

_____. Counseling: The innocent profession or fiddling while Rome burns. *Counseling Psychologist* 1973b, 9: 111-15.

_____. Microcounseling: The counselor as trainer. *Personnel and Guidance Journal* 1973c, 51: 311-16.

_____. Microcounseling and media therapy: State of the art. *Counselor Education and Supervision* 1974a, 13: 172-83.

_____. The clinician as teacher of interpersonal skills: Let's give away what we've got. *Clinical Psychologist* 1974b, 27: 6-9.

_____, and Leppaluoto, J.R. Changes ahead! Implications of the Vail Conference. *Personnel and Guidance Journal* 1975, 53: 747-52.

_____; Normington, C.J.; Miller, C.D.; Morrill, W.H.; and Haase, R.F. Microcounseling and attending behavior: An approach to prepracticum counselor training. *Journal of Counseling Psychology* 1968, 15: 1-12.

Jackson, A.M. Psychotherapy: Factors associated with the race of the therapist. *Psychotherapy: Theory, Research and Practice* 1973, 10: 273-77.

Jackson, M., and Thompson, C.L. The effective counselor: Characteristics and attitudes. *Journal of Counseling Psychology* 1971, 18: 249-53.

Jacob, T. A survey of graduate education in community psychology. *American Psychologist* 1971, 26: 940-44.

Jacobson, G.F. Emergency services in community mental health: Problems and promise. *American Journal of Public Health* 1974, 64: 124-28.

Janes, H.D. The welfare agency role in staff and volunteer training. *Personnel Journal* 8, 47: 420-23.

Jansen, D.G., and Garvey, F.J. High-, average- and low-rated clergymen in a state hospital clinical program. *Journal of Clinical Psychology* 1973, 29: 89-92.

_____ , and _____ . Self-actualization of clergymen rated high and low in clinical competencies. *Counselor Education and Supervision* 1974, 13: 298-302.

_____ ; Robb, G.P.; and Bonk, E.C. Clergymen as counselor trainees: Comparisons with counselors rated most and least competent by their peers. *Journal of Clinical Psychology* 1972, 28: 601-3.

Jarmusz, R.T. Some considerations in establishing a suicide prevention service. *Mental Hygiene* 1969, 53: 351-56.

Jason, L.; Clarfield, S.; and Cowen, E.L. Preventive intervention with young disadvantaged children. *American Journal of Community Psychology* 1973, 1: 50-61.

Johnson, C.A., and Katz, R.C. Using parents as change agents for their children: A review. *Journal of Child Psychology and Psychiatry* 1973, 14: 181-200.

Johnson, C.T. Paraprofessionals bridging the gap. *American Journal of Orthopsychiatry* 1971, 41: 234-35.

Johnson, D.L.; Hanson, P.G.; Rothaus, P.; Morton, R.B.; Lyle, F.A.; and Moyer, R. Human relations training for psychiatric patients: A follow-up study. *International Journal of Social Psychiatry* 1965, 11: 188-96.

_____ ; Leler, H.; Rios, L.; Brandt, L.; Kahn, A.J.; Mazeika, E.; Frede, M.; and Bisett, B. The Houston Parent-Child Development Center: A parent education program for Mexican-American families. *American Journal of Orthopsychiatry* 1974, 44: 121-28.

Johnson, D.W. *Reaching out: Interpersonal effectiveness and self-actualization.* Englewood Cliffs, N.J.: Prentice-Hall, 1972.

Johnson, R. Some casework aspects of using foster grandparents for emotionally disturbed children. *Children* 1967, 14: 46-52.

Joint Commission on Mental Health of Children. *Crisis in child mental health: Challenge for the 1970's.* New York: Harper & Row, 1970.

Joint Commission on Mental Illness and Health. *Action for mental health.* New York: Basic Books, 1961.

Jones, E. Social class and psychotherapy: A critical review of research. *Psychiatry* 1974, 37: 307-20.

Jones, J.E. Types of growth groups. In J.W. Pfeifer and J.E. Jones (eds.), *The 1972 annual handbook for group facilitators.* La Jolla, Calif.: University Associates, 1972.

Jones, M. *The therapeutic community.* New York: Basic Books, 1953.

_____ . *Beyond the therapeutic community.* New Haven, Conn.: Yale University Press, 1968.

Jones, W.L. The A-B-C method of crisis management. *Mental Hygiene* 1968, 52: 87-89.

Kadish, J. Mental health training of police officers. *Mental Hygiene* 1966, 50: 205-10.

Kadushin, L., and Kadushin, A. The ex-addict as a member of the therapeutic team. *Community Mental Health Journal* 1969, 5: 386-93.

Kagan, N. *Influencing human interaction.* East Lansing, Mich.: Instructional Media Center, Michigan State University, 1971.

Kahn, M.W., and Delk, J.L. Developing a community mental health clinic on the Papago Indians reservation. *International Journal of Social Psychiatry* 1973, 19: 299-306.

Kalafat, J., and Tyler, M. The community approach: Programs and implications for a campus mental health agency. *Professional Psychology* 1973, 4: 43-49.

Kale, R.J., Zlutnik, S., and Hopkins, B.L. Patient contributions to a therapeutic environment. In R. Ulrich, T. Stachnik, and J. Mabry (eds.), *Control of human behavior II.* Glenview, Ill.: Scott, Foresman, 1970.

Kalis, B.L. Orientation to community mental health for clinicians in training. *Community Mental Health Journal* 1973, 9: 316-24.

Kanfer, F.H., and Phillips, J.S. *Learning foundations of behavior therapy.* New York: Wiley, 1970.

Kaplan, H.M. Learning to deal with a crisis. *Empire Magazine* November 12, 1972.

Kaplan, S.R., and Roman, S.R. *The organization and delivery of mental health services in the ghetto: The Lincoln Hospital experience.* New York: Praeger, 1973.

Karlins, M., and Abelson, H.I. *Persuasion: How opinions and attitudes are changed.* New York: Springer, 1970.

Karlsruher, A.E. The nonprofessional as a psychotherapeutic agent: A review of the empirical evidence pertaining to his effectiveness. *American Journal of Community Psychology* 1974, 2: 61-76.

Karnes, M.B.; Teska, J.A.; Hodgins, A.S.; and Badger, E.C. Educational intervention at home by mothers of disadvantaged infants. *Child Development* 1970, 41: 925-36.

Karno, M.; Ross, R.N.; and Caper, R.A. Mental health roles of physicians in a Mexican-American community. *Community Mental Health Journal* 1969, 5: 62-69.

Katahn, M. A survey of the interest in continuing education among mental health professionals in the southeastern states. *American Psychologist* 1970, 25: 941-52.

Katz, M. Family crisis training: Upgrading the police while building a bridge to the minority community. *Journal of Police Science and Administration* 1973, 1: 30-35.

Kaufman, M.R. Problems of undergraduate psychiatric teaching. *Seminars in Psychiatry* 1970, 2: 145-61.

_____. The teaching of psychiatry to the nonpsychiatrist physician. *American Journal of Psychiatry* 1971, 128: 610-16.

Kazdin, A.E. Issues in behavior modification with mentally retarded persons. *American Journal of Mental Deficiency* 1973, 78: 134-40.

Kelly, E.W., and Midgette, J.L. Librarian-counselor: A place to begin? *Elementary School Guidance and Counseling* 1972, 7: 188-93.

Kelly, J.G. The mental health agent in the urban community. In *Urban America and the planning of mental health services.* New York: Group for the Advancement of Psychiatry, 1964.

Kent, R.I. Patients help ward operations. *Hospital and Community Psychiatry* 1969, 20: 84.

Kiesler, D.J. Some myths of psychotherapy research and the search for a paradigm. *Psychological Bulletin* 1966, 65: 110-36.

_____. Experimental designs in psychotherapy research. In A.E. Bergin and S.L. Garfield (eds.), *Handbook of psychotherapy and behavior change.* New York: Wiley, 1971.

Kiev, A. *Curanderismo: Mexican-American folk psychiatry.* New York: Free Press, 1968.

_____. *Transcultural psychiatry.* New York: Free Press, 1972.

_____(ed.). *Magic, faith, and healing.* New York: Free Press, 1974.

Kilburn, K.L.; McDole, G.; and Smith, R.E. The Strong Vocational Interest Blank as a measure of success in the training of psychiatric technicians. *Psychological Reports* 1970, 26: 883-86.

Killeen, M., and Schmitz, M. A hotline cools off. *Personnel and Guidance Journal* 1973, 52: 250-52.

Kim, B.C. Asian-Americans: No model minority. *Mental Health Digest* 1973, 5: 46.

Kincaid, M. Identity and therapy in the black community. *Personnel and Guidance Journal* 1969, 47: 884-90.

King, M.; Walder, L.O.; and Pavey, S. Personality change as a function of volunteer experience in a psychiatric hospital. *Journal of Consulting and Clinical Psychology* 1970, 35: 423-25.

Kirk, B.A.; Free, J.E.; Johnson, A.P.; Michel, J.; Redfield, J.E.; Roston, R.A.; and Warman, R.E. Guidelines for university and college counseling centers. *American Psychologist* 1971, 26: 585-89.

Kish, G.B., and Hood, R. Voluntary activity promotes more realistic conceptions of the mentally ill by college students. *Journal of Community Psychology* 1974, 21: 30-32.

_____, and Stage, T. College student mental hospital volunteers: Any benefits to the student or to society? *Journal of Community Psychology* 1973, 1: 13-15.

Kivowitz, J., and Keirn, W. A genetics counseling clinic in a mental health setting. *Hospital and Community Psychiatry* 1973, 24: 156-58.

Klein, D.C., and Ross, A. Kindergarten entry: A study of role-transition. In H.J. Parad (ed.), *Crisis intervention: Selected readings.* New York: Family Service Association of America, 1965.

Kleinman, A.M. Some issues for a comparative study of medical healing. *International Journal of Social Psychiatry* 1973, 19: 159-65.

Knapp, R.H., and Holzberg, J.D. Characteristics of college students volunteering for service to mental patients. *Journal of Consulting Psychology* 1964, 28: 82-85.

Knopp, W.; Johnson, E.W.; Derbyshire, J.S.; and Saltis, L.M. Planning and executing a course in human behavior and relations for first-year medical students. *Journal of Medical Education* 1970, 45: 160-67.

Knott, P.D. On the manpower problem and graduate training in clinical psychology. *American Psychologist* 1969, 24: 675-79.

Knowles, L. Evaluation of P.E.T.: Does improved communication result in better understanding? Unpublished research.

Knox, W.J. Attitudes of psychologists toward alcoholism. *Journal of Clinical Psychology* 1969, 25: 446-50.

_____. Attitudes of psychiatrists and psychologists toward alcoholism. *American Journal of Psychiatry* 1971, 127: 1675-79.

Koegler, R.R., and Williamson, E.R. A group approach to helping emotionally disturbed Spanish-speaking patients. *Hospital and Community Psychiatry* 1973, 24: 334-37.

Kohan, S.; Chung, S.Y.; and Stone, J. Expanding the pharmacists' role in a psychiatric hospital. *Hospital and Community Psychiatry* 1973, 24: 164-66.

Korman, M. National conference on levels and patterns of professional training in psychology: The major themes. *American Psychologist* 1974, 29: 441-49.

Korson, S.M., and Hayes, W.L. Empathic relationship therapy utilizing student nurses: A five-year pilot study. *American Journal of Psychiatry* 1966, 123: 213-16.

Kraft, I.A. Volunteers as social-work technicians in a child psychiatry clinic. *Mental Hygiene* 1966, 50: 460-62.

Krakowski, A.J. The role of medicine in community psychiatry: A proposal. *Psychosomatics* 1970, 11: 13-17.

Kramer, H.C., and Barr, D.J. In-service training for campus police. *Community Mental Health Journal* 1974, 10: 180-84.

Krasner, L. The operant approach in behavior therapy. In A.E. Bergin and S.L. Garfield (eds.), *Handbook of psychotherapy and behavior change.* New York: Wiley, 1971.

_____, and Ullman, L.P. (eds.). *Research in behavior modification: New developments and implications.* New York: Holt, 1965.

Krasnoff, H. A practicum in community organization for psychiatric technicians. *Journal of the Fort Logan Mental Health Center* 1970, 6: 53-60.

Kratochvil, D. Changes in values and interpersonal functioning of nurses in training. *Counselor Education and Supervision* 1969, 8: 104-7.

Kreisman, J.J. The curandero's apprentice: A therapeutic integration of folk and medical healing. *American Journal of Psychiatry* 1975, 132: 81-83.

Kriegman, G.; Harris, M.D.; and Rosinski, E.F. A continuing educational program for paramedical personnel. *Community Mental Health Journal* 1968, 4: 377-87.

Kroeker, L.L.; Forsyth, D.R.; and Haase, R.F. Evaluation of a police-youth human relations program. *Professional Psychology* 1974, 5: 140-54.

Kurtz, R.R., and Grumman, D.L. Different approaches to the measurement of therapist empathy and their relationship to therapy outcomes. *Journal of Consulting and Clinical Psychology* 1972, 39: 106-15.

Laemmel, K. Psychodynamic sensitization for teachers. *Psychology in the Schools* 1969, 6: 204-205.

Lamb, H.R., and Goertzel, V. Ellsworth House: A community alternative to jail. *American Journal of Psychiatry* 1974, 131: 64-68.

Lambie, D.Z., and Weikart, D.P. Ypsilanti-Carnegie infant education project. In J. Hellmuth (ed.), *Disadvantaged child*, vol. 3. New York: Brunner-Mazel, 1970.

Larson, R.S. Can parent classes affect family communications? *School Counselor* 1972, 19: 261-70.

Laufer, L.G. Group therapy, sensitivity training groups and the industrial physician. *Journal of Occupational Medicine* 1968, 10: 124-26.

Lawton, M.P. Correlates of the opinion about mental illness scale. *Journal of Consulting Psychology* 1964, 28: 94.

_____. Personality and attitudinal correlates of psychiatric-aide performance. *Journal of Social Psychology* 1965, 66: 215-26.

_____. Social ecology and the health of older people. *American Journal of Public Health* 974, 64: 257-60.

_____, and Goldman, A.E. Role conceptions of the psychiatric aide. *Genetic Psychology Monographs* 1965, 71: 311-48.

_____, and Lipton, M.B. Student-employees become companions to patients. *Mental Hospitals* 1963, 14: 550-56.

Lazarus, A.A. *Behavior therapy and beyond.* New York: McGraw-Hill, 1971.

Lebow, M.D. Behavior modification in parent-child therapy: A bibliography. *JSAS Catalog of Selected Documents in Psychology* 1973, 3: 12-13.

Lee, D., and Znachko, G. Training psychiatric aides in behavioral modification techniques. *Journal of Psychiatric Nursing and Mental Health Services* 1968, 6: 7-11.

Lee, D.T. Recovery, Inc.: Aide in the transition from hospital to community. *Mental Hygiene* 1971, 55: 194-98.

Lehmann, S. Selected self-help: A study of clients of a community social psychiatry service. *American Journal of Psychiatry* 1970, 126: 1444-54.

Leibowitz, Z., and Rhoads, D.J. Adolescent peer counseling. *School Counselor* 1974, 21: 280-83.

LeMasters, E.E. Parenthood as crisis. In H.J. Parad (ed.), *Crisis intervention: Selected readings.* New York: Family Service Association of America, 1965.

Lentz, R.J., and Paul, G.L. "Routine" vs. "therapeutic" transfer of chronic mental patients. *Archives of General Psychiatry*, 1971, 25: 187-92.

_____; _____; and Calhoun, J.F. Reliability and validity of three measures of functioning with "hard-core" chronic mental patients. *Journal of Abnormal Psychology* 1971, 78: 69-76.

Leon, R.L. Some implications for a preventive program for American Indians. *American Journal of Psychiatry* 1968, 125: 232-36.

Leonard, A.R., and King, E.S. Involving public health nurses in mental health work with patients and families before and after discharge. *Hospital and Community Psychiatry* 1968, 19: 321-24.

Levenson, A.I., and Reff, S.R. Community mental health center staffing patterns. *Community Mental Health Journal* 1970, 6: 118-25.

Levenstein, P. Cognitive growth in pre-schoolers through stimulation of verbal interaction with mothers. *American Journal of Orthopsychiatry* 1970, 40: 426-32.

Levine, M. Scientific method and the adversary model: Some preliminary thoughts. *American Psychologist* 1974, 29: 661-77.

_____ , and Graziano, A.M. Intervention programs in elementary schools. In S.E. Golann and C. Eisdorfer (eds.), *Handbook of community mental health.* New York: Appleton-Century-Crofts, 1972.

Levinson, B.M. The veterinarian and mental hygiene. *Mental Hygiene* 1965, 49: 320-23.

Levis, D.J. Behavioral therapy: The fourth therapeutic revolution? In D.J. Levis (ed.), *Learning approaches to therapeutic behavior change.* Chicago: Aldine, 1970.

Levitz, L.S., and Stunkard, A.J. A therapeutic coalition for obesity: Behavior modification and patient self-help. *American Journal of Psychiatry* 1974, 131: 423-27.

Levy, B.S. Five years after: A follow-up of 50 narcotic addicts. *American Journal of Psychiatry* 1972, 128: 868-72.

Levy, L. The role of a natural mental health service delivery system in dealing with basic human problems. In G.A. Specter and W.L. Claiborn (eds.), *Crisis intervention.* New York: Behavioral Publications, 1973.

Lewis, I.L., and Cleveland, S.E. Nursing students' attitudinal changes following a psychiatric affiliation. *Journal of Psychiatric Nursing* 1966, 4: 223-31.

Liberman, R. The role of physicians in the patient's path to the mental hospital. *Community Mental Health Journal* 1967, 3: 325-30.

_____ . Police as a community mental health resource. *Community Mental Health Journal* 1969, 5: 111-20.

Lief, H.I. Subprofessional training in mental health. *Archives of General Psychiatry* 1966, 15: 660-64.

_____ . New developments in the sex education of the physician. *Journal of the American Medical Association* 1970, 212: 1864-67.

Lifton, W.M. *Working with groups: Group process and individual growth.* New York: Wiley, 1967.

Lillibridge, M. The relationship of a P.E.T. program to change in parents' self-assessed attitudes and children's perceptions of parents. Unpublished doctoral dissertation, 1971.1

Limbacher, W.J. An approach to elementary training in mental health. *Journal of School Psychology* 1967, 5: 225-34.

Lindemann, E. Symptomatology and management of acute grief. *American Journal of Psychiatry* 1944, 101: 141-48.

Lippitt, R. Dimensions of a consultant's job. *Journal of Social Issues* 1959, 15: 5-12.

Lipsitt, P.D., and Steinbruner, M. An experiment in police-community relations: A small group approach. *Community Mental Health Journal* 1969, 5: 172-79.

Locke, B.Z., and Gardner, E.A. Psychiatric disorders among the patients of general practitioners and internists. *Public Health Reports* 1969, 84: 167-74.

Lockwood, J.A., and Dingman, P.R. A small state looks at local casework and mental health. *American Journal of Orthopsychiatry* 1971, 41: 243.

Lombardo, A. A mental health curriculum for the lower grades. *Mental Hygiene* 1968, 52: 570-76.

Long, B.E. Educational change with elementary school psychology curriculum. *Professional Psychology* 1974, 5: 166-74.

Looff, D.H. Appalachian public health nursing: Mental health component in eastern Kentucky. *Community Mental Health Journal* 1969, 5: 295-303.

Lorion, R.P.; Cowen, E.L.; and Kraus, R.M. Contact frequency and duration regularities in a school based mental health project. *Journal of Consulting and Clinical Psychology* 1974, 42: 346-52.

Lourie, R.S.; Rioch, M.J.; and Schwartz, S. The concept of a training program for child development counselors. *Americal Journal of Public Health* 1967, 57: 1754-58.

Lubchansky, I.; Egri, G.; and Stokes, J. Puerto Rican spiritualists view mental illness: The faith healer as a paraprofessional. *American Journal of Psychiatry* 1970, 127: 312-21.

Luborsky, L.; Auerbach, A.H.; Chandler, M.; Cohen, J.; and Bachrach, H.M. Factors influencing the outcome of psychotherapy: A review of quantitative research. *Psychological Bulletin* 1971, 75: 145-85.

Ludwig, A.M., and Marx, A.J. The buddy treatment model for chronic schizophrenics. *Journal of Nervous and Mental Disease* 1969, 148, 528-41.

Lundell, K.T. *Behavior contracting kit for teachers and parents.* Linden, N.J.: Remediation Associates, 1972.

Lurie, A., and Ron, H. Self-help in an aftercare socialization program. *Mental Hygiene* 1971, 55: 467-72.

Lykke, R.L. Consulting with the principal: A must. *Elementary School Guidance and Counseling* 1972, 7: 129.

Lynch, M., and Gardner, E.A. Some issues raised in the training of paraprofessional personnel as clinic therapists. *American Journal of Psychiatry* 1970, 126: 1473-79.

McBride, M. Developing a student volunteer program for residence halls. *Journal of College Student Personnel* 1973, 14: 317-20.

McCarthy, B.W. New approaches to mental health services in colleges and universities. *Psychological Reports* 1970, 27: 420-22.

_____ and Berman, A.L. The development of a student-operated crisis center. *Personnel and Guidance Journal* 1971, 49: 523-28.

_____, and Michaud, P.A. Companions: An adjunct to counseling. *Personnel and Guidance Journal* 1971, 49: 839-41.

McClure, J.N., Jr.; Wetzel, R.D.; Flanagan, T.A.; McCabe, M.; and Murphy, G.E. Volunteers in a suicide prevention service. *Journal of Community Psychology* 973, 1: 397-98.

McCord, J.B., and Packwood, W.T. Crisis centers and hotlines: A survey. *Personnel and Guidance Journal* 1973, 51: 723-28.

McIntyre, R. *For love of children: Behavioral psychology for parents.* Del Mar, Calif.: CRM Books, 1970.

McKinney, J.P., and Keele, T. Effects of increased mothering on the behavior of severely retarded boys. *American Journal of Mental Deficiency* 1963, 67: 556-62.

McNally, H.A., and Drummond, R. Ratings of Carkhuff's facilitative conditions: A second look. *Counselor Education and Supervision* 1974, 14: 73-75.

McNamara, J.R., and Diehl, L.A. Behavioral consultation with a headstart program. *Journal of Community Psychology* 1974, 2: 352-57.

McPheeters, H.L. The middle-level mental health worker: II. His training. *Hospital and Community Psychiatry* 1972, 23: 334-35.

_____; King, J.B.; and Teare, R.J. The middle-level mental health worker: I. His role. *Hospital and Community Psychiatry* 1972, 23: 329-34.

McWilliams, S.A. A process analysis of a school-based mental health program. *Journal of School Psychology* 1972, 10: 367-77.

_____, and Finkel, N.J. High school students as mental health aides in the elementary school setting. *Journal of Consulting and Clinical Psychology* 1973, 40: 39-42.

_____, and Morris, L.A. Community attitudes about mental health services. *Community Mental Health Journal* 1974, 10: 236-42.

Mabel, S. Outcome of patients' assuming a staff function. *Hospital and Community Psychiatry* 1971, 22: 25-28.

Mackay, M.W., and Serrano, A.C. Involving public health nurses in mental health care. Part II: Crisis intervention for troubled families. *Hospital and Community Psychiatry* 1968, 19: 324-26.

Maclennan, B.W. Special problems in training the non-professional. In B.G. Guerney (ed.), *Psychotherapeutic agents: New roles for nonprofessionals, parents, and teachers.* New York: Holt, 1969.

_____, Klein, W.; Pearl, A.; and Fishman, J. Training for new careers. *Community Mental Health Journal* 1966, 2: 135-41.

Madsen, C.H., Jr.; Madsen, C.K.; Saudargas, R.A.; Hammond, W.R.; and Smith, J.B. Classroom raid (rules, approval, ignore, disapproval): A cooperative approach for professionals and volunteers. *Journal of School Psychology* 1970, 8: 180-85.

Magaro, P.A., and Staples, S.B. Schizophrenic patients as therapists: An expansion of the prescriptive treatment system based upon pre-morbid adjustment, social class and A-B status. *Psychotherapy: Theory, Research and Practice* 1972, 9: 352-58.

Magoon, T.M., and Golann, S.E. Non-traditionally trained women as mental health counselors/psychotherapists. *Personnel and Guidance Journal* 1966, 44: 788-92.

_____; _____; and Freeman, R.W. *Mental health counselors at work.* London: Pergamon Press, 1969.

Maholick, L.T. A delivery system for local mental health services. *American Journal of Public Health* 1972, 62: 364-69.

_____; Shapiro, D.S.; and Crumbaugh, J.C. The Bradley Center community-wide mental health assessment program: An introduction. *Psychological Reports* 1960, 6: 358.

Maierle, J.P. The politics of supporting paraprofessionals. *Professional Psychology* 1973, 4: 313-20.

Malan, D.H. The outcome problem in psychotherapy research. *Archives of General Psychiatry* 1973, 29: 719-29.

Malcolm, A.H. Bartenders being trained to provide counseling as well as drinks. *New York Times*, October 13, 1974.

Mandeville, P.F., and Maholick, L.T. Changing points of emphasis in training the community's natural counselors. *Mental Hygiene* 1969, 53: 208-15.

Mann, P.A. Establishing a mental health consultation program with a police department. *Community Mental Health Journal* 1971, 7: 118-26.

March, M. The neighborhood center concept. *Public Welfare* 1968, 26: 97-111.

Margolis, P.M., and Bonstedt, T. What is community psychiatry? *Diseases of the Nervous System* 1970, 31: 251-58.

Marler, D.C. The nonprofessionalization of the war on mental illness. *Mental Hygiene* 1971, 55: 291-94.

Marston, A.R. It is time to reconsider the Graduate Record Examination. *American Psychologist* 1971, 26: 653-55.

Martin, F. Teacher inservice training in classroom use of contingency management. *Psychology in the Schools* 1973, 10: 226-30.

Martinez, C., and Martin, H.W. Folk diseases among urban Mexican-Americans. *Journal of the American Medical Association* 1966, 196: 161-64.

Mason, R.; Holt, F.D.; and Newsome, G. Human nature and authoritarianism in seminary students and counselor trainees. *Personnel and Guidance Journal* 1969, 47: 689-92.

Matarazzo, J.D. Changing concepts: Care and caregivers—three points of view. *Mental Hygiene* 1968, 52: 165-67, 197-98.

Matarazzo, J.D. A national mental health manpower showcase conference: NAMH leads the way. *Mental Hygiene* 1970, 54: 333-36.

_____. Some national developments in the utilization of nontraditional mental health manpower. *American Psychologist* 1971, 26: 363-72.

Matarazzo, R.G. Research on the teaching and learning of psychotherapeutic skills. In A.E. Bergin and S.L. Garfield (eds.), *Handbook of psychotherapy and behavior change.* New York: Wiley, 1971.

Mathis, J. A teaching problem in psychiatry: One solution. *Journal of Medical Education* 1965, 40: 882-84.

Matthews, R.A., and Rowland, L.W. *How to recognize and handle abnormal people: A manual for the police officer.* New York: National Association for Mental Health, 1960.

Mayer, J., and Myerson, D.J. Training the physician in alcoholism therapy. *Journal of Medical Education* 1972, 47: 296-97.

Mayo, J.A. The significance of socio-cultural variables in psychiatric treatment of black outpatients. *Comprehensive Psychiatry* 1974, 15: 471-82.

Mazza, J., and Pumroy, D.K. A review of evaluation of behavior modification programs. *Psychological Record* 1975, 25: 111-21.

Means, B.L. Levels of empathic response. *Personnel and Guidance Journal* 1973, 52: 23-28.

Megenity, D.D.; Russell, K.R.; and Kerkoski, J. Undergraduate college students as child-care workers in a state hospital. *Hospital and Community Psychiatry* 1972, 23: 223-25.

Mehr, J. Evaluating nontraditional training for psychiatric aides. *Hospital and Community Psychiatry* 1971, 22: 315-18.

_____; Truckenbrod, P.; and Fisher, W. Core-competence training manual. *JSAS Catalog of Selected Documents* 1973, 3: 90.

Meltzoff, J., and Kornreich, M. *Research in psychotherapy.* New York: Atherton Press, 1970.

Mendel, W.M. Psychiatric consultation education—1966. *American Journal of Psychiatry* 1966, 123: 150-55.

_____, and Rapport, S. Outpatient treatment for chronic schizophrenic patients: Therapeutic consequences of an existential view. *Archives of General Psychiatry* 1963, 8: 190-96.

_____; Wexler, M.; and Brotman, S. Group psychotherapy as a technique for teaching psychiatry to medical students. *Journal of Medical Education* 1964, 89: 497-501.

Mental Hygiene News. Foster grandparents program flourishes at Gouverneur. 1973, 44: 5.

Mesmer, R.E.; Roueche, M.S.; Hagberg, F.G.; and Bergman, L.A. Pastoral counseling seminars for rural clergymen. *Hospital and Community Psychiatry* 1971, 22: 61-62.

Meyer, E.J. Lawyer in a mental hospital: The New York experiment. *Mental Hygiene* 1969, 53: 14-16.

Meyer, H.J. Sociological comments. In C. Grosser, W.E. Henry, and J.G. Kelly (eds.), *Nonprofessionals in the human services*. San Francisco: Jossey-Bass, 1969.

Miller, C.D.; Morrill, W.H.; Ivey, A.E.; Normington, C.J.; and Uhlemann, M.R. Microcounseling: Techniques in assessing clients' attitudes toward guidance tests. *Counselor Education and Supervision* 1973, 13: 14-23.

Miller, D. Alternatives to mental patient rehospitalization. *Community Mental Health Journal* 1966, 2: 124-28.

Miller, G.E. Continuing education for what? *Journal of Medical Education* 1967, 42: 320-26.

Miller, H. *A mental health education program for North Dakota's beverage handlers*. Bismark, N.Dak.: North Dakota Mental Health Association, 1973.

Miller, S.I., and Schoenfeld, L. Grief in the Navajo: Psychodynamics and culture. *International Journal of Social Psychiatry* 1973, 19: 187-91.

Mira, M. Results of a behavior modification training program for parents and teachers. *Behavior Research and Therapy* 1970, 8: 309-11.

Mischel, W. *Personality and assessment*. New York: Wiley, 1968.

Mitchell, K.M.; Rubin, S.E.; Bozarth, J.D.; and Wyrick, T.J. Effects of short-term training on residence hall assistants. *Counselor Education and Supervision* 1971, 10: 310-18.

Mitchell, L.E. Nonprofessionals in mental health. In C. Grosser, W.E. Henry, and J.G. Kelly (eds.), *Nonprofessionals in the human services*. San Francisco: Jossey-Bass, 1969.

Mitchell, W.E. Amicatherapy: Theoretical perspectives and an example of practice. *Community Mental Health Journal* 1966, 2: 307-14.

Moore, B.L., and Bailey, J.S. Social punishment in the modification of a pre-school child's "autistic-like" behavior with a mother as therapist. *Journal of Applied Behavior Analysis* 1973, 6: 497-507.

Moore, M. Training professionals to work with paraprofessionals. *Personnel and Guidance Journal* 1974, 53: 308-12.

Moreland, J.R.; Ivey, A.E.; and Phillips, J.S. An evaluation of microcounseling as an interviewer training tool. *Journal of Consulting and Clinical Psychology* 1973, 41: 294-300.

Morrill, R.G. Group identity, marginality, and the nonprofessional. *Archives of General Psychiatry* 1968, 19: 404-12.

Morrill, W.H., and Hurst, J.C. A preventative and developmental role for the college counselor. *Counseling Psychologist* 1971, 2: 90-95.

_____; Oetting, E.R.; and Hurst, J.C. Dimensions of counselor functioning. *Personnel and Guidance Journal* 1974, 52: 354-59.

Morris, K.D. Behavioral change: A concomitant of attitude change in nursing students. *Nursing Research* 1964, 13: 132-38.

Moser, A.J. Training nonprofessional behavioral change agents. *Journal of School Psychology* 1973, 11: 251-55.

Mueller, B.J., and James, B.J. Social work practice and community mental health. *Community Mental Health Journal* 1972, 8: 178-88.

Mueller, J.; Cameron, K.; and Joransen, D. Community caretakers as mental health casefinders. *Mental Hygiene* 1971, 55: 214-18.

Mumford, E. Promises and disaffections in mental health programs in schools. *Psychology in the Schools* 1970, 7: 20-29.

Musante, G.J. Staff evaluations of the technician role. *Professional Psychology* 1974, 5: 214-16.

Myers, A.E.; Myers, G.E.; Tapp, M.A.; and Tapp, J.T. Helping the ex-addict. *Personnel and Guidance Journal* 1972, 50: 817-22.

Myers, K., and Clark, D.H. Results in a therapeutic community. *British Journal of Psychiatry* 1972, 120: 51-57.

Myrick, R.D., and Moni, L.S. The counselor's workshop: Teacher in-service workshops. *Elementary School Guidance and Counseling* 1972a, 7: 156-61.

_____, and _____. The counselor's workshop: Helping children disclose themselves. *Elementary School Guidance and Counseling* 1972b, 7: 55-58.

_____, and _____. The counselor's workshop: Helping humanize education. *Elementary School Guidance and Counseling* 1972c, 7: 295-99.

Nadler, D. Affecting the learning climate through magic circles. *Elementary School Guidance and Counseling* 1973, 8: 107-11.

Naftulin, D.H.; Donnelly, F.A.; and Wolkon, G.H. Psychiatry education programs for nonpsychiatrist physicians: A 10-year perspective. *Comprehensive Psychiatry* 1974, 15: 133-39.

Nash, K.B. The group psychotherapist and the training of the new mental health worker: What else is new? *International Journal of Group Psychotherapy* 1974, 24: 32-41.

_____, and Mittlefehedt, V. The training of supervisors of new professionals. *American Journal of Orthopsychiatry* 1974, 44: 284-85.

National Clearinghouse for Drug Abuse Information. Narcotics: Some questions and answers. Washington: U.S. Government Printing Office, 1971.

National Institute on Alcohol Abuse and Alcoholism. Alcoholism and its treatment. Washington: U.S. Government Printing Office, 1972.

Naylor, H.H. Professional leadership for volunteer development. In E. Berlatsky (ed.), *Social work practice.* New York: Columbia University Press, 1969.

Neisworth, J.T.; Deno, S.L.; and Jenkins, J.R. *Student motivation and classroom management: A behavioristic approach.* Lemont, Pa.: Behavior Technics, 1973.

Neki, J.S. Guru-chela relationship: The possibility of a therapeutic paradigm. *American Journal of Orthopsychiatry* 1973, 43: 755-66.

Neleigh, J.R.; Newman, F.L.; Madore, C.E.; and Sears, W.F. Training nonprofessional community project leaders. *Community Mental Health Journal* 1971, Monograph No. 6.

Nelson, R. Support personnel in elementary school guidance. *Elementary School Guidance and Counseling* 1968, 2: 303-6.

Nelson, S.H., and Torrey, E.F. The religious functions of psychiatry. *American Journal of Orthopsychiatry* 1973, 43: 362-67.

Newbrough, J.R. Community psychology: A new specialty in psychology? In D. Adelson and B.L. Kalis (eds.), *Community psychology and mental health: Perspectives and challenges.* Scranton, Pa.: Chandler, 1970.

New Human Services Newsletter. Mental health associates: 150 programs. 1973, 2: 2.

Newman, L.E., and Steinberg, L. Consultation with police on human relations training. *American Journal of Psychiatry* 1970, 126: 1421-29.

Nicholas, J.R., and Ransohoff, W. "Tandem" teaching to nonpsychiatrist physicians. *American Journal of Psychiatry* 1965, 122: 489-94.

Nichtern, S.; Donahue, G.T.; O'Shea, J.; Marans, M.; Curtis, M.; and Brody, C. A community educational program for the emotionally disturbed child. *American Journal of Orthopsychiatry* 1964, 34: 705-13.

Norman, E.L., and Forti, T.J. A study of the process and the outcome of mental health consultation. *Community Mental Health Journal* 1972, 8: 261-70.

Nyman, L. Some odds on getting into Ph.D. programs in clinical and counseling psychology. *American Psychologist* 1973, 28: 934-35.

O'Connell, B. Labor's role in community mental health. *Mental Hygiene* 1968, 52: 239-43.

O'Connell, W.E. Community confrontations: A challenge to psychotherapeutic practice. *Journal of Individual Psychology* 1969, 25: 38-47.

O'Dell, S. Training parents in behavior modification: A review. *Psychological Bulletin* 1974, 81: 418-33.

Odgers, J.C. Cause for concern. *Counselor Education and Supervision* 1964, 4: 17-20.

O'Donnell, E.J. The professional volunteer versus the volunteer professional. *Community Mental Health Journal* 1970, 6: 236-45.

O'Donnell, J.A. The relapse rate in narcotic addiction: A critique of follow-up studies. In D.M. Wilner and G.G. Kassebaum (eds.), *Narcotics.* New York: McGraw-Hill, 1965.

Oetting, E.R. Developmental education of counseling psychology. *Journal of Counseling Psychology* 1967, 14: 382-85.

_____; Cole, C.W.; and Adams, R. Problems in program evaluation: A ministers' workshop. *Mental Hygiene* 1969, 53: 214-17.

_____, and Hawkes, F.J. Training professionals for evaluative research. *Personnel and Guidance Journal* 1974, 52: 434-38.

O'Leary, K.D.; O'Leary, S.; and Becker, W.C. Modification of a deviant sibling interaction pattern in the home. *Behavior Research and Therapy* 1967, 5: 113-20.

Orlando, N.J. The mental patient as therapeutic agent: Self-change, power, and caring. *Psychotherapy: Theory, Research and Practice* 1974, 11: 58-62.

Oxhorn, J.L. A collaborative mental health program in the early prevention of adjustment difficulties in the elementary school. *Journal of School Psychology* 1965, 4: 1-5.

Ozarin, L.D., and Thomas, C.S. Advocacy in community mental health programs. *American Journal of Public Health* 1972, 62: 557-59.

Ozarin, L.D.; Taube, C.; and Spaner, F.E. Operations indices for community mental health centers. *American Journal of Psychiatry* 1972, 128: 1511-15.

Padilla, A.M., and Ruiz, R.A. *Latino mental health: A review of literature.* Washington: U.S. Government Printing Office, 1973.

Page, S., and Yates, E. Fear of evaluation and reluctance to participate in research. *Professional Psychology* 1974, 5: 400-8.

Palumbo, A., and Kurtz, P.D. *Helping children: A positive approach for home and school.* Lemont, Pa.: Behavior Technics, 1973.

Panyan, M.; Boozer, H.; and Morris, N. Feedback to attendants as a reinforcer for applying operant techniques. *Journal of Applied Behavior Analysis* 1970, 3: 1-4.

Parad, H.J. (ed.), *Crisis intervention: Selected readings.* New York: Family Service Association of America, 1965.

_____, and Rapoport, L. Advanced social work educational programs in community mental health. In S.E. Golann and C. Eisdorfer (eds.), *Handbook of community mental health.* New York: Appleton-Century-Crofts, 1972.

Pasework, R.A. Follow-up study of a summer work study program on mental health and retardation. *Journal of Community Psychology* 1974, 2: 28-30.

_____; Hall, W.T.; and Grice, J.E. Patients' perception of clergy as group psychotherapists. *Pastoral Counselor* 1969, 7: 18-19.

Patterson, C.H. Subprofessional functions and short-term training. *Counselor Education and Supervision* 1965, 4: 144-46.

Patterson, G.R. Behavioral intervention procedures in the classroom and in the home. In A.E. Bergin and S.L. Garfield (eds.), *Handbook of psychotherapy and behavior change.* New York: Wiley, 1971a.

_____. *Families: Applications of social learning to family life.* Champaign: Ill.: Research Press, 1971b.

_____, and Gullion, M.E. *Living with children: New methods for parents and teachers.* Champaign, Ill.: Research Press, 1968.

_____; McNeal, S.; Hawkins, N.; and Phelps, R. Reprogramming the social environment. *Journal of Child Psychology and Psychiatry* 1967, 8: 181-95.

_____, and Reid, J.B. Reciprocity and coercion: Two facets of social systems. In C. Neuringer and J. Michael (eds.), *Behavior modification in clinical psychology.* New York: Appleton-Century-Crofts, 1970.

_____; Shaw, D.A.; and Ebner, M.J. Teachers, peers, and parents as agents of change in the classroom. In F.A. Benson (ed.), *Modifying deviant social behaviors in various classroom settings.* Eugene: University of Oregon Press, 1969.

Patterson, N.B., and Patterson, T.W. A companion therapy program. *Community Mental Health Journal* 1967, 3: 133-36.

Pattison, E.M., and Elpers, J.R. A developmental view of mental health manpower trends. *Hospital and Community Psychiatry* 1972, 23: 325-28.

_____; Lapins, N.A.; and Doerr, H.A. Faith healing: A study of personality and function. *Journal of Nervous and Mental Disease* 1973, 157: 397-409.

Paul, G.L.; McInnis, T.L.; and Mariotto, M.J. Objective performance outcomes associated with two approaches to training mental health technicians in milieu and social-learning programs. *Journal of Abnormal Psychology* 1973, 82: 523-32.

Payne, I.R.; Rasmussen, D.M.; and Shinedling, M.M. *Weight control and commitment-action training.* Provo, Utah: Weight Control Institute, 1971.

Pearl, A., and Riessman, F. *New careers for the poor: The nonprofessional in human services.* New York: Free Press, 1965.

Peck, H. A candid appraisal of the community mental health center as a public health agency: A case history. *American Journal of Public Health* 1969, 59: 459-69.

_____. The community's role in mental health training: Conformity or autonomy. *American Journal of Orthopsychiatry* 1974, 44: 266-67.

_____; Kaplan, S.; and Roman, M. Prevention, treatment and social action: A strategy of intervention in a disadvantaged urban area. *American Journal of Orthopsychiatry* 1966, 36: 57-69.

Peck, R.F. Why should we teach elementary school children about the principles of human behavior? *Journal of School Psychology* 1967, 5: 235-37.

Peine, H.A., and Munro, B.C. Behavioral management of parent training programs. *Psychological Record* 1973, 23: 459-66.

Peplau, H.E. Nursing education and community mental health. In S.E. Golann and C. Eisdorfer (eds.), *Handbook of community mental health.* New York: Appleton-Century-Crofts, 1972.

Perkins, D.V., and Thompson, J.R. An assessment of physicians' attitudes toward community mental health. *Community Mental Health Journal* 1974, 10: 282-91.

Perlmutter, F. Prevention and treatment: A strategy for survival. *Community Mental Health Journal* 1974, 10: 276-81.

_____, and Durham, D. Using teenagers to supplement casework service. *Social Work* 1965, 10: 41-48.

_____, and Silverman, H.A. Conflict in consultation-education. *Community Mental Health Journal* 1973, 9: 116-22.

Perry, R.J. The effect of long-term experience on the attitudes of psychiatric aides. *Journal of Community Psychology* 1974, 2: 166-73.

Persons, R.W.; Clark, C.; Persons, M.; Kadish, M.; and Patterson, W. Training and employing undergraduates as therapists in a college counseling service. *Professional Psychology* 1973, 4: 170-78.

Peterson, B. Parent effectiveness training and change in parental attitudes. Unpublished research.

Peterson, B.G. Parent effectiveness training. *School Counselor* 1969, 16: 367-69.

Peterson, D.R. The doctor of psychology program at the University of Illinois. *American Psychologist* 1968, 23: 511-16.

Pettinelli, V.D. Coordinating a volunteer program. *Mental Hygiene* 1971, 55: 516-18.

Pfeiffer, E. Patients as therapists. *American Journal of Psychiatry* 1967, 123: 1413, 1418.

Phelan, J.F. Developing new professional categories of volunteers in child welfare services. *Child Welfare* 1966, 45: 214-17.

Phillips, C.E. A study of marriage counselor's MMPI profiles. *Journal of Marriage and the Family* 1970, 32: 119-30.

Pierce, R., and Drasgow, J. Teaching facilitative interpersonal functioning to patients. *Journal of Counseling Psychology* 1969, 16: 295-98.

Piercy, F., and Brush, D. Effects of P.E.T. on empathy and self-disclosure. Unpublished research, 1971.

Pinkus, R.B., and Korn, J.H. The pre-professional option: An alternative to graduate work in psychology. *American Psychologist* 1973, 28: 710-18.

Pino, C.J. Relation of a trainability index to T-group outcomes. *Journal of Applied Psychology* 1971, 55: 439-42.

Plaut, T.F. *Alcohol problems: A report to the nation by the Cooperative Commission on the Study of Alcoholism.* New York: Oxford University Press, 1967.

_____. Prevention of alcoholism. In S.E. Golann and C. Eisdorfer (eds.), *Handbook of Community Mental Health.* New York: Appleton-Century-Crofts, 1972.

Polak, P., and Jones, M. The psychiatric nonhospital: A model for change. *Community Mental Health Journal* 1973, 9: 123-32.

Pomerleau, O.F.; Bobrove, P.H.; and Harris, L.C. Some observations on controlled social environments for psychiatric patients. *Journal of Behavior Therapy and Experimental Psychiatry* 1972, 3: 1-7.

_____; _____; and Smith, R.H. Rewarding psychiatric aides for the behavioral improvement of assigned patients. *Journal of Applied Behavior Analysis* 1973, 6: 383-90.

Portnoy, S.M.; Biller, H.B.; and Davids, A. The influence of the child case worker in residential treatment. *American Journal of Orthopsychiatry* 1972, 42: 719-22.

Poser, E.G. The effect of therapists' training on group therapeutic outcome. *Journal of Consulting Psychology* 1966, 30: 283-89.

_____. Fundamentals of behavior therapy: An introductory teaching aid. *Canadian Psychiatric Association Journal* 1970, 15: 487-92.

Posinsky, S.H. Yurok shamanism. *Psychiatric Quarterly* 1965, 39: 227-43.

Powell, M. A program leading to a master of science degree in community mental health. *Community Mental Health Journal* 1969, 5: 215-18.

Proshansky, H.M. For what are we training our graduate students? *American Psychologist* 1972, 27: 205-12.

Pryer, M.W.; Distefano, M.K.; and Poe, M.B. Effects of training programs on psychiatric attendants. *Mental Hygiene* 1966, 50: 66-70.

Rabkin, J.G. Opinions about mental illness: A review of the literature. *Psychological Bulletin* 1972, 77: 153-71.

Ralph, D.E. Attitudes toward mental illness among two groups of college students in a neuropsychiatric hospital setting. *Journal of Consulting and Clinical Psychology* 1968, 32: 98.

Randall, O.A. Emerging patterns of planned recreation for the elderly. *Public Welfare* 1971, 29: 389-92.

Rapoport, L. Working with families in crisis: An exploration in preventive intervention. In H.J. Parad (ed.), *Crisis intervention: Selected readings.* New York: Family Service Association of America, 1965.

Rappaport, J. College students and chronic patients: Current directions in outcome, selection, and training. Paper presented at the Annual VA Conference, New Orleans, Louisiana, 1973a.

_____. Personal communication, October 1973b.

_____, and Chinsky, J.M. Behavior ratings of chronic hospitalized patients: Cross-situational and cross-rater agreement. *Journal of Consulting and Clinical Psychology* 1970, 34: 394-97.

_____, and _____. Accurate empathy: Confusion of a construct. *Psychological Bulletin* 1972, 77: 400-4.

_____; _____; and Cowen, E.L. *Innovations in helping chronic patients: College students in a mental institution.* New York: Academic Press, 1971.

Rappaport, J.R.; Gross, T.; and Lepper, C. Modeling, sensitivity training, and instruction: Implications for the training of college student volunteers and for outcome research. *Journal of Consulting and Clinical Psychology* 1973, 40: 99-107.

Rath, S.F., and David, A.C. Teenage companions work with disturbed children. *Hospital and Community Psychiatry* 1973, 24: 624-26.

Raush, H.L. Research, practice, and accountability. *American Psychologist* 1974, 29: 678-81.

_____, and Rausch, C.L. *The halfway house movement: A search for sanity.* New York: Appleton-Century-Crofts, 1968.

Reding, G.R., and Goldsmith, E.F. The nonprofessional hospital volunteer as a member of the psychiatric consultation team. *Community Mental Health Journal* 1967, 3: 267-72.

Regester, D.C. Community mental health—for whose community? *American Journal of Public Health* 1974, 64: 886-93.

Reiff, R. Mental health manpower and institutional change. *American Psychologist* 1966, 21: 540-48.

_____. Social intervention and the problem of psychological analysis. *American Psychologist* 1968, 23: 524-31.

_____. Dilemmas of professionalism. In C. Grosser, W.E. Henry, and J.G. Kelly (eds.), *Nonprofessionals in the human services.* San Francisco: Jossey-Bass, 1969.

_____. Community psychology, community mental health and social needs:

The need for a body of knowledge in community psychology. In I. Iscoe and C.D. Spielberger (eds.), *Community psychology: Perspectives in training and research.* New York: Appleton-Century-Crofts, 1970.

Reiff, R. Community psychology and public policy. In G. Rosenblum (ed.), *Issues in community psychology and preventive mental health.* New York: Behavioral Publications, 1971.

_____. Comment. *Professional Psychology* 1972, 3: 337-39.

_____, and Riessman, F. The indigenous nonprofessional: A strategy of change in community action and community mental health programs. *Community Mental Health Journal* 1965, Monograph No. 1.

Reinherz, H. Group leadership of student volunteers. *Mental Hospitals* 1962, 13: 600-3.

_____. College student volunteers as case aides in a state hospital for children. *American Journal of Orthopsychiatry* 1963, 33: 544-46.

Reiser, M. The police department psychologist. *Police* 1970, 14: 24-26.

Reiser, M.F. Psychiatry in the undergraduate medical curriculum. *American Journal of Psychiatry* 1973, 130: 565-67.

Reres, M.E. A survey of the nurse's role in psychiatric outpatient clinics in America. *Community Mental Health Journal* 1969, 5: 382-85.

Rettig, E.B. *ABC's for parents: An educational workshop in behavior modification.* San Marino, Calif.: Associates for Behavior Change, 1973.

Rhead, C.; Abrams, A.; Trosman, H.; and Margolis, P. The psychological assessment of police candidates. *American Journal of Psychiatry* 1968, 124: 1575-80.

Rice, J.K., and Rice, D.G. Implications of the women's liberation movement for psychotherapy. *American Journal of Psychiatry* 1973, 130: 191-96.

Richan, W.C. A theoretical scheme for determining roles of professional and nonprofessional personnel. *Social Work* 1961, 6: 22-28.

Richards, H., and Daniels, M.S. Sociopsychiatric rehabilitation in a black urban ghetto. 2. Innovative treatment roles and approaches. *American Journal of Orthopsychiatry* 1969, 39: 662-76.

Richmond, C. Expanding the concepts of the halfway house: A satellite housing program. *International Journal of Social Psychiatry* 1970, 16: 96-102.

Rie, H.E. Therapeutic tutoring for underachieving children. *Professional Psychology* 1974, 5: 70-75.

Riessman, C.K. The supply-demand dilemma in community mental health centers. *American Journal of Orthopsychiatry* 1970, 40: 858-69.

Riessman, F. The "helper" therapy principle. *Social Work* 1965, 10: 27-32.

_____. A neighborhood-based mental health approach. In E.L. Cowen, E.A. Gardner, and M. Zax (eds.), *Emergent approaches to mental health problems.* New York: Appleton-Century-Crofts, 1967a.

_____. Strategies and suggestions for training nonprofessionals. *Community Mental Health Journal* 1967b, 3: 103-10.

_____. What is the relation between poverty and mental health? *Psychiatric Research Reports of the American Psychiatric Association* 1967c, 21: 35-49.

_____ ; Cohen, J.; and Pearl, A. (eds.). *Mental health of the poor.* New York: Free Press, 1964.

_____ , and Hallowitz, E. The neighborhood service center: An innovation in preventive psychiatry. *American Journal of Psychiatry* 1967, 123: 1408-13.

_____ , and Popper, H.I. *Up from poverty: New career ladders for nonprofessionals.* New York: Harper & Row, 1968.

_____ , and Schribner, S. The utilization of mental health services by workers and low income groups: Causes and cures. *American Journal of Psychiatry* 1965, 121: 798-801.

Rioch, M.J. Training the mature woman for a professional role. *American Association of University Women Journal* 1962, 55: 236-39.

_____. Changing concepts in the training of therapists. *Journal of Consulting Psychology* 1966, 30: 290-92.

_____. Pilot projects in training mental health counselors. In E.L. Cowen, E.A. Gardner, and M. Zax (eds.), *Emergent approaches to mental health problems.* New York: Appleton-Century-Crofts, 1967.

_____. Comment. *Professional Psychology* 1972, 3: 334-35.

_____ ; Elkes, C.; Flint, A.A.; Usdansky, B.S.; Newman, R.G.; and Silber, E. National Institute of Mental Health pilot study in training mental health counselors. *American Journal of Orthopsychiatry* 1963, 33: 678-89.

Risley, T.R. The effects and side effects of punishing autistic behaviors of a deviant child. *Journal of Applied Behavior Analysis* 1968, 1: 21-34.

Rittelmeyer, L.F. Continuing education in psychiatry for physicians. Report of a four-year experience. *Journal of the American Medical Association* 1972, 220: 710-14.

Robertson, R.N.; Maholick, L.T.; and Shapiro, D.S. The parish minister as counselor: A dilemma and challenge. *Pastoral Psychology* 1969, 22: 48-52.

Robertson, R.L., and Shriver, B.M. The general practitioner training program of the National Institute of Mental Health: Fiscal years 1959-1962. *Journal of Medical Education* 1964, 39: 925-34.

Robinson, D. On call for crises. *Good Housekeeping* 1971, 92: 167-68.

Robinson, H.B., and Robinson, M.M. *The mentally retarded child: A psychological approach.* New York: McGraw-Hill, 1965.

Robinson, L., and Podnos, B. Resistance of psychiatrists in treatment of alcoholism. *Journal of Nervous and Mental Disease* 1966, 143: 220-25.

Rockland, L.H. Psychiatric consultation to the clergy: A report on a group experience. *Mental Hygiene* 1969, 53: 205-7.

Roen, S.R. Teaching the behavioral sciences in the elementary grades. *Journal of School Psychology* 1967, 5: 205-16.

_____. Evaluative research and community mental health. In A.E. Bergin and

S.L. Garfield (eds.), *Handbook of psychotherapy and behavior change*. New York: Wiley, 1971.

Roeske, N.A. The junior medical student as diagnostician of the family of an emotionally disturbed child. *Journal of Medical Education* 1972, 47: 51-56.

Rogeness, G.A., and Bednar, R.A. Behavior and attitude change in children in a mental health tutoring program. *Journal of Community Psychology* 1973a, 1: 204-8.

_____ , and _____ . Teenage helper: A role in community mental health. *American Journal of Psychiatry* 1973b, 130: 933-36.

Rogers, C.R. The necessary and sufficient conditions of therapeutic personality change. *Journal of Consulting Psychology* 1957, 21: 95-103.

Rolde, E.J.; Fersch, E.; Kelly, F.J.; Frank, S.; and Guberman, M. A law enforcement training program in a mental health center catchment area. *American Journal of Psychiatry* 1973, 130: 1002-5.

Romano, J. The teaching of psychiatry to medical students. *American Journal of Psychiatry* 1973, 130: 559-62.

Romond, A.M.; Forrest, C.K.; and Kleber, H.D. Follow-up of participants in a drug dependence therapeutic community. *Archives of General Psychiatry* 1975, 32: 369-74.

Rosen, B.M.; Locke, B.Z.; Goldberg, I.D.; and Babigian, H.M. Identification of emotional disturbance in patients seen in general medical clinics. *Hospital and Community Psychiatry* 1972, 23: 364-70.

Rosenbaum, M. Some comments on the use of untrained therapists. *Journal of Consulting Psychology* 1966, 30: 292-94.

_____ , and Berger, M. (eds.), *Group psychotherapy and group function*. New York: Basic Books, 1963.

Rosenblatt, A. Interest of older persons in volunteer activities. *Social Work* 1966, 11: 87-94.

_____ , and Mayer, J.E. Help seeking for family problems: A survey of utilization and satisfaction. *American Journal of Psychiatry* 1972, 128: 1136-40.

Rosenblum, G. Mental health retools for the seventies. *Massachusetts Mental Health Journal* 1972, 2: 5-16.

_____ . Advanced training in community psychology: The role of training in community systems. *Community Mental Health Journal* 1973, 9: 63-67.

_____ , and Hassol, L. Training for new mental health roles. *Mental Hygiene* 1968, 52: 81-86.

Rosenthal, M.S., and Biase, D.V. Phoenix House: Therapeutic communities for drug addicts. *Hospital and Community Psychiatry* 1969, 20: 26-30.

Ross, A.O. Continuing professional development in psychology. *Professional Psychology* 1974, 5: 122-28.

Rothaus, P., and Hanson, P.G. Path of inquiry in mental illness and problem-centered self-descriptions. *Community Mental Health Journal* 1965, 1: 29-36.

_____ ; _____ ; Johnson, D.L.; Lyle, F.A.; and Moyer, R. The anticipation and management of crisis on an open psychiatric ward. *Journal of Applied Behavioral Science* 1966, 2: 431-47.

_____ ; Morton, R.B.; Johnson, D.L.; Cleveland, S.E.; and Lyle, F.A. Human relations training for psychiatric patients. *Archives of General Psychiatry* 1963, 8: 572-81.

Rothman, B. Social work education. In C. Grosser, W.E. Henry, and J.G. Kelly (eds.), *Nonprofessionals in the human services.* San Francisco: Jossey-Bass, 1969.

Rouse, B.M., and Farb, J. Training adolescents to use behavior modification with the severely handicapped. *Exceptional Children* 1974, 40: 286-88.

Ruiz, P. Consumer participation in mental health programs. *Hospital and Community Psychiatry* 1973, 24: 38-40.

_____ , and Behrens, M. Community control in mental health: How far can it go? *Psychiatric Quarterly* 1973, 47: 317-24.

_____ , and Langrod, J. Psychiatrists and folk healers: A scientific dialogue. *American Journal of Orthopsychiatry* 1974, 44: 268-69.

_____ ; Vazquez, W.; and Vazquez, K. The mobile unit: A new approach in mental health. *Community Mental Health Journal* 1973, 9: 18-24.

Runquist, M.P., and Behar, L.B. Prevention of mental health problems: Meeting needs or imposing values? *American Journal of Orthopsychiatry* 1974, 44: 269-70.

Rusalem, H. Ombudsmen for patients at a mental health center. *Hospital and Community Psychiatry* 1973, 24: 680-81.

Rushing W.A. The hospital nurse as mother surrogate and bedside psychologist: A sociological appraisal. *Mental Hygiene* 1966, 50: 71-80.

Rybak, W.S.; Sadnavitch, J.M.; and Mason, B.J. Psycho-social changes in personality during foster grandparents program. *Journal of the American Geriatrics Society* 1968, 16: 956-59.

Sabshin, M. The anticommunity mental health "movement." *American Journal of Psychiatry* 1969, 126: 1005-12.

Saltmarsh, R.E. Development of empathic interview skills through programmed instruction. *Journal of Counseling Psychology* 1973, 20: 375-77.

Salzinger, K.; Feldman, R.S.; and Portnoy, S. Training parents of brain injured children in the use of operant conditioning procedures. *Behavior Therapy* 1970, 1: 4-32.

Sanders, R. New manpower for mental hospital service. In E.L. Cowen, E.A. Gardner, and M. Zax (eds.), *Emergent approaches to mental health problems.* New York: Appleton-Century-Crofts, 1967.

_____ ; Smith, R.S.; and Weinman, B.S. *Chronic psychoses and recovery.* San Francisco: Jossey-Bass, 1967.

Sandler, I.N. Characteristics of women working as child aides in a school-based preventive mental health program. *Journal of Consulting and Clinical Psychology* 1972, 39: 56-61.

Sandusky, R.M. The pharmacist as staff educator and consultant. *Hospital and Community Psychiatry* 1973, 24: 844-45.

Sarason, S.B. *The psychological sense of community: Prospects for a community psychology.* San Francisco: Jossey-Bass, 1974.

Sasaki, Y. Psychiatric study of the shaman in Japan. *Transcultural Psychiatric Research* 1967, 4: 15-17.

Sata, L.S. A mental health center's partnership with the community. *Hospital and Community Psychiatry* 1972, 23: 242-45.

_____ ; Perry, D.A.; and Cameron, C.E. Store-front churches in the inner city. *Mental Hygiene* 1970, 54: 256-60.

Savino, M.; Stearns, P.; Merwin, E.; and Kennedy, R. The lack of services to the retarded through community mental health programs. *Community Mental Health Journal* 1973, 9: 158-68.

Scarlett, W.G. The clergyman's role and community mental health. *Mental Hygiene* 1970, 54: 378-81.

Schacter, S. Some extraordinary facts about obese humans and rats. *American Psychologist* 1971, 26: 129-37.

Scheibe, K.E. College students spend eight weeks in a mental hospital: A case report. *Psychotherapy: Theory, Research and Practice* 1965, 2: 117-120.

_____ ; Kulik, J.A.; Hersch, P.D.; and LaMacchia, S. College students on chronic wards. *Community Mental Health Journal* 1969, Monograph No. 5.

Schilling, K. The peer counseling program in the residence halls of the University of Florida. *Journal of the American College Health Association* 1974, 22: 182-84.

Schindler-Rainman, E. Are volunteers here to stay? *Mental Hygiene* 1971, 55: 511-15.

Schofield, W. *Psychotherapy: The purchase of friendship.* Englewood Cliffs, N.J.: Prentice-Hall, 1964.

Schulberg, H.C. Private practice and community mental health. *Hospital and Community Psychiatry* 1966, 17: 363-66.

_____ . Challenge of human service programs for psychologists. *American Psychologist* 1972, 27: 566-73.

Schulman, J.L.; Ford, R.C.; and Busk, P. A classroom program to improve self-concept. *Psychology in the Schools* 1973, 10: 481-87.

_____ ; _____ ; _____ ; and Kaspar, J.C. Evaluation of a classroom program to alter friendship practices. *Journal of Educational Research* 1973a, 67: 99-102.

_____ ; _____ ; _____ ; _____ . Mental health in the schools. *Elementary School Journal* 1973b, 74: 48-56.

Scott, D., and Goldenberg, H.L. The phenomenon of self-perpetration in Synanon-type drug treatment programs. *Hospital and Community Psychiatry* 1973, 24: 231-33.

Selig, A.L. Prevention of mental illness and community organization: A review and annotated bibliography. *JSAS Catalog of Selected Documents in Psychology* 1973, 3: 57.

Selzer, M.L., and Benedek, E.P. Lawyers' use of psychiatry. *American Journal of Psychiatry* 1965, 122: 212-13.

Shacknow, J., and Matorin, S. Community psychiatry welcomes the nonprofessional. *Psychiatric Quarterly* 1969, 43: 492-511.

Shane, P.G. The police: Social controllers or service deliverers? *American Journal of Orthopsychiatry* 1974, 44: 197-98.

Shapiro, A.K. Placebo effects in medicine, psychotherapy, and psychoanalysis. In A.E. Bergin and S.L. Garfield (eds.), *Handbook of psychotherapy and behavior change.* New York: Wiley, 1971.

_____ , and Struening, E. Defensiveness in the definition of placebo. *Comprehensive Psychiatry* 1973, 14: 107-20.

Shapiro, D.S. Mental health professionals' hang-ups in training mental health counselors. *Mental Hygiene* 1970, 54: 364-69.

_____ , and Maholick, L.T. A systematic approach to mental health assessment and counseling. *Mental Hygiene* 1962, 46: 393-99.

_____ , and _____ . A community mental health program revisited. *Psychological Reports* 1967, 20: 289-90.

_____ ; _____ ; and Robertson, R.N. Mental health training for ministers. *American Journal of Public Health* 1967, 57: 518-22.

Shaw, R., and Eagle, C.J. Programmed failure: The Lincoln Hospital story. *Community Mental Health Journal* 1971, 7: 255-63.

Sheeley, W.F. The general practitioner's contribution to community psychiatry. In L. Bellak (ed.), *Handbook of community mental health.* New York: Grune & Stratton, 1964.

_____ . Methodology in postgraduate psychiatric education. *American Journal of Psychiatry* 1965, 122: 494-97.

Shelly, J.A., and Bassin, A. Daytop Lodge: A new treatment approach for drug addicts. *Corrective Psychiatry* 1965, 11: 186-95.

Sheppard, W.C.; Shank, S.B.; and Wilson, D. *How to be a good teacher: Training social behavior in young children.* Champaign, Ill.: Research Press, 1972.

Sheridan, K.; Sheridan, E.P.; Shack, J.; Walker, R.E.; Egan, G., and Lavigne, J. A training program for small-group leaders: 1. Overview. *Journal of Community Psychology* 1973, 1: 3-7.

Shiloh, A. Psychiatric patients as research interviewers in the mental hospital. *Mental Hygiene* 1969, 53: 443-45.

Shubert, O.W., and Fulton, R.T. An in-service training program of communication. *Mental Retardation* 1966, 4: 27-28.

Siegel, J.M. Mental health volunteers as change agents. *American Journal of Community Psychology* 1973, 1: 138-58.

Siegel, R.L. The training and use of mental health associates in the Veterans Administration. *Hospital and Community Psychiatry* 1974, 25: 295-98.

Signell, K.A. Kindergarten entry: A preventive approach to community mental health. *Community Mental Health Journal* 1972, 8: 60-70.

_____, and Scott, P.A. Mental health consultation: An interaction model. *Community Mental Health Journal* 1971, 7: 288-302.

_____, and _____. Training in consultation: A crisis of role transition. *Community Mental Health Journal* 1972, 8: 149-60.

Sikes, M.P., and Cleveland, S.E. Human relatives training for police and community. *American Psychologist* 1968, 23: 766-69.

Silverman, P.R. Services to the widowed: First step in a program of preventive intervention. *Community Mental Health Journal* 1967, 3: 37-44.

_____. The Widow-to-Widow Program: An experiment in preventive intervention. *Mental Hygiene* 1969, 53: 333-37.

_____. The widow as a caregiver in a program of preventive intervention with other widows. *Mental Hygiene* 1970, 54: 540-47.

_____. Widowhood and preventive intervention. *Family Coordinator* 1972, 21: 95-102.

Singer, P.; Araneta, E.; and Aarons, L. Integration of indigenous healing practices of the Kali cult with Western modalities in British Guiana. *Transcultural Psychiatric Research* 1967, 4: 65-67.

Skovholt, T.M. A new manpower boom. *Mental Hygiene* 1973, 57: 28-30.

Slem, C.M., and Cotler, S. Crisis phone services: Evaluation of a hotline program. *American Journal of Community Psychology* 1973, 1: 219-27.

Sloan, P. Volunteer orientation and training as a public relations asset for a mental health center. Paper presented at the Annual Meeting of the Rocky Mountain Psychological Association, May 1973.

Sloane, R.B., and Horvitz, D.F. Pastoral counseling. *Mental Hygiene* 1971, 55: 539-43.

Sloop, E.W., and Quarrick, E. Technician performance: Reliability and validity. *Professional Psychology* 1974, 5: 216-18.

Small, S.M. Limitations and values of evaluation techniques in psychiatric education. *American Journal of Psychiatry* 1975, 132: 52-55.

Smith, A.B. Humanism and behavior modification: Is there a conflict? *Elementary School Journal* 1973, 74: 59-67.

Smith, J.A. For God's sake, what do these women want? *Personnel and Guidance Journal* 1972, 51: 133-36.

Smith, J.J. Psychiatric hospital experience and attitudes toward "mental illness." *Journal of Consulting and Clinical Psychology* 1969, 33: 302-06.

Smith, J.M., and Smith, D.E. *Child management: A program for parents and teachers.* Ann Arbor, Mich.: Ann Arbor Publishers, 1966.

Smitson, W.S. Foster mothers and mental patients: An exploratory study of interpersonal relationships. *Mental Hygiene* 1970, 54: 251-55.

Snow, D.L., and Brooks, R.B. A school consultation program in behavior modification. *Journal of School Health* 1974, 44: 130-35.

Snyder, J.A. The use of gatekeepers in crisis management. *Bulletin of Suicidology* 1971, 8: 39-44.

Sobey, F. *The nonprofessional revolution in mental health.* New York: Columbia University Press, 1970.

Sokol, R.J., and Reiser, M. Training police sergeants in early warning signs of emotional upset. *Mental Hygiene* 1971, 55: 303-7.

Sommer, J.J. Work as a therapeutic goal: Union-management clinical contributions to a mental health. *Mental Hygiene* 1969, 53: 263-68.

Southern Regional Education Board: *The community college in mental health training.* Atlanta, Ga.: Southern Regional Education Board, 1966.

Specter, G.A., and Claiborn, W.L. *Crisis intervention.* New York: Behavioral Publications, 1973.

_____, and Cowen, E.L. A pilot study in stimulation of culturally deprived infants. *Child Psychiatry and Human Development* 1971, 1: 168-77.

Sperber, Z., and Reiser, M. Utilizing nonprofessional aides in the treatment of psychotic children at an outpatient clinic. *Psychotherapy: Theory, Research and Practice* 71, 8: 224-30.

Spielberger, C.D., and Iscoe, I. Graduate education in community psychology. In S.E. Golann and C. Eisdorfer (eds.), *Handbook of community mental health.* New York: Appleton-Century-Crofts, 1972.

Staats, A.W.; Minke, K.A.; and Butts, P. A token-reinforcement remedial reading program administered by black therapy-technicians to problem black children. *Behavior Therapy* 1970, 1: 331-53.

Staton, E.E.; Tiller, C.B.; and Weyler, E.H. Teens who care: Potential mental health manpower. *Mental Hygiene* 1969, 53: 200-04.

Stearn, M. The relationship of P.E.T. to parent attitudes, parent behavior and child self-esteem. Unpublished doctoral dissertation, 1970.

Steele, R.L. A manpower resource for community mental health centers. *Journal of Community Psychology* 1974, 2: 104-7.

Steenland, R. Paraprofessionals in counseling centers. *Personnel and Guidance Journal* 1973, 51: 417-18.

Stein, L.J.; Test, M.A.; and Marx, A.J. Alternative to the hospital: A controlled study. *American Journal of Psychiatry* 1975, 132: 517-22.

Steisel, I.M. Paraprofessionals—questions from a traditionalist. *Professional Psychology* 1972, 3: 331-34.

Stepansky, P.E., and Stepansky, W. Training primary physicians as psychotherapists. *Comprehensive Psychiatry* 1974, 15: 141-51.

Stephan, P.G. Clergymen as counselors. Unpublished doctoral dissertation, University of Michigan, 1971.

Stewart, H. Kindling of hope in the disadvantaged: A study of the Afro-American healer. *Mental Hygiene* 1971, 55: 96-100.

Stiavelli, R.E., and Shirley, D.T. The Citizenship Council: A technique for managing behavior disorders in the educationally handicapped class. *Journal of School Psychology* 1968, 6: 147-56.

Stocking, M.; Rothney, W.; Grosser, G.; and Goodwin, R. Psychpathology in the pediatric hospital—implications for the community health. *American Journal of Public Health* 1972, 62: 551-56.

Stollak, G.E. The experimental effects of training college students as play therapists. *Psychotherapy: Theory, Research and Practice* 1968, 5: 77-80.

_____. An integrated graduate-undergraduate program in the assessment, treatment, and prevention of child psychopathology. *Professional Psychology* 1973a, 4: 158-69.

_____. Education for early childhood consultation. Paper presented at the Annual Meeting of the American Psychological Association, Montreal, 1973b.

_____; Green, L.; Scholom, A.; Schreiber, J.; and Messe, L.A. The process and outcome of play encounters between undergraduates and clinic-referred children: Preliminary findings. Paper presented at the Meeting of the Society for Psychotherapy Research, Philadelphia, 1973.

Stone, J.L., and Crowthers, V. Innovations in program and funding mental health services for blue-collar families. *American Journal of Psychiatry* 1972, 128: 1375-80.

Stotsky, B.A. The physician's role in a nursing home. *Medical Insight* 1972, 4: 22-25.

_____, and Rhetts, J.E. Changing attitudes toward the mentally ill in nursing homes. *Nursing Research* 1966, 15: 175-77.

_____, and _____. Functional significance of attitudes toward the mentally ill among nursing home personnel. *Journal of Social Psychology* 1967, 71: 79-85.

Stoudenmire, J.A. Mental health education for supervisors. *Mental Hygiene* 1972, 56: 52-56.

_____; Clark, D.A.; and Fleming, E.E. Evaluating a mental health seminar for foremen in industry. *Journal of Community Psychology* 1974, 2: 176-78.

Stover, L., and Guerney, B.G. The efficacy of training procedures for mothers in filial therapy. *Psychotherapy: Theory, Research and Practice* 1967, 4: 110-15.

Streeter, N.M., and Owens, W.E. Partners in ministering—a psychiatrist and a pastor. *Community Mental Health Journal* 1970, 6: 292-99.

Stringer, L.A. Children at risk: 1. The unready for school. *Elementary School Journal* 1973a, 73: 364-73.

_____. Children at risk: 2. The teacher as change agent. *Elementary School Journal* 1973b, 73: 424-33.

Strom, K.R. New thrusts in clinical education and training for clergymen. *International Journal of Social Psychiatry* 1973, 19: 207-13.

Strupp, H.H. *Psychotherapy and the modification of abnormal behavior.* New York: McGraw-Hill, 1971.

_____. Is the time right for comparisons of therapeutic techniques? *Psychotherapy and Social Science Review* 1972, 6: 17-22.

Stuart, R.B. Behavioral control of overeating. *Behavior Research and Therapy* 1967, 5: 357-65.

_____, and Davis, B. *Slim chance in a fat world: Behavioral control of obesity.* Champaign, Ill.: Research Press, 1972.

Stunkard, A.J. New therapies for the eating disorders: Behavior modification of obesity and anorexia nervosa. *Archives of General Psychiatry* 1972, 26: 391-98.

_____; Levine, H.; and Fox, S. The management of obesity: Patient self-help and medical treatment. *Archives of Internal Medicine* 1970, 125: 1067-72.

Sue, D.W., and Sue, S. Counseling Chinese Americans. *Personnel and Guidance Journal* 1972, 50: 637-44.

Sullivan, R. Violence, like charity, begins at home. *The New York Times Magazine*, November 24, 1968.

Sydnor, G.L.; Akridge, R.L.; and Parkhill, N.D. *Human relations: A manual for trainers.* West Monroe, Louisiana: Human Resources Development Training Institute, 1973.

Tahmisian, J.A., and McReynolds, W.T. Use of parents as behavioral engineers in the treatment of a school-phobic girl. *Journal of Counseling Psychology* 1971, 18: 225-28.

Talbott, J.A., and Talbott, S.W. Training police in community relations and urban problems. *American Journal of Psychiatry* 1971, 127: 894-900.

Taplin, J.R. Crisis theory: Critique and reformulation. *Community Mental Health Journal* 1971, 7: 13-23.

Tapp, J.T., and Spanier, D. Personal characteristics of volunteer phone counselors. *Journal of Consulting and Clinical Psychology* 1973, 41: 245-50.

Tavormina, J.B. Basic models of parent counseling: A critical review. *Psychological Bulletin* 1974, 81: 827-35.

_____. Relative effectiveness of behavioral and reflective group counseling with parents of mentally retarded children. *Journal of Consulting and Clinical Psychology* 1975, 43: 22-31.

Terrell, D.L.; McWilliams, S.A.; and Cowen, E.L. Description and evaluation of group-work training for nonprofessional aides in a school mental health program. *Psychology in the Schools* 1972, 9: 70-75.

Tharp, R.G., and Wetzel, R.J. *Behavior modification in the natural environment.* New York: Academic Press, 1969.

Thomas, E.J. Introduction. In E.J. Thomas (ed.), *Behavior modification procedure: A sourcebook.* Chicago: Aldine, 1974.

Thomas, P.; Frisone, G.; and Lipson, D. An evaluation of parent drug education. *Mental Hygiene* 1971, 55: 456-60.

Thompson, J.R., and Fiddleman, P. Counseling outreach in a dormitory. *Personnel and Guidance Journal* 1973, 51: 734-38.

Thune, J.; Tine, S.; and Booth, F.E. Retraining older adults for employment in community services. *Gerontologist* 1964, 4: 5-9.

Tinling, D.C. Voodoo, root work, and medicine, *Psychosomatic Medicine* 1967, 29: 483-91.

Toban, E. Perceived skill of professional and nonprofessional community health workers. *Journal of Consulting and Clinical Psychology* 1970, 34: 308-13.

Toepfer, C.; Reuter, J.; and Maurer, C. Design and evaluation of an obedience training program for mothers of preschool children. *Journal of Consulting and Clinical Psychology* 1972, 39: 194-98.

Tolor, A., and Lane, P.A. An experimental approach to the treatment of disturbed school-aged children. *Journal of School Psychology* 1968, 6: 97-103.

Tolson, H. Counseling the "disadvantaged." *Personnel and Guidance Journal* 1972, 50: 735-38.

Tomlinson, T.M.; Barthol, R.P.; and Groot, H. Responses of non-professional therapists to chronic schizophrenics. *Psychotherapy: Theory, Research and Practice* 1969, 6: 256-60.

Torrey, E.F. The case for the indigenous therapist. *Archives of General Psychiatry* 1969, 20: 365-73.

_____ . What Western psychotherapists can learn from witchdoctors. *American Journal of Orthopsychiatry* 1972, 42: 69-76.

_____ . The mind game: Witchdoctors and psychiatrists. New York: Bantam Books, 1973.

Tourney, G. A history of therapeutic fashions in psychiatry, 1800-1966. *American Journal of Psychiatry* 1967, 124: 784-96.

Tramontana, J. A review of research on behavior modification in the home and school. *Educational Technology* 1971, 11: 61-64.

Trickett, E.; Kelly, J.; and Todd, D. The social environment of the high school: Guidelines for individual change and organizational redevelopment. In S.E. Golann and C. Eisdorfer (eds.), *Handbook of community mental health.* New York: Appleton-Century-Crofts, 1972.

Truax, C.B. The training of nonprofessional personnel in therapeutic interpersonal relationships. *American Journal of Public Health* 1967, 57: 1778-91.

_____ . An approach to counselor education. *Counselor Education and Supervision* 1970, 10: 4-15.

_____ . The meaning and reliability of accurate empathy ratings: A rejoinder. *Psychological Bulletin* 1972, 77: 397-99.

_____ , and Carkhuff, R.R. *Toward effective counseling and psychotherapy: Training and practice.* Chicago: Aldine, 1967.

_____ ; _____ ; and Douds, J. Toward an integration of the didactic and experiential approaches to the training in counseling and psychotherapy. *Journal of Counseling Psychology* 1964, 11: 240-47.

_____ ; and Lister, J.L. Effectiveness of counselors and counselor aides. *Journal of Counseling Psychology* 1970, 17: 331-34.

_____ , and Mitchell, K.M. The psychotherapeutic and psychonoxious: Human encounters that change behavior. In M. Feldman (ed.), *Studies in psychotherapy and behavioral change.* Vol. 1. *Research in individual psychotherapy.* Buffalo: State University of New York Press, 1968.

_____, and _____. Research on certain therapist interpersonal skills in relation to process and outcome. In A.E. Bergin and S.L. Garfield (eds.), *Handbook of psychotherapy and behavior change*. New York: Wiley, 1971.

True, J.E., and Young, C.E. Associate degree programs for human services workers. *Personnel and Guidance Journal* 1974, 53: 304-7.

_____; _____; and Packard, M.E. *A national survey of associate degree programs in mental health*. Columbia, Md.: Center for Human Services Research, Johns Hopkins University, 1972.

Tseng, W.S. Psychiatric study of shamanism in Taiwan. *Archives of General Psychiatry* 1972, 26: 561-65.

_____, and McDermott, J.F. Psychotherapy: Historical roots, universal elements, and cultural variations. *American Journal of Psychiatry* 1975, 132: 378-84.

Tucker, B.J.; Megenity, D.; and Vigil, L. Anatomy of a campus crisis center. *Personnel and Guidance Journal* 1970, 48: 343-48.

Tucker, G.J., and Reinhardt, R.F. Psychiatric attitudes of young physicians: Implications for teaching. *American Journal of Psychiatry* 1968, 124: 986-90.

_____, and _____. Psychiatric attitudes of young physicians: II. The effects of postgraduate training and clinical practice. *American Journal of Psychiatry* 1969, 126: 167-70.

Tureen, L.L., and Wortman, M. A program, sponsored by a labor union, for treatment and prevention of psychiatric conditions. *American Journal of Orthopsychiatry* 1965, 35: 594-97.

Uhlenhuth, E.H., and Duncan, D.B. Subjective change with medical student therapists: I. Course of relief in psychoneurotic outpatients. *Archives of General Psychiatry* 1968a, 18: 428-38.

_____, and _____. Subjective change with medical student therapists: II. Some determinants of change in psychoneurotic outpatients. *Archives of General Psychiatry* 1968b, 18: 532-40.

Ullmann, L.P., and Krasner, L. *A psychological approach to abnormal behavior*. Englewood Cliffs, N.J.: Prentice-Hall, 1969.

Upcraft, M.L. Undergraduate students as academic advisors. *Personnel and Guidance Journal* 1971, 49: 827-31.

Vaillant, G.E. A 20-year follow-up of New York narcotic addicts. *Archives of General Psychiatry* 1973, 29: 237-41.

Van Camp, S.S. A human relations curriculum. *Childhood Education* 1973, 50: 273-76.

Vander Kolk, C.J. Comparison of two mental health counselor training programs. *Community Mental Health Journal* 1973, 9: 260-69.

Van Stone, W.W., and Gilbert, R. Peer confrontation groups: What, why, and whether. *American Journal of Psychiatry* 1972, 129: 583-88.

Varenhorst, B.B. Training adolescents as peer counselors. *Personnel and Guidance Journal* 1974, 53: 271-75.

Vaughn, R.M.; Teitelbaum, S.; and Kumpan, H. A research project in psychiatric aide training. *American Journal of Psychiatry* 1962, 119: 555-59.

Verinis, J.S. The ex-patient as a lay therapist: Attitudes of group members toward him. *Psychotherapy: Theory, Research and Practice* 1970a, 7: 161-63.

_____. Therapeutic effectiveness of untrained volunteers with chronic patients. *Journal of Consulting and Clinical Psychology* 1970b, 34: 152-55.

Vernallis, F.F., and St. Pierre, R.G. Volunteer workers' opinions about mental illness. *Journal of Clinical Psychology* 1964, 20: 140-43.

Vernon, W.M. *Motivating children: Behavior modification in the classroom.* New York: Holt, 1972.

Vidaver, R.M. The mental health technician: Maryland's design for a new health career. *American Journal of Psychiatry* 1969, 125: 1013-23.

_____, and Carson, J.E. A new framework for baccalaureate careers in the human services. *American Journal of Psychiatry* 1973, 130: 474-78.

Visotsky, H.M. Spillage of manpower. *Psychiatry Digest* 1970, 31: 13-16.

Vitalo, R.L. Teaching improved interpersonal functioning as a preferred mode of treatment. *Journal of Clinical Psychology* 1971, 27: 166-71.

Volkman, R., and Cressey, D.R. Differential association and the rehabilitation of drug addicts. *American Journal of Sociology* 1963, 64: 129-42.

Vontress, C.E. Cultural barriers in the counseling relationship. *Personnel and Guidance Journal* 1969, 48: 11-17.

Wade, R.; Jordan, G.; and Myers, G. Sociopsychiatric rehabilitation in a black urban ghetto. 3. The view of the paraprofessional. *American Journal of Orthopsychiatry* 1969, 39: 677-83.

Wagenfeld, M.O. The primary prevention of mental illness: A sociological perspective. *Journal of Health and Social Behavior* 1972, 13: 195-203.

Wagner, E.E., and Dobbins, R.D. MMPI profiles of parishioners seeking pastoral counseling. *Journal of Consulting Psychology* 1967, 31: 83-84.

Wagner, F.F. Suicide prevention and social clubs. *International Journal of Social Psychiatry* 1965, 11: 116-19.

Wagner, M.K. Parent therapists: An operant conditioning method. *Mental Hygiene* 1968, 52: 452-55.

Wagonfeld, S., and Wolowitz, H.M. Obesity and the self-help group: A look at TOPS. *American Journal of Psychiatry* 1968, 125: 249-52.

Wahler, R.G. Oppositional children: A quest for parental reinforcement control. *Journal of Applied Behavior Analysis* 1969, 2: 159-70.

_____; Winkel, G.H.; Peterson, R.F.; and Morrison, D.C. Mothers as behavior therapists for their own children. *Behavior Research and Therapy* 1965, 3: 113-24.

Waite, R.R. The negro patient and clinical theory. *Journal of Consulting Psychology* 1968, 32: 427-33.

Walsh, J.A. Converting clinicians to consultants: An in-service training seminar. *Journal of Community Psychology* 1973, 1: 292-94.

_____ ; Schneider, G.A.; Phelan, T.W.; Shattan, S.P.; and Fuhrmann, D.E. Organizational development through a staff workshop. *Journal of Community Psychology* 1974, 2: 24-27.

Ward, E.J. A gift from the ghetto. *Personnel and Guidance Journal* 1970, 48: 753-56.

Ware, J.E.; Strassman, H.D.; and Naftulin, D.H. A negative relationship between understanding interviewing principles and interview performance. *Journal of Medical Education* 1971, 46: 620-22.

Waring, E.M. Psychiatric illness in physicians: A review. *Comprehensive Psychiatry* 1974, 15: 519-30.

Watters, T.A. Teaching non-psychiatric physicians to handle psychiatric problems. *American Practitioner* 1960, 11: 111-15.

Watts, A. *Psychotherapy East and West.* New York: Mentor Books, 1963.

Weilhofen, H. All things to all people. *Mental Hygiene* 1972, 56: 12-17.

Weiner, L. The psychiatric home treatment service and the role of nonprofessional agents in community mental health. *Dissertation Abstracts International* 1966, 26: 1612-13.

Weinman, B.; Kleiner, R.; Yu, J.H.; and Tillson, V.A. Social treatment of the chronic psychotic patient in the community. *Journal of Community Psychology* 1974, 2: 358-65.

_____ ; Sanders, R.; Kleiner, R.; and Wilson, S. Community based treatment of the chronic psychotic. *Community Mental Health Journal* 1970, 6: 13-21.

Weiss, B.S.; Roberts, P.; and Wolford, J. The uninvolved: A study of services for former mental patients. *International Journal of Social Psychiatry* 1969, 15: 223-29.

Weissman, H.N., and Steward, M. Pre-school consultation: Follow-up intervention. *Journal of Community Psychology* 1973, 1: 379-82.

Weisstein, N. Psychology constructs the female. In V. Gornick and B. Moran (eds.), *Woman in sexist society.* New York: Basic Books, 1971.

Werkman, S.L.; Landau, S.; and Wakefield, H. Medical students view clinical psychiatry. *American Journal of Psychiatry* 1973, 130: 562-65.

Westberg, G.C. The parish pastor's finest hour. *Journal of Religion and Health* 1970, 9: 171-84.

Whalen, C.K., and Henker, B.A. Creating therapeutic pyramids using mentally retarded patients. *American Journal of Mental Deficiency* 1969, 74: 331-37.

_____ , and _____ . Pyramid therapy in a hospital for the retarded: Methods, program evaluation and long-term effects. *American Journal of Mental Deficiency* 1971a, 75: 414-34.

_____ , and _____ . Play therapy conducted by mentally retarded inpatients. *Psychotherapy: Theory, Research and Practice* 1971b, 8: 236-45.

Whittaker, J.K. Training child care staff: Pitfalls and promises. *Mental Hygiene* 1970, 54: 516-19.

Whittington, H.G. The police: Ally or enemy of the comprehensive community mental health center? *Mental Hygiene* 1971, 55: 55-59.

Wiener, D.N. *Classroom management and discipline*. Itasia, Ill.: F.E. Peacock, 1972.

Wigfall, S., and Mace, A.H. A paraprofessional speaks to training issues. *American Journal of Orthopsychiatry* 1972, 42: 278-79.

Willcox, A.F. The new professionals: Practical aspects of the use of new careerists in public service agencies. *Mental Hygiene* 1970, 54: 347-56.

Williams, D.L., and Kremer, B.J. Pastoral counseling students and secular counseling students: A comparison. *Journal of Counseling Psychology* 1974, 21: 238-42.

Wilson, J.R. The distinction between pastoral care, pastoral counseling and psychotherapy. *International Journal of Social Psychiatry* 1973, 19: 192-206.

Wilson, W., and Calhoun, J.F. Behavior therapy and the minority client. *Psychotherapy: Theory, Research and Practice* 1974, 11: 317-25.

Winer, J.A.; Dinello, F.A.; Pasca, A.; and Weingarten, S. Innovations at university mental health services. *Journal of the American College Health Association* 1974, 22: 281-83.

Winters, W.A., and Arent, R. The use of high school students to enrich an elementary guidance and counseling program. *Elementary School Guidance and Counseling* 1969, 3: 198-205.

Wittes, G., and Radin, N. *Helping your child to learn: The reinforcement approach*. San Rafael: Dimensions Publishing Company, 1969.

Wittman, M. Social work manpower for the health services: Problems and prospects. *American Journal of Public Health* 1974, 64: 370-75.

Wittmer, J., and Lister, J.L. The Graduate Record Examination, 16 PF Questionnaire, and counseling effectiveness. *Counselor Education and Supervision* 1971, 10: 293.

Wogan, M. Investigation of a measure of empathic ability. *Psychotherapy: Theory, Research and Practice* 1969, 6: 109-12.

Wolcott, O. Function of mental health aides in a psychiatric clinic. *International Journal of Social Psychiatry* 1969, 15: 302-6.

Wolff, T. Undergraduates as campus mental health workers. *Personnel and Guidance Journal* 1969, 48: 294-304.

_____. Helping students change the campus. *Personnel and Guidance Journal* 1974, 52: 552-56.

Wolff, W.T., and Merrens, M.R. Behavioral assessment: A review of clinical methods. *Journal of Personality Assessment* 1974, 38: 3-16.

Wolkon, G.H.; Karmen, M.; and Tanaka, H.T. Evaluation of a social rehabilitation program for recently released psychiatric patients. *Community Mental Health Journal* 1971, 7: 312-22.

Wollersheim, J.P. Hospital treatment innovation via in-service training projects. *Psychological Reports* 1973, 33: 58.

Wolpe, J. *The practice of behavior therapy*. New York: Pergamon Press, 1969.

Woods, T.L. A professional's nonprofessional experience: Suggestions for supervisors. *Mental Hygiene* 1971, 55: 298-302.

Wrenn, R.L., and Mencke, R. Students who counsel students. *Personnel and Guidance Journal* 1972, 50: 687-89.

Wylan, L.; Dolloff, P.; and Becker, A. Training paraprofessional community mental health workers. *Massachusetts Journal of Mental Health* 1972, 2: 18-29.

Yablonsky, L. *The tunnel back: Synanon.* New York: Macmillan, 1965.

Yates, A.J. *Behavior therapy.* New York: Wiley, 1970.

Zabarenko, L. Education of the graduate physician: Attempts at evaluation. *American Journal of Psychiatry* 1965, 122: 500-03.

Zabarenko, R.N.; Merenstein, J.; and Zabarenko, L. Teaching psychological medicine in family practice office. *Journal of the American Medical Association* 1971, 218: 392-96.

Zacker, J. Understanding one's clients: An attempt to improve sensitivity and morale in police recruits. *Psychological Reports* 1972, 31: 999-1008.

_____. Is opposition to social intervention resistance or coping? *Professional Psychology* 1974, 5: 198-205.

_____, and Bard, M. Adaptive resistance to change in a community. *Journal of Community Psychology* 1973a, 1: 44-49.

_____, and _____. Effects of conflict management training on police performance. *Journal of Applied Psychology* 1973b, 58: 202-8.

Zax, M., and Cowen, E.L. Early identification and prevention of emotional disturbance in a public school. In E.L. Cowen, E.A. Gardner, and M. Zax (eds.), *Emergent approaches to mental health problems.* New York: Appleton-Century-Crofts, 1967.

_____, and _____. *Abnormal psychology: Changing conceptions.* New York: Holt, 1972.

_____; _____; Izzo, L.D.; Madonia, A.J.; Merenda, J.; and Trost, M.A. A teacher-aide program for preventing emotional disturbances in young school children. *Mental Hygiene* 1966, 50: 406-15.

Zelhart, P.F., and Davis, M.S. Therapeutic conditions and physician-patient interactions: With comment on criticisms of Truax's scales. *International Journal of Social Psychiatry* 1973, 19: 70-76.

Zifferblatt, S.M. *Improving study and homework behaviors.* Champaign, Ill.: Research Press, 1970.

Zimmerman, E.H., and Zimmerman, J. The alteration of behavior in a special classroom situation. *Journal of the Experimental Analysis of Behavior* 1962, 1: 59-60.

Zolik, E.S., and Stotsky, B. Relationships between problem labeling and treatment referrals by laymen. *Community Mental Health Journal* 1966, 2: 114-20.

Zuithoff, D. Community psychiatry and social action: A survey. *American Journal of Psychiatry* 1970, 126: 1621-27.

252

Zunker, V.G., and Brown, W.F. Comparative effectiveness of student and professional counselors. *Personnel and Guidance Journal* 1966, 44: 738-43.

Author Index

Subject Index

About the Authors

Michael Gershon is a clinical psychologist at Psychological Associates, a private psychological counseling and consulting firm in Warwick, Rhode Island. He received his undergraduate training at Boston University, the Ph.D. at the University of Rhode Island in 1976. He served his internship in 1973 at the Fort Logan Mental Health Center, the Jefferson County Mental Health Center, and the Malcolm X Mental Health Center, in Denver. His major areas of interest include preventive mental health, psychosomatic medicine, and paraprofessional training.

Henry B. Biller is professor of psychology at the University of Rhode Island. He was a Phi Beta Kappa, Magna Cum Laude graduate from Brown University, 1962; a United States Public Health Service predoctoral fellow at Duke University, 1962-1965; a clinical psychology intern at the Emma Pendleton Bradley Hospital, 1965-1966; and a United States Public Health predoctoral research fellow at Duke, 1966-1967. After receiving the Ph.D. in psychology from Duke in 1967 he was a faculty member at the University of Massachusetts (1967-1969) and at George Peabody College (1969-1970). His academic positions have included participation in University-affiliated mental health facilities (University of Massachusetts Child Guidance Clinic; George Peabody College Child Study Center; University of Rhode Island Psychology Clinic). He is a consultant at the Emma Pendleton Bradley Hospital and is a Fellow of the American Psychological Association. In addition to having written numerous articles, he is the author of *Father, Child and Sex Role* (Lexington Books, D.C. Heath, 1971), *Paternal Deprivation* (Lexington Books, D.C. Heath, 1974), and coauthor with Dennis Meredith of *Father Power* (McKay, 1974).